WAR
AND THE
ROYAL
HOUSES
OF
EUROPE

WAR
AND THE
ROYAL
HOUSES
OF
EUROPE

IN THE TWENTIETH CENTURY

ANTHONY DEVERE-SUMMERS

ARMS AND
ARMOUR

I dedicate this book to my wife, Lisa

Arms and Armour Press
An Imprint of the Cassell Group
Wellington House, 125 Strand, London WC2R 0BB

Distributed in the USA by Sterling Publishing Co. Inc.,
387 Park Avenue South, New York, NY 10016-8810.

Distributed in Australia by Capricorn Link (Australia) Pty. Ltd,
2/13 Carrington Road, Castle Hill, NSW 2154.

British Library Cataloguing-in-Publication Data:
a catalogue record for this book is available from the British Library

ISBN 1-85409-310-X

Designed and edited by DAG Publications Ltd.
Designed by David Gibbons; edited by Gerald Napier;
printed and bound in Great Britain by
Hartnolls Limited, Bodmin, Cornwall

CONTENTS

CONTENTS

INTRODUCTION

I have been interested in European monarchy for many years and the aim of this book is to tell the fascinating story of the decline of an institution, which until the twentieth century was the predominant form of government in Europe. The First and Second World Wars were fundamental to that decline, but history is littered with war and social upheaval, so why should these conflicts have proved an exception to the norm ?

The horrendous cost to human life in the First World War was unacceptable to the people who lost the struggle and received nothing in exchange for that sacrifice. Armed with a greater respect for individual liberty than their forefathers they challenged the military tradition and sabre rattling concept of government that had led to the war. Their monarchies were very much part of that tradition, and they paid the ultimate price in defeat.

The victors were equally preoccupied by fatality rates and harshly penalised those nations responsible for the carnage. This created far more animosity than probably existed before the war and gave rise to some ruthless dictatorships amongst the defeated nations. They in turn spread their ideology across international borders, adding to human misery and bringing about the Second World War.

The monarchies that fell at the end of the Second World War were victims of either fascism or communism, and only participated in the Second World War by default. Although weakened by the loss of the mighty empires in 1918 which dealt a severe blow to the invincibility of monarchy, they were not unpopular with the ordinary people and only lost power when their opponents resorted to dishonest plebiscites, and intimidation of the masses. Monarchy was not the root cause of the Second World War.

The success of monarchy is demonstrated by those that have been retained in Western Europe. It is a solution that should not be dismissed in Eastern Europe where the Iron Curtain has at last fallen and monarchic restoration is a possibility. I would like to think that this is the most important message to come out of the book.

ACKNOWLEDGEMENTS

The book spans many countries and many years. This has involved considerable research and I would like to thank Theo Aronson, Margaret and Pamela Davis, Robin Piguet and Charlotte Zeepvat for their advice and/or research material. I also extend my appreciation to the Palace of Monaco, the Royal Norwegian Embassy, the Imperial War Museum, and Norwich Central Library for their assistance.

I would particularly thank Eileen Grimes for the hours spent proof reading the book, and my wife Lisa, for the support she has shown throughout the project.

Anthony Devere-Summers
14 April 1996

CHAPTER ONE. STARTING PISTOL

The recent fighting in Bosnia-Herzegovina is but a continuation of the violent history of the Balkans. To understand why people died on the streets of Sarajevo one must go back to ancient or medieval days, when the Balkan states possessed Balkan empires in succession to each other. A period of freedom ocurred before they were enslaved by Ottoman rule in the fifteenth century. In the nineteenth century, Ottoman power was in decline allowing the states to regain their independence. This did not bring back to them the splendours of empire, and with only so much territory to go around, they immediately began to jostle with one another for superiority within the region. It led to bloody infighting as Ottoman rule had made the Balkan peoples proud and ruthless warriors. The European powers, notably Austria-Hungary, France, Great Britain, Germany, Italy, and Russia sought to exert a calming influence by despatching their princes to the Balkans. For example Prince Wilhelm of Denmark went to Greece in 1863, Prince Karl of Hohenzollern-Sigmaringen to Roumania in 1866, Prince Ferdinand of Saxe-Coburg and Gotha travelled in turn to Bulgaria in 1887, and Prince Wilhelm of Wied was sent to Albania in 1914. However, these newfound monarchs wished to win, and retain the loyalty of their new subjects. A number were to experience long reigns, and through genuine commitment to their new countries, they came to represent national aspirations without recourse to the European powers.

Bismarck labelled the Balkans the 'powder keg of Europe' and there was universal concern when the Balkan states went to war in 1912 and 1913. In the first of the wars, the Balkan states achieved the unthinkable and united to push the frontiers of the Ottoman Empire back to the outskirts of Constantinople, modern day Istanbul. Officially the war lasted from 17 October 1912 to 30 May 1913, but much time was taken up with the peace negotiations, and the odd bastion of Turk resistance such as Adrianople. Otherwise, Serbia, Bulgaria, Greece, and Montenegro managed to conquer Macedonia, Western Thrace and Albania in one decisive blow, radically altering the map of Europe. When the powers attempted to bring the states back into line by first promising to impose reform upon Turkey, and then taking the view that Ottoman rule in Europe was nothing to do with the Balkan states they received one response – Ottoman Europe was inhabited by Greeks, Bulgars, and Serbs, and not by Germans, Frenchmen, or Englishmen.

Balkan audacity was soon to be undermined by their own success. The rapid fall of the Ottoman army either brought forth unexpected territory, or provided the opportunity for the different states to recover parts of their long lost empires, both of which turned the allies in on themselves. This allowed the European powers to impose restraint on the peace process for example by removing Serbia and Montenegro from Albania in deference to Austro-Hungarian and Italian influence in the region.

Russia and Great Britain also ensured that Constantinople, the Muslim capital of Turkey and the ancient Christian capital of the Byzantine Empire, remained in Ottoman hands. This greatly upset King Ferdinand of Bulgaria who entertained the rather grand design of restoring the city to Christianity and basking in the glory of the Christian world. The Great Powers had long ridiculed his claim to Constantinople, and not without some encouragement from Ferdinand himself, who had commissioned his portrait in the robes of a Byzantine emperor. But the first Balkan War gave him the chance to prove them all wrong, and the Bulgarian Army very nearly took the city. The European powers only just snatched Constantinople from his grasp when a cholera epidemic in the Bulgarian Army forced the king to the peace table. His humour hardly increased when he found that his allies had in the meantime carved up the territory around him, including Greece who took his second target Salonika and solemnly restored the mosques to the Christian church.

King Ferdinand therefore went to war with his allies on 30 June 1913, but he found himself facing Roumania and Turkey as well. The former feared for Bulgarian domination of the Balkans and made an unprovoked attack, whilst the latter saw the opportunity for retaliation. Bulgaria was therefore completely encircled by the enemy and was forced to sue for peace as early as 31 July. The Treaty of Bucharest gave Adrianople back to Turkey. Parts of the Dobrudja were ceded to Roumania, and Macedonia was left to Serbia and Greece. Bulgaria was left with absolutely nothing to show for the First Balkan War, which is something Russia for one sought to avoid with the unsuccessful yet correct argument that Bulgarian resentment would only fester and later re-emerge to the detriment of Balkan stability. It certainly influenced King Ferdinand in his decision that Bulgaria should become the only Balkan state to join forces with Germany in the First World War.

The Greeks had just cause to be pleased with their conquests, including Mount Olympus in Macedonia, the home of the Greek gods of antiquity. Salonika was the jewel in the crown, although King Giorgios I, formerly Prince Wilhelm of Denmark, was assassinated there on 18 March 1913. His killer was a drunken beggar who did not appear to have carried out the murder for political ends, although he committed suicide before he could be probed further at his trial. The king was out for an afternoon walk with just one aide-de-camp when he was shot. Strangely enough, his brother, King Frederik VIII of Denmark, had died a little under a year earlier whilst on a solitary walk through the streets of Hamburg. With no one in attendance it was not until the next day that the Danish royal family were alerted to his unidentified body in the city mortuary.

King Konstantinos I of the Hellenes thought that his moment to die had come when on his entry to Salonika he noticed armed Turks amongst the jubilant Greek population. They did not move to change the course of history, but following the death of his father his household went to great lengths to protect him whilst he lived in Salonika, and with guards lining the walls around his palace, he reminded them that he was not born to be the Tsar of Russia. He was, nevertheless, reassured to have taken the city on the patronal festival of St Demetrius, a military hero of a bygone age. Such festivals did appear to have a calming influence on the combatants. As tension increased between the allies in the build up to the Second Balkan War, King Konstantinos won Bulgarian praise when he attended mass to celebrate King Ferdinand's saint's day in April 1912. In return, the Bulgarians paraded before the Greek king on his saint's day in May.

By contrast the atmosphere was a little more strained when King Konstantinos visited his closest ally the Crown Prince Aleksander of Serbia. Monastir was a Serb conquest but was also a town with a large Greek population and their enthusiastic welcome for the king did not go unnoticed by Serbia. The king also found it difficult to comprehend the successful command of the crown prince who was only 24 years old and a mere lieutenant general. Serbia believed the war to be a Christian crusade and divine providence is said to have taken a hand when the Serbs retook the plain of Kossovo. The area is partly covered by white pebbles reputed to be Christian bread turned to stone before the hungry Muslim invader. When the Serbs returned to Kossovo they found large quantities of rationed biscuits abandoned by the Turks. It was almost as if the stones had turned back to bread.

Nevertheless, the Serbs' mission was incomplete. The Central Powers had denied the Serbs Albania and their newly-won access to the Adriatic Sea, whilst the Austro-Hungarian annexation of Bosnia-Herzegovina in 1908 deprived them of territory which had belonged to Serbia in medieval times. When the Central Powers had resurrected an independent kingdom of Serbia in 1878, they had given it boundaries better suited to nineteenth century diplomacy, and this simply replaced a longing for independence with a desire for the 'Greater Serbia' of old. The struggle with His Imperial and Apostolic Majesty Kaiser Franz-Josef of Austria-Hungary was no Christian crusade, but Serbia entertained some pretty nasty terrorist organisations, and in the assassination of Archduke Franz-Ferdinand, the fight was to prove equally ruthless.

The archduke was the heir to the Habsburg throne and therefore a particular target for Serb extremists. The Austro-Hungarian Empire was in decay, although not to the extent of the Ottoman Empire, and Archduke Franz-Ferdinand was anxious to consolidate his inheritance before he too was ejected from the Balkans. It was anticipated that upon his accession he would placate his Slav subjects by giving them greater autonomy within the empire. This would hinder Serb ambitions in Bosnia-Herzegovina, and as Kaiser Franz-Josef ambled through his seventh decade, Belgrade was acutely aware of the archduke impatiently marking time at the foot of the throne. A Serb terrorist group called the Black Hand therefore decided to take action, which was bad news for Archduke Franz-Ferdinand as the very same organisation had brutally murdered their own king and queen in 1903.

King Aleksander Obrenovic had been perceived to have been too lenient with Austria-Hungary, and his unpopular marriage to Madame Draga Mashin, a woman with a reputation for dubious morals and meddling in state affairs, had given the Black Hand the opportunity to walk into the palace, hack their victims to pieces, and throw their mutilated bodies from an upstairs window into the gardens below. It had been a brutal attack that brought a comparison to the Ripper murders in London. The Black Hand included many army officers and this had given them ready access to the palace. A loyal sergeant had raised the alarm giving King Aleksander and Queen Draga time to hide in a secret closet behind their bedroom wall. There they remained for some time until the queen, looking outside from a window within the closet, confused a rebel officer for a loyal guard, and in shouting for help, alerted the Black Hand to their true location.

The bloodstained throne passed to Prince Petar Karadjordjevic, a descendant of Karadjord, or Black George, who rose against Ottoman rule and helped pave the way for independence. The Serb people did not oppose his accession and even presented him with a crown made of cannon metal used in battle by Karadjord. It is not clear to what extent the new king had been involved in the coup d'etat, and the stigma of the murders was to remain with him for many years. The situation hardly improved when in 1909 his eldest son, Crown Prince Jord was declared unfit for the throne amid rumours that he had kicked his valet to death. The involvement of army officers gave rise to the charge of state terrorism and Austria-Hungary was to capitalise on this on the assassination of the archduke.

In the summer of 1914, Bosnia-Herzegovina hosted the annual army manoeuvres and Franz-Ferdinand was in attendance in his capacity as Inspector-General of the Armed Forces. At the end of the manoeuvres he was to pay a ceremonial visit to the Bosnian capital of Sarajevo. Unfortunately the date fixed for the visit, 28 June, was the anniversary of the Ottoman destruction of Greater Serbia and to the Serb anarchist this only added insult to injury. The archduke attempted to postpone the journey when discontent to the timing of the visit was made known, but Kaiser Franz-Josef who had in 1910 returned from Sarajevo unharmed, instructed his nephew to proceed as planned. However, to encourage him, the kaiser gave permission for his nephew, who was to celebrate his fourteenth wedding anniversary on the same day, to take his morganatic wife along with him on her first official function inside the empire. Still the archduke wavered over the visit but the kaiser's word was final and he duly went to Sarajevo.

The former Countess Sophie Chotek von Chotkova und Wogin was a lady in waiting at court, and as her rather grand title might suggest, she came from an aristocratic background. Nevertheless, in accordance with Habsburg etiquette she was not qualified to marry an archduke. However, Franz-Ferdinand had insisted upon the marriage, and he eventually won the right to wed Countess Sophie. It was not all that long ago that his cousin the Crown Prince Rudolf, had committed suicide for the love of Baroness Marie Vetschera and Franz-Josef was wary of a similar situation. The archduke had won the first battle, but he was not to win the war. Although his wife was elevated to the title of Duchess von Hohenburg, she was not to be an archduchess, and this denied her the right to accompany her husband on official functions. They were, however, making headway. In contrast to the majority of Habsburg marriages, theirs was a success and it was with dignity that the duchess withstood the abuse of court officialdom. To make their point, the courtiers ensured that whenever the archduke left his palace the Royal Guard would stand down and leave the duchess undefended until her husband returned, an humiliation the archduke could not forget as inspector-general of armed forces.

Security was lacking even for the archduke, when the couple made their ceremonial entry into Sarajevo. Few soldiers lined the route and the worst of Franz-Ferdinand's fears were very quickly realised. No sooner had they driven into Sarajevo than an anarchist threw a bomb at their car. It just missed, bouncing from the folded canopy at the back of the car on to the road behind. The explosion injured the occupants of the next vehicle and left a large hole in the road. At the City Hall where the welcoming ceremony took place, contingency plans were made to protect them from further attack but all proved ineffectual. Arrangements were made for the duchess to return home but she would not go without her husband. Extra military protection was discussed but in the end only two officers were assigned to the running boards on either side of the car. Finally, the route of the procession was changed but no one thought to tell the chauffeur who went off in the wrong direction after the archduke and duchess had taken leave of the dignitaries at the City Hall. In a moment of panic an aide brought the car to a halt in the middle of the road, and as the chauffeur went to turn the vehicle around, another assassin by the name of Gavrilo Princip stepped forward and shot them dead.

Scant regard appears to have been given to the demise of the duchess who the Court continued to ridicule in death. At their lying in state, it was noticeable that Sophie's coffin was at a lower level to Franz-Ferdinand's and in comparison to the archducal orders around his casket, there lay before the Duchess a fan, the traditional sign of a lady in waiting. However, the murder of the archduke was taken seriously. Not because he was any more popular than his wife, but because he was the heir to the throne and a harsh ultimatum was delivered to the Serbian Government.

Austria-Hungary provided a long list of demands that basically came down to two issues. State sponsored subversion was to be ended and the entry of Austrian police to Serb territory for the arrest and trial of those responsible for this and other crimes against the empire was to be allowed. It was a deliberately harsh ultimatum designed to provoke a belligerent response, but to everyone's surprise Serbia sent a conciliatory reply agreeing to everything other than Austrian police on her territory. This met with short sharp shrift in Vienna where the authorities were determined upon confrontation, and a month after his nephew was killed, Kaiser Franz-Josef went to war with Serbia.

Austro-Hungarian pride was dealt an immediate blow with the failure of not one, but three military expeditions into Serbia. Belgrade remained at liberty for all bar thirteen days, whilst Sarajevo was very nearly lost to the

Serb Army. Only with German and Bulgarian assistance did the Austrians send the Serb Army scuttling across the snow-covered mountains of Albania to the Greek island of Corfu, and only after they themselves had become the butt of German humour. General Potiorek who won acclaim for a rare Austro-Hungarian victory was the target of one popular joke which went something like this: 'Do you know the new Viennese dance called the Potiorek? It is quite original, you take two steps forward and six steps back!' Lese-majesty was very nearly committed with another joke aimed at Kaiser Franz-Josef himself. 'Why does the old Austrian Kaiser always carry his head bowed so low? He is looking for Belgrade which the army laid at his feet'.

Whereas Kaiser Franz-Josef failed to inspire a decisive victory, King Petar I of Serbia, who was almost as ancient as the Austrian emperor, did encourage his men in their prolonged resistance to Austro-Hungarian forces. At one point when the outlook was bleak and the soldiers were beginning to waver, the king appeared in the trenches with his own rifle and ammunition. He gave permission for anyone who doubted Serb success to leave and find safety elsewhere, but he for one intended to stay and fight. As a result, the troops remained in place and turned the battle to their advantage. It was therefore very difficult to evacuate King Petar from Serbia and he had made it known that he would fight to the end so that when the enemy came they would find a deserted country and a dead king. His eldest son Prince Aleksander decided otherwise. He was regent and commander-in-chief of the army, and when he gave the order for court, government and army to leave, his father went as well.

In doing so the prince regent saved a number of leading figures from a directive by Archduke Friedrich who became the military governor of Serbia. He instigated a witch-hunt against those suspected of anti-Austrian activities prior to, and during, the war. Army officers were hauled from prisoner of war camps and tried for the murder of Archduke Franz-Ferdinand, whilst civilians who had resisted the occupation were tied to crosses. This ensured Austria-Hungary was tried and condemned by world opinion for terrorising the Serb people in the same way as Germany had mistreated the citizens of Belgium. Bulgaria was no more benevolent towards the Serbs in the territory occupied by her troops. It forced men of military age to join the Bulgarian Army and fight their Serb brothers. This led to the mutiny of approximately 20,000 Serb recruits who fought the Bulgarians for two weeks. Of the 6,000 mutineers captured by the Bulgarians, 2,000 were machine gunned to death and buried in a mass grave. The remaining 4,000 were sent to Asia Minor where, as guests of the Ottoman Empire, they were given hard labour.

The Albanian mountains were covered in snow but it was not the first time the king had been forced to beat a hasty retreat in arctic conditions. During the rule of the Obrenovic dynasty his home had been in France, and in his younger days he had been trained at the military academy of St Cyr. He therefore fought for France in the Franco-Prussian War and narrowly avoided capture by swimming the width of the River Loire. It was at the height of winter and the water was very cold which left him with the Legion of Honour and chronic rheumatism. The latter did not bode well for a march across the Albanian mountains and the king was carried part of the way on a stretcher. Nevertheless, he had impeccable credentials for an ally of France and his son met with equal favour in Russia, where Prince Aleksander had been educated at the prestigious Corps des Pages in St Petersburg. Defeat might have detracted from his victories in the Balkan Wars but Prince Aleksander did take advantage of exile to rid Serbia of the Black Hand whose ringleaders were executed by firing squad in 1917. Only with the Serb Army confined to Corfu and effectively under Entente jurisdiction did the prince have the ability to move against the organisation.

He likewise achieved the unification of the Serbs, Croats, and Slovenes, under the Karadjordjevic Dynasty, a new kingdom in which the different peoples were given equal rights under a parliamentary democracy elected by universal suffrage and secret ballot. Freedom of religion and expression were also guaranteed, the latter aided by the use of both the Cyrillic and Latin alphabets. This was a model state for a people who had suffered Ottoman or Austro-Hungarian rule, but in the euphoria it was overlooked that Belgrade had finally achieved the Greater Serbia of old and through the Karadjordjevic Dynasty the Serbs were to exert considerable influence on the development of the kingdom. Differences very quickly surfaced, and in 1928, seven years after Prince Aleksander's accession to the throne, he was obliged to suspend the constitution and rule by decree until 1931. By then he had given the country the name of Yugoslavia but unity could not be found in a new name and he found to his cost that it was not easy to change the map of the Balkans.

The new kingdom also absorbed the Montenegrins, the slav people of Kara-Dagh, or Black Mountain. This was a trifle awkward because it ended the 58-year reign of Aleksander's maternal grandfather King Nikola of Montenegro, a colourful figure who always wore national dress which included a round cap, braided jacket with baggy sleeves, broad knee breeches, white stockings and ankle boots. His people were fierce warriors who had only just started to take prisoners alive and stopped exhibiting enemy skulls in the capital of Cettinje. They were, however, a primitive race, as demonstrated by their legal system which included no lawyers and courtrooms, but a tree of justice under which the king tried the villains. This backwardness allowed the Serbs to get the better of the Montenegrins, and the loss of sovereignty brought an end to the Petrovic Dynasty which had ruled the small country since 1696; no mean achievement for a Balkan dynasty and one that initially governed Montenegro through five celibate bishops. King Nikola had no such inhibitions and of his nine children, five daughters married into the Serbian, Italian, Hessian and Russian royal houses. However none was able to help him retain his throne. Princess Zorka of Serbia was long since dead, and the Hessian and Russian monarchies were also to fall in the First World War. His daughter Queen Elena of Italy did attempt to make amends in the Second World War with a restoration of the dynasty to Italian occupied Montenegro but nothing came of her plan.

15

CHAPTER TWO. CALL TO ARMS

Bismarck was nervous of the Balkan 'powder keg' because around it rested an enormous armoury which could set Europe ablaze. Life outside the Balkans was no less hostile, if more refined, and the majority of nations were intent on imperialism. Indeed the strength of the Great Powers lay within their empires. The climate of the pre-war years can best be gauged by the entangled web of alliances that grew to govern the military and diplomatic activity of the day, most notably the Triple Alliance of Germany, Austria-Hungary and Italy, and the Triple Entente of Great Britain, France and Russia.

The Triple Alliance was concluded as a result of Austro-German apprehension of Russia and Italo-German tension with France. The initial treaty between Austria and Germany was signed in 1879, and committed the signatories to military cooperation in the event of a Russian attack on either empire. This was broadened in 1882 to include Italy and a similar accord over France. Although the contents of the treaties were a closely guarded secret, their very existence unnerved the other powers, but their anxiety only increased when Kaiser Wilhelm II dismissed Prince von Bismarck from office in 1890. Although Bismarck was the architect of the Triple Alliance, his nineteen years in office and the jealous guard he placed upon his prerogatives, ensured that there was no one of sufficient calibre to replace him. As a result, German foreign policy was clumsy and erratic, winning few friends.

The kaiser, who had ascended the throne in 1888, sought to fill the power vacuum himself, but he failed to win the confidence of his European neighbours. There were three reasons for this. The first was his insistence on ruling Germany in the guise of 'Supreme Warlord' which did not suggest peaceful intent; the second was his support for colonialisation, and the third was his lack of diplomacy, even though he possessed intelligence and charm. War secured Hohenzollern might, and it did not go unnoticed that Kaiser Wilhelm II, who was commissioned into the Foot Guards at ten years of age, had embraced the profession with an enthusiasm unknown to a dynasty of soldier kings since Frederick the Great in the eighteenth century. He was never happier than when in the presence of heel-clicking adjutants and goose stepping guardsmen, and he was forever shown to the outside world reviewing military parades, directing army manoeuvres, or launching new warships.

The German Empire was initially confined to a collection of German speaking principalities and dukedoms within Europe. Having achieved a prominent position in Europe, Germany looked to establish world authority in an overseas Empire, and very quickly acquired German South-West Africa, Tanganyika, Togoland, the Cameroons, German New Guinea, and German Samoa. Bismarck accomplished this without a navy, but Kaiser Wilhelm II saw the necessity for a fleet to police the empire. However, the number of battleships built exceeded this mandate, and allowed Germany to engage in gunboat diplomacy. There was always the possibility that colonial tension could upset

the balance of power in Europe and this is exactly what happened; not en
a surprise when it is remembered that Great Britain, France, Italy, the Ne
lands, Belgium and Portugal were all represented in Africa.

Kaiser Wilhelm II was a grandson of Queen Victoria, and generally l
in high esteem by the British public, but relations with Great Britain dete
rated over South Africa. The Transvaal region was occupied by Dutch settl
and the British were unable to gain full control of the territory. The First B
War of 1880-1881 was won by the Dutch who created the Transvaal Repub
under President Stephanus Kruger. His position was subsequently strengt
ened by the commercial development undertaken by Germany. In 189.
Doctor Leander Jameson of the British South Africa Company led an abortiv
raid into the Transvaal. His defeat protected German interests ther
prompting the kaiser to send President Kruger a telegram of congratulations
The message caused an uproar in London and, during the Second Boer War
of 1899-1902 which brought a British victory, there was an atmosphere of
distrust between Britain and Germany which harmed their relationship elsewhere.

Reflecting on the Kruger telegram, his second cousin Princess Alice,
Countess of Athlone, summed up the kaiser's impact on Anglo-German relations:

> It was not easy to understand everything Wilhelm did because he
> was flamboyantly vain and temperamentally unstable. Without
> being blind to the consequences of his actions, he seemed unable
> to resist an opportunity of throwing his weight about if it helped
> magnify his importance and the might of the empire whose
> destiny, with God's connivance, it was his duty to shape. Invari-
> ably, he regretted his impetuosity and tried, not often success-
> fully, to repair the harm caused by his rashness.[1]

The Triple Alliance, which to an extent was concluded through German insecurity, now gave the Reich the confidence to stand her ground on colonial
issues, although in reality, Germany was the alliance. Italy had joined the
Triple Alliance when she was particularly upset with France over the annexation of Tunis, and as time wore on, and her anger abated, her long term
commitment to the treaty was questionable.

The kaiser also cast doubt on the value of Italian participation in the
alliance with his disparaging treatment of 'the dwarf', King Vittorio-Emanuele
III, who was barely five feet tall, and therefore the butt of endless Wilhelmine
jokes. He did, however, take things to the extreme when in total disregard to
the king's sensitivity about his size, the kaiser took with him on a state visit
to Italy the tallest guards regiment in his army. That apart, there were similarities between the two monarchs. Kaiser Wilhelm also had a physical hand-
icap in his withered arm, and like Germany, Italy had recently gained national
unity under one crown.

Italy was of use to Germany in so much as she guaranteed assistance in the event of a French invasion, a commitment Austria-Hungary would not give. It was important to Vienna that the Great Powers continued to recognise that the empire was essential to the balance of power. Russia on the other hand did threaten her Balkan territories, and weakened as she was by the nationalist demands of her minority races, Austria-Hungary had cause to fear Russian intrigue. The one major attempt Kaiser Franz-Josef had made to put his empire in order was the union with Hungary in 1867, when the ancient kingdom was given equality with Austria. Thereafter, Franz-Josef rigidly abided by dualism regardless of the protestations of his other subject peoples.

The Austro-German treaty placed the Russians at such a disadvantage that they turned to France for support. Autocratic Russia and republican France were an unlikely combination but a surprisingly successful one. The close relationship was emphasised when Tsar Nikolai II made an official visit to Paris and honoured the memory of the Emperor Napoleon I, the same emperor who had dared to invade Russia, by visiting the tomb at Les Invalides. The Parisians gave the tsar a unexpectedly warm welcome. As King Louis XVI (1774–1792) could testify they were not sympathetic to autocracy, and when in 1871, a Bourbon restoration was all but assured, the Comte de Chambord dashed all hopes with a rejection of the revolutionary tricolour. Bourbon fortunes rose with the defeat of the Emperor Napoleon III in the Franco-Prussian War. The conflict was to leave very deep divisions between the two countries. Harsh indemnities, and the annexation of the border region of Alsace-Lorraine were injustices the French swore to revenge. Kaiser Wilhelm II attempted to woo Tsar Nikolai away from France but met with little success. The nearest he ever came to achieving this was the so called Treaty of Bjorko, an appeal to dynastic kinship which ended in farce.

The sight of the German imperial yacht *Hohenzollern*, or its Russian counterpart the *Standard*, cruising off the Coast of Finland was nothing unusual as both emperors enjoyed annual cruises in the picturesque fjords. Normally these visits did not coincide but in 1905 the two yachts could be seen off Bjorko. It was classed as a family reunion between royal cousins and no ministers of state were in attendance. During the meeting the kaiser produced a draft treaty binding the two empires together and laid it before the tsar amid a nostalgic look to the past, no doubt with a mind to the unsuccessful Dreikaiser Bund (Three Emperors League between Russia, Austria-Hungary and Germany) of 1873. Influenced by Kaiser Wilhelm's sentimentality, Tsar Nikolai placed his signature to the document. The treaty contradicted their obligations to their respective allies, and prompted a ministerial revolt back home, ensuring that it was never ratified.

In light of such folly, one can perceive Tsar Nikolai II to be a weak ruler. Without question this mild-natured man was not suited to absolutism, although he would have made a good constitutional monarch like his cousin King George V, to whom he bore a close resemblance. The tragedy was his inability to make the transfer. The tsar was conscious of his inheritance, and one he was deter-

mined to preserve for the next generation of Romanovs. Limited monarchy was incompatible with that legacy but it was to his misfortune that his people thought otherwise, and there developed an ugly struggle which at times reached the very threshold of the Winter Palace in St Petersburg.

In 1905, industrial workers demanding better factory conditions staged a peaceful demonstration before the Winter Palace. The tsar was out of St Petersburg at the time and in his absence the authorities sent the troops in and turned the demonstration into a bloodbath. The day became known as Bloody Sunday, and the tsar, who was not violent by nature, gained the reputation of Bloody Nikolai. Bloody Sunday inaugurated a year of violent demonstrations, a revolution, which threatened the very existence of the regime. Although the tsar was to survive, confidence in his rule was severely dented, and nowhere more so than abroad.

His French ally had good reason to question the strength of the partnership with Russia. Political weakness was compounded by military defeat in the Far East which helped contribute to the unrest in Russia. The Russo-Japanese War of 1904-1905, a result of conflicting aims in Manchuria, had identified severe weaknesses in the Russian war machine. The defence of Port Arthur and the land battles of the Yalu, Telissu, Liao-Yang and Mukden saw the loss of approximately 97,000 troops, whilst the sea battle of Tsushima destroyed the Baltic Fleet altogether. The same fleet had on its outward journey to Manchuria mistaken British trawlers fishing in the North Sea as a Japanese patrol and to the outrage of the British government sent the fishing boats to the bottom of the sea. Relations between Great Britain and Russia were quickly repaired by a fine imposed on Russia by the Court of Arbitration sitting in the Hague.

Ironically, the Court had been the one positive result of two peace conferences called by the tsar in 1899 and 1907. Europe believed the tsar's motive to be his inability to finance modern weaponry for Russia, but Tsar Nikolai was actually influenced by a Russian writer called Ivan Bliokh, who assessed the capabilities of modern weapons and the human misery they would cause. It was as much as Europe could do not to laugh at him outright to his face, and Queen Wilhelmina of the Netherlands made the following comment after she had opened the Peace Palace which was to be the home of the Court of Arbitration:

> I had little hope that conventions agreed at peace conferences would be observed in the case of serious conflict, although I had not imagined the extent to which they would be ignored in the near future.[2]

French mediation also brought Britain and Russia together in search of another ally to bolster the alliance with Russia. The Anglo-French Entente Cordiale was ratified in 1904, and three years later France, Russia and Great Britain came together in the Triple Entente, which provided a formidable counterbalance to the Triple Alliance of Germany, Austria-Hungary and Italy. Just as France and Russia were old adversaries, so France and Britain were not historically the best of friends, but the new alliance stood the test of time, ignoring German attempts to undermine the agreement. The Treaty of Bjorko was an example to hand, but another of far greater significance was the tussle over Morocco.

The sultanate was in crisis when at the beginning of the century France stepped in to guide her finances and strengthen law enforcement. Kaiser Wilhelm II moved to challenge French influence with a visit to Sultan Abd al-Aziz in 1905, and a highly charged speech in defence of Moroccan sovereignty. Tension between France and Germany prompted the Algeciras Conference. Sympathy was with France and although lip service was given to German demands for international access to Moroccan finance, France retained control of customs and excise. She likewise retained an influential role in the police force, although a Swiss inspector general was appointed to appease Germany. Algeciras did not therefore mollify Germany and the situation once again deteriorated when a new sultan, who was besieged by unfriendly tribesmen, invited French troops to Morocco. Germany reacted by sending a gunboat to the port of Agadir, which remained in place until France gave part of the French Congo to Germany, in exchange for a German withdrawal from Morocco. Gunboat diplomacy had paid off and, in Berlin, it justified the expansion of the Imperial Navy. In London, it confirmed Admiralty fears for the British Empire, and the Royal Navy's mastery of the seas.

The tension that existed throughout Great Britain also penetrated Buckingham Palace, although at the palace it was largely due to a personality clash between King Edward VII and his nephew Kaiser Wilhelm II. The king resented the kaiser's arrogance, and particularly with regard to his family, which on one occasion saw Wilhelm place his own sister under house arrest for riding a bicycle in public. King Edward had long rebelled against his Germanic upbringing and the stiff collar environment of the German courts. He was more in tune with the glamour and gaiety of France, and he had made a valuable contribution towards the Entente Cordiale. This led Kaiser Wilhelm to believe that his uncle was scheming against Germany, particularly when he delayed an official visit to Berlin until his reign was nearly over, and he had visited most of the other courts in Europe. It would, however, be incorrect to say that his dislike of Wilhelm represented a complete Germanophobia, nor that it greatly influenced government policy. The relationship between the two royal houses improved with the accession of King George V in 1910, but by then the die was cast.

King George V and Queen Mary went to Berlin to attend the wedding of Princess Viktoria Louise of Prussia in 1913. The groom was Prince Ernst August of Hanover, and the marriage ended a feud between the two royal houses dating from the Austro-Prussian War of 1866. The Hanoverian royal house, whose kings numbered George the First, Second, and Third of Great Britain, had supported the Habsburgs and was denied the throne by the victorious Hohenzollerns. Although the Hanoverian throne was not restored, the kaiser did give his new son-in-law the Duchy of Brunswick which had passed in name to the Hanoverians as early as 1884. Reconciliation at the very heart of the Hohenzollern Empire could have been a powerful symbol to the outside world, but few people took note.

There were bitter recriminations in Berlin against King George V when Britain went to war against Germany in 1914. The kaiser's brother, Prince Heinrich of Prussia, was in Britain immediately before the outbreak of world war. He had seen the king before his departure and in the course of the audience he asked him what Great Britain would do in the event of a continental war. King George replied that Great Britain had no quarrel with anyone and he hoped for neutrality. He then added if Germany went to war with France and Russia, then neutrality would be difficult, but his government would do everything to avert a European war. This was interpreted in Berlin as a declaration of neutrality, but as the king had hinted, war with Britain's allies would change things, and this was the drawback of the intricate network of alliances, for when one went to war, they all went to war. Great Britain fought through her commitment to France, and not only through the invasion of Belgium. Two days before Germany crossed the Belgian border, the British government undertook to use the Royal Navy to protect the French coast from German attack. However, the violation of Belgian neutrality was fundamental to the process because it brought parliament and public opinion behind a declaration of war, and made it easier to send troops to the continent.

Germany did attempt to prevent an Austro-Hungarian declaration of war against Serbia. Kaiser Wilhelm II argued that the moderate response received from Belgrade cancelled the military option, but Germany was in a moral dilemma, because Austria-Hungary had given her ally unqualified support since their alliance, and now she wanted the same commitment in return. Germany therefore took the decision to mobilise alongside Austria-Hungary. German mobilisation could not cope with indecision and once the army was on the move there was no going back, as Kaiser Wilhelm II found to his cost at the eleventh hour. The cause of his last minute doubts was the threat of war with Russia, who had announced her intention to defend the Serbs. Russia and Germany both declared war on 1 August 1914. France followed suit two days later in support of Russia. Great Britain went to war on 4 August in support of her French ally, and Belgium. Italy remained neutral until 23 August 1915, whereupon she joined the Entente Powers. The war soon escalated beyond the original parties to the Triple Alliance and Triple Entente, transforming the conflict into the First World War. The Ottoman Empire and Bulgaria were to side with Germany, whilst the Entente Powers ended the war with nineteen allies including the United States of America, Japan, Brazil and Haiti.

References:

1. *For My Grandchildren*, HRH Princess Alice, Countess of Athlone.
2. *Lonely But Not Alone*, HRH Princess Wilhelmina of the Netherlands.

CHAPTER THREE. THE FIRST WORLD WAR

As the world joined in the conflict, so the fighting spread across the globe. In 1914, the war was concentrated in Europe with fighting in Belgium, and France on the Western Front, and East Prussia, Russian Poland, Hungary and Serbia to the east. However, Ottoman entry to the war saw bloodshed in Egypt, Mesopotamia and the Caucasus, whilst the majority of German colonies fell to the Entente. Only German East Africa, the Cameroons, and some of German South-West Africa remained to the kaiser. Meanwhile on the high seas, there was the Battle of Heligoland Bight and the Battle of the Falkland Isles. Another important factor in the spread of war throughout the world was the support of the British dominions for the mother country, and India, Canada, South Africa, Australia, and New Zealand, all committed troops to the war, many fighting on the Western Front.

In 1915, the Western Front experienced the second battle at Ypres and two major Entente offensives in Artois and Champagne. There was also an increase of activity in the Balkans with the Bulgarian declaration of war, and Italy invaded Austria. The ill-fated Dardanelles campaign got under way in Asia Minor, and with Russian Poland almost totally in Austro-Hungarian hands, the Central Powers marched on the Baltic States. Meanwhile there was increased fighting in Mesopotamia and Egypt, and the fall of German South-West Africa.

The following year saw concerted efforts to break the deadlock in France, and amongst the battles fought were those of Verdun and the Somme. Austro-Italian fortunes fluctuated in the Trentino, and Russia launched a successful counter-attack in Poland. In the Balkans, Roumania invaded Hungary, whilst Austria-Hungary conquered Montenegro and Northern Albania. A breakaway movement in Greece defied the neutrality of the Athens government and joined with the Entente forces in Salonika. In Arabia the Turks were expelled from Mecca and Jiddah, and the Cameroons were finally lost to Germany. The naval Battle of Jutland took place off the Danish coast. 1917 was not a good year for the Entente who saw the near total collapse of the Italian Front, the surrender of Roumania, and the fall of Imperial Russia. The one bright spot was the entry into the war of the United States of America. However, the British did enjoy success in the Near East with the capture of Gaza, Jaffa, and Jerusalem.

1917 may have not been a good year for the Entente, but 1918 was to prove disastrous for the Central Powers. It started well with the Treaty of Brest-Litovsk which finally removed Bolshevik Russia from the war. This gave Poland and the Baltic States to the Central Powers and enabled a full-scale transfer of troops to the West. The Germans also launched a successful attack on the Western Front and there followed the Battle of St Quentin, the Battle of the Lys, and the Second Battle of the Marne, which all went in their favour. However, fortunes were reversed by the summer, and the Battles of Amiens,

Bapaume and the Scarpe placed the Germans back on the defensive. The further Battles of the Hindenburg Line, Flanders, Selle, and Sambre saw their defeat. Meanwhile, similar onslaughts in the Balkans, and on the Italian Front, forced Bulgaria and Austria-Hungary out of the war. The destruction of the Turkish army in Palestine likewise brought about the surrender of the Ottoman Empire.

CHAPTER FOUR. BELGIUM

The Schlieffen Express

The brutality of Balkan Warfare had long ceased to shock the outside world, but the violation of Belgian neutrality and the systematic terrorisation of the Belgian people was to have an enormous bearing upon world opinion. Entente propaganda was to distort the violent onslaught, and a photograph in the London Daily Mail of German officers carrying off gold and silver treasures from Belgian houses transpired to be a pre-war picture of officers showing off their trophies at the military steeplechase at Grünwald. Nevertheless, there were valid reasons for a German diplomat in Brussels to comment, 'I know the German Army. It will be like laying a baby on the track before a locomotive.'[1] An American journalist by the name of Richard Harding Davis, wrote that the German Army moved into the city as smoothly and compactly as an American train called the Empire State Express, but he very quickly came to witness an ugly undertone to the endless grey columns that marched past him.' Hour after hour passed and there was no halt, no breathing time, no open spaces in the ranks, the thing became uncanny, inhuman.'[2]

He noted the ghostly effect of the grey-green uniforms which saw the soldiers almost disappear against a background of grey cobbled streets and stone shop fronts. At a hundred yards it was difficult for him to see the cavalry passing under the trees below his window and the horses appeared to be without riders. Only the steady chant of the infantry song 'My Fatherland, My Fatherland' told of troop movements. At times 2,000 men were singing in unison with each line of the song separated by three steps. Then there were the large siege guns, with creaking wheels and clanking chains.

It was the infamous Schlieffen Plan in all its might. This was a strategy devised by General Alfred von Schlieffen for a war on two fronts and one that would quickly eliminate France prior to full Russian mobilisation by simply marching around the Alsace-Lorraine fortifications, through Belgium, and across the almost open Franco-Belgian border to Paris. A not entirely unrealistic objective given the cumbersome nature of the Russian war machine, and the backwardness of the Belgian Army which still commissioned dog-drawn machine-guns.

It failed, however, because Russia mobilised a lot quicker than expected and forced Germany to transfer soldiers to the east. The German High

Command also greatly underestimated the leadership of King Albert I of the Belgians who inspired a more than perfunctory defence of his kingdom. Like everyone else the generals in Berlin thought the king better suited to the Royal Academy of Letters, Art and Science than the Military Academy. As a young man he had trained in the armed forces and came third in his class when he graduated, but he did not take to 'square bashing'. On one occasion he had been ordered to march backwards and forwards once too often, and actually told the instructor to be quiet. The officer was furious but royal immunity protected him from arrest.

The American Minister recalled a court ball at which the king appeared in black evening dress amongst officers in brightly coloured uniforms, bedecked with gold lace and medals; a far cry from the hundred and one uniforms worn by his cousin the German kaiser. When Albert did wear uniform it was always the same, rather plain, outfit of a lieutenant general, and in khaki he looked very much the civilian called to arms. However, his image was to be transformed overnight when he rode on a charger to parliament to give a categoric 'no' to the German ultimatum demanding access to France through Belgian territory. Without question it was the most momentous occasion of his reign, and the finest detail was recorded for posterity, from his firm stride and clanking sword, to the pince-nez on the end of his nose. The world suddenly took notice as he declared, 'Everywhere, in Flanders and in Wallonia, in town and country, one thought alone fills our hearts – patriotism; one single vision fills our minds – our threatened independence; one duty alone steels our energy-obstinate resistance.'[3] Then to the rapturous applause of the deputies, and the cheering of the flag-waving people outside, he left to prepare for war.

Shortly afterwards the king went to army headquarters in a high speed motorcade, the officers in his suite resplendent in their bonnets commemorating independence from the Netherlands in 1830. Under Article 68 of the Constitution King Albert was obliged to assume total command of the armed forces in time of war. For years he had worked behind the scenes to strengthen the country's defences but the politicians, who controlled the military in time of peace, simply referred to the Franco-Prussian War when Belgian neutrality had been respected. Now Albert had to pick up the pieces and defend his kingdom the best he could. Liège was an example of what could have been. Perched high above the Meuse, it guarded against a German invasion, and was therefore of immense strategic value. In a moment of weakness, parliament had bowed to pressure from the Crown and in 1887 constructed a complex network of underground fortifications around the city. The domes for the gun turrets were the only visible signs above ground. A formidable obstacle, even in 1914, but by then the world of soldiering had passed the Belgians by and their outdated armour proved no match for the Big Bertha siege guns of the Germans.

The impact of the enormous 'Big Bertha' class guns upon an unsuspecting people, is described by the Infanta Eulalia of Spain, who found herself at the wrong end of the barrel whilst in Paris. In what she was to refer to as a 'curious illness of the war', the infanta wrote of the rush of air from the shells. 'Once, when I was driving to my dentist, a shell fell near by and the current of air was so strong that my hat was literally lifted off my head, the hat-pins were carried away like straws in the wind, and a piece of my hair was actually torn from my scalp.'[4]

The fortress held out for ten valuable days against overwhelming odds. When wave after wave of troops failed to capture it the Germans resorted to some bizarre schemes, including an attempt to kidnap Commandant Gerard Leman by a group of men masquerading as British troops. Finally, the siege guns were brought in to pound the Belgian garrison into submission, and although the Germans were to find General Leman unconscious under the rubble, the majority of his men had withdrawn to fight another day. Germany was therefore forced to weaken the attack on Paris so as to fight the Belgians on their flank. The German Army sought revenge on the civilian population and if Liège represented the valour of the Belgian people, then Louvain epitomised their agony, and the price of their glory. Louvain is a town steeped in history and until 1914 was one rich in architecture. To protect this valuable piece of heritage from cannon fire, the Belgian Army evacuated the town before the German forces arrived but this did not stop them burning the place to the ground and destroying the university with its world-famous library of manuscripts from the Middle Ages. They maintained that the burgomaster's son had shot a German general but the burgomaster had no son, and no general had disappeared from the battlefront.

It was a nightmare and one all too familiar elsewhere. The people of Andenne lost 211 people in retaliation for the Belgian Army blowing up the bridge over the Meuse. In Tamines, 384 townspeople died following resistance from the French Army. The same happened in Dinant where 665 people perished. A pattern soon developed whereby the Germans would enter a town peacefully enough. They would demand food and forage and then move on. Suddenly they would return with a vengeance destroying men and livestock, brick and mortar.

King Albert was greatly affected by the atrocities but the fortitude with which he faced one bloody deed after another was an inspiration to the most downtrodden of people. German efforts to lay the blame at the king's feet went unheeded and the loyalty of his people was shown in a concerted effort to beat the censor on the king's birthday. With all demonstrations of loyalty strictly forbidden, the gentlemen of Brussels decided to wear tall hats as a mark of respect and on the royal birthday the boulevards were unusually packed with men in tall hats. This was a mark of respect known to all but the German authorities, and an ingenuous display of solidarity rivalled only by the macaroni that appeared in shop windows the day Italy declared war on the Central Powers. One visitor to Belgian Headquarters oddly enough appealed to public imagination when he compared the king to a viking; the description of Albert with moustache grown long, a fixed sadness in his face and a steady flame in the eye was the romantic image now common to his name.

Public opinion was mirrored by the armed forces who appreciated the king's presence at the front. He had an even-handed approach to discipline and once when he came across an off-duty officer with his wife in an area she should not otherwise have been, the king chose to overlook the matter as the queen was also at the front. On the other hand he would not tolerate any slackness on duty and officers who led their men in retreat without authorisation were quickly court-martialled. Discipline was essential because the military outlook was bleak. The sheer might of the German war machine kept the Belgians on the defensive, apart from the odd sortie here and there. Although further stands were made at the fortresses of Namur and Antwerp, it was not long before the king's army found themselves with their backs to the sea. All that was left to them was a small stretch of land between the Yser Canal and the coast.

The Schlieffen Express came to rest in the mud of Flanders. Cannon fire only aggravated the conditions created by climate and terrain. In places the mud was reported to be nine feet deep and drowning in mud was a common occurrence. The Belgians helped defend the Yser by opening sluice gates and blocking drainage systems to flood the land occupied by the enemy. German agony was highlighted in letters home. One soldier told how he had to stand in water day and night, with survival dependent on the sandbags packed around his legs. There was no escaping the rising water line, for above the dugouts the gunfire rattled between the opposing trenches and it was not wise to put one's head above the parapets.

Whilst the army remained on Belgian soil there was hope for those under German occupation and many young men crossed the line to enlist. In scenes reminiscent of the best prisoner of war epics to adorn the cinema screens, many swam to freedom amid a hail of bullets, whilst others thrust hollow barrels through electric fencing and crawled to liberty. Around 34,000 men passed through the Netherlands in the first winter of the war; the lucky ones were to return four years later having served their king and country. The alternative was slave labour in Germany. On the pretext of relieving the economic hardships caused by the Entente blockade, the German authorities forcibly removed thousands of unemployed men to the Fatherland. There they were worked all hours of the day and were fed on a diet of acorns, black bread and turnip soup. When they were too weak, or ill, to work they were sent home in cattle trucks but many died on the way. Some of the labour camps in Germany were situated alongside Belgian prisoner of war camps and the soldiers did their best to smuggle their Red Cross parcels to the deportees.

Edith Cavell was an English nurse who had worked in Brussels since 1907 as Directress of the capital's very first nursing school, L'Ecole Belge d'Infirmières Diplômées, where Queen Elisabeth had once been treated for a broken arm.

At the outbreak of war, the expertise of the school was used to treat casualties from both military camps. Edith Cavell remained at her post despite the dangers that her presence in Belgium posed. The Germans appeared to have a particular hatred of the British. Brand Whitlock, the American Minister in Brussels, noted that despite all the terrible things that the Germans did to the Belgian and French people, there was not the intense and personal hatred that they held for the British.

Genuine concern was therefore expressed with the news of Nurse Cavell's arrest on 5 August 1915. She stood accused of hiding British and French soldiers in her house, and of helping Belgians of military age to escape to the Netherlands. This placed her in violation of paragraph 68 of the German Military Penal Code which carried the death sentence for anyone aiding the enemy.

The trial did little to allay fears, and when Nurse Cavell was brought before a military tribunal at 8.00am on the morning of the 7 October 1915, she was seated along with 34 other prisoners in a semi-circle which prevented them from communicating with their lawyers or seeing the witnesses for the prosecution. The proceedings were held in private and it was only afterwards that details of the trial emerged. Asked by the judge if she had helped British soldiers trapped behind enemy lines to reach the Netherlands after the battles of Mons and Charleroi, Nurse Cavell admitted that she had. They were English, and she would help her own. She then committed a fatal error which almost certainly condemned her to death. When a judge referred to the English being ungrateful, Edith Cavell bravely corrected him. 'The English are not ungrateful'. When asked how she knew this she innocently replied. 'Because some have written to me from England to thank me for my help'[5]. To help people to a neutral country was one thing but to help them back to a hostile country was an altogether more serious offence.

On 11 October Nurse Cavell was told that she had been sentenced to death. She was to be shot early the next morning. Nurse Cavell faced death with enormous fortitude. She did not regret her actions and was glad for the restful weeks in prison at the end of a busy life. It is said that she faced the firing squad without being bound or blindfolded. She was given royal recognition when King Albert visited her grave at the end of the war and later, when her body was taken home to Great Britain, Queen Alexandra attended the memorial service at Norwich Cathedral.

Amid the vast network of airfields, military barracks, ammunition dumps and hospitals on the Yser lived the king and queen. For the remainder of the war, home was a simple red brick villa on the sea front at La Panne. It was sparsely furnished, and deliberately so. To the queen's mind, to make it any more comfortable would have been to acknowledge it as anything but a temporary residence and that would never have done. Besides, like the king, she was too busy with the war, tending the wounded and comforting the dying. Queen Elisabeth was fully qualified to wear the uniform of an Ambulancière of the Red Cross. Her father Karl Theodore, Duke in Bavaria, was a leading eye specialist of his day, and Elisabeth had been associated with medicine from an early age, often accompanying the duke as he went about his work. The queen was therefore active in her leadership of the Belgian Red Cross, and her patronage played an important part in the advance of medicine, most notably in plastic surgery. It was certainly beneficial to have an influential patron, for when medical supplies ran low, it was not unknown for Queen Elisabeth to replenish stocks with a quick call to Harrods in London.

Together, King Albert and Queen Elisabeth exuded a calmness that belied the turbulence around them, and there is no better illustration of this than in the *Daily Mail*:

> It is All Saints Day; the time is 7.30 in the morning; the scene a narrow lane between the sand dunes by the side of a little brick church. The lane is quite empty when, around the corner, came a solitary couple walking side by side. It was the King of the Belgians and his Queen, walking to early mass at the little church. Thirty yards behind them followed a single officer, but except for that, a stranger would have detected no more of the artificial signs of kingship in the pair other than the husband was unusually young for a general.[6]

Normally, the public were treated to more daring exploits such as the time when the king joined the renowned Belgian pilot, Captain Jacquets, in a reconnaissance flight over the front line. Although it was reported that no enemy planes rose to challenge them, there was anti-aircraft fire to contend with. To King Albert it was perhaps no more of a risk than standing on the ground, as the royal family were often targets of enemy bombing raids, but here again the queen took it all in her stride, finding some of the bomb craters to have ideal acoustics for playing the violin.

The Entente bombing of Belgian towns in occupied territory was an issue that brought the king into conflict with his own side. Another was the spy mania that prompted the Entente to request the evacuation of entire communities in unoccupied territory. The king linked the two when he was in contact with the French commanders. 'These attacks irritate the people and encourage them to lend an ear to German agitators. The French troops should appear to everyone as the forces of liberation animated by an ideal of gallantry and generosity.'[7]

By far the most contentious issue was the command of the Belgian Army. When the French suggested that the king delegate command to one of his generals, it earned them a stinging rebuke. 'The sovereign, with the agreement of the government, intends to retain the command of the Belgian Army, whatever its strength. But, recognising the necessity for unity of action between the Allies, he would be happy if the Generalissimo should act with the Belgian Army in the same way as he does with the British Army and communicate directly with its chief.' When the British went a stage further and suggested that the Belgian Army be placed under their control, King Albert commented to General Nivelle. 'One sees quite well that small countries must beware of the big ones, even when the latter call themselves Allies !'[8]

Belgium consists of two regions, Flemish speaking Flanders to the north and the predominantly French speaking Wallonia in the south; two diverse regions united by the monarchy. It was therefore just as well that King Albert retained his command because Flemish unrest broke out in the army towards the end of the war and the king was called upon to restore order. French was the principal language of the service and this upset the Flemings who demanded equality, but the government was undecided on the matter viewing the unruly, yet non-violent, demonstrations as the work of frivolous intellectuals. The king, however, was anxious to retain a united front against the enemy, and with force ruled out to end the unrest, he turned to the politicians for a workable solution. Two Crown Council meetings failed to resolve the issue, so the king convened a third in which the ministers were given only a morning to make up their minds. The result was a Flemish speaking military academy for Flanders, along with a committee to promote and safeguard the use of the Flemish language in the Army.

King Albert was right to press for a quick solution because Germany had already attempted to play Fleming against Walloon by dividing the country into two administrative regions, one comprising the provinces of Antwerp, Limbourg, East and West Flanders, Brussels and Louvain, the second consisting of the Walloon provinces of Hainaut, Liège, Luxembourg, Namur and Nivelles. Each region was to have its own council, the first in Brussels and the second in Namur. A Flemish delegation went to Berlin where Chancellor Bethmann-Hollweg spoke of the similarities between the Flemish and German peoples ending with a call for unity between them. 'In the midst of a bloody struggle Germans and Flemish might remember that the bitter fight against the encroachments of the Latin race should lead them to the same end.'[9] For his part, the kaiser was prepared to lay 'the corner stone of the edifice of the Flemish national autonomy which the Flemish people were not able to conquer for themselves.' However, King Albert really had no cause for concern, because the majority of Flanders rejected the German overtures and waited for the day when they could negotiate a deal with their fellow countrymen, free from violence or intimidation.

King Albert I helped them regain their freedom and on 22 November 1918, Brussels resounded to another, altogether happier, parade. The royal family was home and the people cheered with wild enthusiasm as the king and queen rode on horseback at the head of the Belgian Army. With them was Prince Leopold of Belgium and Prince Albert of Great Britain. Both were to be king for the Second World War but fate ensured they were not to enjoy the close relationship that their fathers experienced.

References:
1, 3, 5 and 9. *Belgium Under the German Occupation*, Brand Whitlock.
2. *The Faber Book of Reportage.*
4. *Courts and Countries After the War*, the Infanta Eulalia of Spain.
6. *Albert the Brave, King of the Belgians*
7 and 8. *The War Diaries of Albert I, King of the Belgians*, General R. van Overstraeten.

CHAPTER FIVE. SPAIN

The King, the Washerwoman and the Nurse

King Alfonso XIII was known for his bravery under fire. Much publicity has been given to the bomb outrage at his wedding, in which Queen Victoria Eugenie's bridal gown was sprayed with the blood of attendants and horses killed in the blast, but less attention has been paid to another attempt upon his life which was made on 13 April 1913. The king had just attended a military parade and was riding back to the palace when a lone gunman emerged from the crowd and shot at him with a revolver. The king was unhurt but he did not retreat in face of the attack. Instead he rode at the would be assassin, who seized the bridle of the king's horse and fired a second shot which singed the king's glove and grazed the horse. With that King Alfonso used the horse to knock the man to the ground and a policeman disarmed the assailant. Although there was the possibility that the man had a colleague in the crowd, the king insisted on attending to his horse, and when he found only a superficial wound he returned to the saddle, reassuring the crowds that everything was alright. 'Señores, it is nothing. Viva España !'[1]

Fortunately he was not required to show his mettle on the battlefields of the First World War. Spain knew her military limitations following the loss of Cuba and the Philippines in the Spanish-American War of 1898, and was fully committed to maintaining her remaining colony in Morocco, which was under threat from an unfriendly native called Abd-El-Krim. Spain therefore remained neutral throughout the conflict, placing King Alfonso in an excellent position to help people such as the washerwoman from Gironde in France, whose husband was missing following the Battle of Charleroi in August 1914. She had therefore written to the King of Spain to ask if he could find out whether her husband was dead or alive. King Alfonso managed to trace the soldier to a prisoner of war camp in Germany, and was able to pass the good news on to the wife. The wider implications of the letter were not lost upon the king. Throughout Europe there existed a vast number of prisoners of war who were humiliated in defeat, bored in captivity, and separated by battle from their families. He therefore decided to work for their wellbeing, and despatched Spanish observers to 4,000 prison camps throughout Europe. The information they collated enabled King Alfonso to trace missing prisoners, pass mail in and out of the camps, lobby for the repatriation of the sick, and rescue the condemned from execution.

Entente press coverage stimulated considerable interest in his work, and 40 people were employed by the Palace to answer the enormous volume of mail received by the king. Their salaries, and the postage generated by the secretariat, was estimated to have cost Pts1,000,000 and this was paid for by King Alfonso from his personal wealth. Many of the replies were in his own hand, and the smallest detail did not escape his attention. When Sylviane Sartor, a little girl from Paris wrote to the king asking him to have her uncle transferred to Switzerland because he was dying of hunger in a prison camp and this was making her mother ill, he replied in his own hand asking for the uncle's details so that he might enquire whether the man could be moved to Switzerland. He also gave Patrick from Addlestone in Surrey the Spanish stamps he asked for when he wrote to thank the king for looking after British prisoners. In all, King Alfonso was to assist 8,000 British soldiers but the magnitude of his task can be gauged by the 122,000 French and Belgian troops that were also helped.

The king's ambassadors abroad were to all intents and purposes members of the secretariat. He involved them in the rescue of people who had been condemned to death and in this respect the Spanish Minister in Belgium, the Marquis de Villalobar was called upon to extricate Nurse Edith Cavell from the firing squad. It was midnight on 11 October 1915 before the death sentence on Nurse Cavell became common knowledge and the Marquis de Villalobar had but a few hours in which to save her.

He immediately went to see Baron von der Lancken-Wakenitz, head of the German Political Ministry in Brussels. The baron was at the theatre with his staff but at the insistence of the marquis he returned to the ministry where Villalobar put his case. She was not a spy and should not die like a spy. He agreed that she had acted against German interests, but she was a woman of charity who had cared for German soldiers. The baron accepted the arguments and made contact with the governor general, Colonel-General Baron von Bissing, but he refused a plea of clemency. At this point the Marquis de Villalobar cast aside diplomatic courtesy and in a raised voice made it abundantly clear to the baron he was bringing about another Louvain, another act that would serve no useful purpose other than to alienate world opinion. It made no difference and he left behind him a red faced Baron von der Lancken-Wakenitz. By now it was even too late for King Alfonso to make a personal appeal to Kaiser Wilhelm .

Edith Cavell was not the only person to help Entente soldiers escape, she was but one link in the chain. A variety of people had therefore stood trial alongside her including an architect, a school teacher, a pharmacist, and the Comtesse de Belleville who were also sentenced to death. The architect Philippe Baucq died alongside Nurse Cavell, but the other death sentences were delayed enabling King Alfonso to plead successfully with the kaiser for Comtesse de Belleville's sentence to be commuted to imprisonment, which of course meant until the occupation was over. The same might well have happened to Nurse Cavell had she not been rushed to the firing squad.

Almost two years to the day, the Entente's execution of a Dutch woman by the name of Margaretha Geertruida was not without recrimination, and had a Spanish twist to the tale. To the world at large she was known as Mata Hari, a renowned beauty who had been linked to Crown Prince Wilhelm of Germany. Other admirers were at the German ministry in Madrid, and she was in Spain when the French Secret Service intercepted a German message to say that their agent 'H21' was going to Paris with a cheque for Frs5,000. Shortly afterwards Mata Hari appeared in Paris with a cheque for that amount. She was arrested and stood trial accused of supplying Germany with information on French shipping, tank designs, and troop mutinies. For this she was paid Frs5,000. Mata Hari maintained that payment was for sexual favours and not for spying. Furthermore, the prosecution could not substantiate the allegations at the request of the defence. Nevertheless, the court found her guilty and sentenced her to death. A number of months passed before her execution and this allowed time for an unsuccessful plea for clemency to the President of France, whereupon on 15 October 1917, she was taken from her cell, given the customary drop of rum and shot.

In the autumn of 1917 King Alfonso telegraphed his representatives in London, Paris, Petrograd, Rome, Berlin, Vienna, Constantinople, Bucharest, Sofia and the Hague, instructing them to lobby for the transfer of tuberculosis sufferers from the prison camps to Switzerland before the winter set in.

Earlier that year, 9,000 Spanish cities, towns and villages petitioned King Alfonso XIII to accept the Grand Cross of the Order of Beneficence for his humanitarian work during the war. It placed the king in rather an awkward position because it meant that he would have to bestow the cross upon himself. He, nevertheless, accepted the honour but sought to share it with the Spanish people, addressing the following message to them:

> Accepting the Cross, I do so because the Spanish people desire it, and it is always my dearest wish to listen to their heart's desire. Yet it is not I who ought to wear this decoration, but Spain; the honour should be bestowed upon the Spanish flag. I therefore propose that this honour which you wish me to wear shall in future be borne upon the standard of the Regiment that bears my name. [The Alfonso XIII Infantry Regiment of Cazadores and Vitoria]. In this way my name, your thought for me, and Spain shall be ever united.[2]

Although Spain had escaped the carnage of world war, she was not to avoid the social upheaval of the interwar years, and in 1931 King Alfonso XIII and Spain parted company. He did not live to see the restoration of the monarchy in 1975, but there is something enduring about the Spanish Bourbons in life and death.

During the winter of 1920, King Alfonso went to the royal catacombs to see if it was true that the burial chamber possessed powers of preservation. This rather eerie mission was centred upon the remains of King Felipe II who died in 1598. His portrait was placed beside his coffin so as to compare his mortal remains with his living image. The coffin was then opened and to everyone's surprise the king's face was identical to the picture although his hair had grown very long.

References:
1 and 2. *Don Alfonso XIII*, HRH Princess Pilar of Bavaria and Major Desmond Chapman-Huston.

CHAPTER SIX. LUXEMBOURG

A Grand Duchess Meets Her Waterloo

Modern day Luxembourg was created at the Congress of Vienna in 1815. The Emperor Napoleon I had been defeated at the Battle of Waterloo, and his enemies, notably Great Britain, Prussia, Austria and Russia were anxious to check French power in the future. Luxembourg had over the years been a frontier post for the empires of Burgundy, Spain, Austria and France, and had grown into a formidable fortress on a par with Gibraltar, making it a much coveted prize within Europe. Cautious not to tip the balance of power in favour of any one nation, the Congress of Vienna gave control of the Luxembourg fortress to Prussia, but entrusted sovereignty to Holland, and for the next 75 years, the King of the Netherlands was also the Grand Duke of Luxembourg.

This arrangement worked well until France, under the Emperor Napoleon III, created further tension over control of the fortress. The Treaty of London in 1867, defused the situation with the removal of Prussian troops and the destruction of the fortress. Thereafter little interest was paid in Luxembourg. The Franco-Prussian War bypassed her borders and no objections were raised when in 1890 the Grand Duchy separated from the Netherlands and established an independent dynasty under a German prince, Duke Adolphe of Nassau-Weilburg. However, interest was renewed in Luxembourg when the Schlieffen Plan saw Germany occupy the Grand Duchy on 2 August 1914.

Grand Duke Adolphe had died in 1905, and after the short reign of his son Grand Duke Guillaume IV (1905-1912), the defence of Luxembourg fell to the twenty-year-old Grand Duchess Marie-Adelaide, whose inauguration had taken place on the 97th anniversary of the Battle of Waterloo. The Grand Duchess had sworn to observe the fifth article of the constitution which was to maintain national independence and safeguard individual liberty. At her disposal was a part-time army of 300 men, headed by a Major Van Dyck. At the first sign of the German army, he had placed himself on the main bridge leading into Luxembourg City, but as if to acknowledge the futility of armed resistance, he did not carry a firearm. His task was to confirm that the violation of territory was a mistake and to accept an apology. This was certainly the tone set by the Prime Minister M. Eyschen when he told parliament 'Prussian officers and soldiers today occupied the station of Ulflingen and have torn up rails on our territory. They belong apparently to the 69th Treves regiment. I can only infer that this is a mistake and await apologies.'[1] It was not, and Luxembourg was obliged to settle down under German rule.

This was not an entirely new experience for the Luxembourg people. They had at the intervention of the European Powers housed a Prussian Garrison from 1815 to 1867, and after the Prussian soldiers had left, there had remained strong economic ties which saw German control of the railway system in Luxembourg into the First World War. When their troops returned they simply had to put them onto a train which travelled into Luxembourg City with the blinds drawn. However, the Entente Powers felt that the Grand Duchy had taken to German occupation with all too much ease. They felt that this was certainly the case for the Grand Duchess whom the French Prime Minister M. Clemenceau dubbed 'la princesse Boche'. Marie-Adelaide was condemned for a string of offences which included receiving the German commandant at the time of the invasion, entertaining the kaiser to tea upon an impromptu visit to the Grand Duchy, attending her grandmother's funeral in Frankfurt and consenting to the engagement of her sister Princess Antonia to Crown Prince Rupprecht of Bavaria. The Grand Duchess was therefore in a very precarious position when Germany was beaten and the Entente Powers entered Luxembourg on 21 November 1918.

The initial encounter was not without success. The American Army was the first upon the scene and Grand Duchess Marie-Adelaide was invited by General Pershing to review his men from the palace balcony. To the Grand Duchess there was no distinction between the arrival of the American Army and that of the German Army, which had already left Luxembourg before the Entente arrival. 'They blame me for having received German generals who were already in the country as war occupants and against whom our little army was powerless, and now they would have me receive the Allied generals come into the Duchy who are practically in the same position in Luxembourg, viewed from the standpoint of our neutrality and our independence.'[2] However, it was soon to become clear that the Americans were far more sympathetic to Luxembourg than the French, who followed them in the next day. France was seriously considering the annexation of Luxembourg and when a delegation from Luxembourg went to Paris to establish economic ties they were left in no doubt that the Grand Duchess, the embodiment of national independence, should go.

The movement against the Grand Duchess was made easier by the political instability within Luxembourg. M. Eyschen had dominated politics for many years, and with little interference from the crown. Grand Duke Adolphe had been an elderly ruler who had come to the throne at the age of 73 and Grand Duke Guillaume had been a sick ruler who had rarely ventured from his bed. However, Grand Duchess Marie-Adelaide was young, in good health and deeply religious. The prime minister therefore came up against unforseen opposition when he placed before the Grand Duchess a parliamentary bill that would weaken the influence of the Church in education, and he died of a heart attack in 1915 whilst battling with his sovereign over policy. A number of her citizens blamed Marie-Adelaide for his sudden death, and saw her opposition as ingratitude for a man who had brought her family to Luxembourg. The debate at the end of the war reopened old wounds, and with no strong political leadership to emerge following his death the Grand Duchess was vulnerable to criticism, particularly from the left who were encouraged by the success of the bolsheviks in Russia.

To the more moderate politicians it was obvious that the dynasty guaranteed the independence of Luxembourg, and although they were prepared to sacrifice Grand Duchess Marie-Adelaide, they would fight to retain the dynasty. The next in line of succession was Princess Charlotte, but her engagement to Prince Felix of Bourbon-Parma caused problems. To the French she had repeated the mistake made by Princess Antonia because Prince Felix was the brother of Kaiserin Zita of Austria-Hungary. However, the Luxembourg government won grudging support when they pointed out that he was a Bourbon and not a Habsburg, and that in the war he had been stationed far from France on the Eastern Front. France was also reminded that although the dynasty was of recent German origin, Prussia had deposed Grand Duke Adolphe as the Duke of Nassau when he sided with Kaiser Franz-Josef in the Austro-Prussian War of 1866. A large petition from the Luxembourg people in favour of the dynasty provided for the accession of Princess Charlotte when Grand Duchess Marie-Adelaide abdicated on 15 January 1919.

A proclamation prepared by the outgoing Grand Duchess ended with the words 'May the Luxembourg people, with the aid of Divine Providence, advance towards a future of peace and prosperity; may they retain inviolate their national traditions and the immeasurable treasure of their independence.'[3] Grand Duchess Charlotte maintained the theme of prosperity and national unity when she spoke at her inauguration the next day. 'I understand this oath to mean that I place above all things the welfare of the people of Luxembourg, that I will live their life, partake both of their joys and of their sorrows, that I will work for and with Luxembourg....That from our united endeavours may come for our land a period of prosperity, of interior and exterior happiness.'[4] It was a number of months before her words were to become reality. France did not grant official recognition to Grand Duchess Charlotte despite her earlier assurances, and Belgium was also talking of annexation, a sentiment that had lain dormant since Belgium failed to take Luxembourg with her when she broke with the Netherlands in 1830. Europe was in suspense as to who would act first, and to everyone's surprise it was Luxembourg which broke the deadlock by holding a referendum on the independence of the country, and by implication the future of the dynasty.

All the options were laid before the Luxembourg people, and on 28 September 1919 the ballot paper gave them the following choices:

Retention of Grand Duchess Charlotte.
Retention of the Nassau-Weilburg dynasty with a new Grand Duchess.
Replacement of the existing dynasty with a new dynasty.
Introduction of a republic.
Union with France.
Union with Belgium.

Grand Duchess Charlotte won an overwhelming majority and France and Belgium were forced to back down before such a public display of national sentiment. This ensured the Grand Duchess would have a long and successful reign, which lasted 45 years.

References:

1, 2, 3 and 4. *Marie-Adelaide Grand Duchess of Luxembourg*, Edith O'Shaughnessy.

CHAPTER SEVEN. MONACO

War of Words

It has often been said that the Monagasque Army has more bandsmen than it does foot soldiers, and it is not surprising therefore that the Principality of Monaco has never widely featured in the journals of European warfare. However, a Grimaldi prince has always taken advantage of his younger, more cavalier days to display his martial prowess, before the restrictions of sovereignty befall him. In recent history the Princes Albert I, Louis II, and Rainier III, all fought under the French Tricolour to earn themselves the Legion of Honour in the Franco-Prussian War, and the First and Second World Wars respectively.

Neutrality was otherwise the order of the day but at the very outset of war in 1914, the House of Grimaldi was innocently drawn into the conflict. To begin with Prince Albert was a guest of Kaiser Wilhelm II at the Kiel Regatta, and was on board the Imperial Yacht when the launch pulled alongside with the momentous news of Archduke Franz-Ferdinand's assassination. He witnessed the gayness of the Edwardian era disappear as quickly as the colour from the kaiser's face, and at the same time, his own efforts to secure peace.

The Franco-Prussian War had taught the prince a lot and, when the already poor relationship between the two powers deteriorated even further towards the end of the nineteenth century, he actively sought to defuse the situation. His friendship with the kaiser and his close contact with the French government were to his advantage, and he endeavoured to mediate whenever a crisis came along, such as Morocco, but met with limited success. Aboard the kaiser's yacht he was under no illusion as to the significance of the telegram, or for that matter, the might of the German militarists. It is doubtful, however, that he envisaged the war of words that was to follow over the next few months.

Prince Albert owned a château in France that was requisitioned by the Duke of Württemberg for his headquarters. An advance guard took possession of the château pending the duke's arrival, and overnight set about emptying the wine cellar. The following day the duke appeared, only to find empty and broken bottles strewn along the drive in the path of his cavalry. The French blamed the drunken behaviour of his men, whilst the Germans interpreted it as an act of sabotage. The commune in which the château was situated was therefore ordered to pay the equivalent of £20,000 or face destruction.

Nevertheless, the Duke of Württemberg may well have been sensitive to the fact that the prince and the kaiser were friends because the initial order did not name the château :

September 19, 1914.
Quartier-General de L'Armée.

Monsieur le Maire, Commune de Sissonne.
It has been proved by evidence that the road leading from Sissonne to the next railway station, Montaigu, has been covered with broken glass at intervals of fifty metres on this 18th of September, which was undoubtably done to impede the move-ment of automobiles. I hold the Commune of Sissonne responsible for this hostile act by its inhabitants, and I punish it with a fine of 500,000f. This sum must be paid before the 15th October to the Treasury on this post. The Inspector of the Post, now at the village of Montcornet, is charged with the carrying out of this order.

(signed) General-in-Chief of the Army, von Bülow.

The Mayor had other ideas. The commune simply could not afford the entire amount and he attempted to contact the Prince of Monaco but was initially blocked by the Germans. On the 5 October 1914, General von Krupka wrote: 'The result of the Mayor's decision in council today to call upon HSH the Prince of Monaco for aid is not possible because of the conditions of the war. The fine must be found in the district.' Nevertheless, when the deadline expired without full payment, von Krupka put pen to paper again:

St Quentin,
October 15, 1914.

Monsieur le Maire,
The Commander-in-Chief of the Post allows a delegation of the Commune of Sissonne composed of two persons to go to Monaco with a view to obtaining from HSH the Prince of Monaco the sum required to cover the fine. The delegation must leave on the 16th of the month, will receive a pass, and by automobiles put at its disposal will reach a German railway station, from which it must leave at once by train and proceed through Switzerland without delay.

I am also ordered by his Excellency to tell you that the remaining part of the fine must be paid before November 1. The delegation is instructed to mention this decision to HSH the Prince of Monaco, adding that, if this sum is not paid, besides other acts the Château of the Prince and the Commune of Marchais will be demolished and burnt.

(signed) von Krupka.

Mission accomplished, the delegation returned with a letter from Prince Albert to General von Bülow:

Monaco,
October 22, 1914.

Monsieur le Général,
To avoid for the Commune of Sissonne and for that of Marchais the rigorous fate with which you have threatened them, I on my honour pledge myself to remit to HM the Emperor Wilhelm, if the war ends without intentional damage to my residence or to the two communes, the sum necessary to complete the 500,000f, which Sissonne is fined by you. As a Sovereign Prince I will treat with the Sovereign who during fifteen years called me his friend and made me a Knight of the Black Eagle. My conscience and my dignity bring me far beyond any feeling of fear and my energy will bring me beyond all regret, but if you destroy the Castle of Marchais, which is a centre of science interesting to the whole world and of charity – if you reserve for this jewel of archaeology and history the fate of the Cathedral of Reims without any hostile act against you on its part, the world will judge between you and me. I address to your Excellency the expression of my highest consideration.

(signed) Albert, Sovereign Prince of Monaco.

The prince proved equally forthright in a letter to the kaiser:

Monaco,
October 22, 1914.

I forward to your Majesty several documents concerning an affair very grave and urgent.

General von Bülow has occupied for a month and a half my residence of Marchais, situated five kilometres from the village of Sissonne. The General has fined 1500 inhabitants of this poor ruined village 500,000f, of which they are unable to pay more than a fourth part. Moreover, he sent me two delegates, bringing documents in which he threatens to destroy my residence and the village of Marchais, besides that of Sissonne, in case I would not take on my shoulders, and this before the end of October, the aforementioned sum. This is how a Prussian General acts towards a Sovereign Prince who was during forty years the friend of Germany and who has received from every country of the world tokens of respect and gratitude of his work.

I answered the demand of General von Bülow saying that I pledged myself on my honour to complete the said 500,000f, because I wish to prevent a horrible action, coldly accomplished, but as a Sovereign Prince I put this question before the judgement of the Emperor, declaring that the aforesaid sum will be paid when the Château de Marchais shall be freed from the risk of intentional destruction.

I am, with great respect, your Majesty, your devoted servant and cousin.

(signed) Albert, Sovereign Prince of Monaco.

The kaiser never replied but the château was not destroyed, and with the ultimate defeat of Germany, the Prince of Monaco was not required to pay the fine. Fortunately for a prince whose palace in Monte Carlo overlooked one of the most famous casinos in the world, he played a good hand and backed a winner.

References:
Quotations are taken from *King Edward, the Kaiser, and The War* by Edward Legge and verified by the Palace of Monaco.

CHAPTER EIGHT. GREAT BRITAIN

Changing the Guard at Buckingham Palace

A meeting of the Privy Council declared war with Germany on 4 August 1914. The king spoke of 'a terrible catastrophe' but few seemed to agree with him. As the Life Guards mobilised for war, vast crowds gathered outside Buckingham Palace in almost festive spirit. Time and time again the king and queen were called to the balcony, to which they responded on no less than three occasions, before the crowds finally stopped singing and dancing and went home at 1.30am. Few seemed to imagine the terrible onslaught to follow, and this included members of the royal family.

Princess Alexander of Teck was astounded by the enthusiasm of the public but was later to admit that, when her husband reported for duty, she like the other regimental wives, 'watched the men of Kitchener's Army marching about and training on Salisbury Plain. We were all very light-hearted. No one had the faintest idea what it all meant at the time, or any premonition of the tragedies in store for the troops or ourselves.'[1]

The death of Prince Maurice of Battenberg in action on 27 October 1914, only too quickly brought home the agony of war but in many respects his death merely served to remind the royal family of the rigours of battle. Maurice was a lieutenant in the 60th (King's Royal) Rifles, the very same regiment in which his cousin, Prince Christian Victor of Schleswig-Holstein, was serving when killed during the Boer War. Both were grandsons of Queen Victoria.

The younger generation of the royal family viewed the war with a sense of trepidation and excitement. Prince Albert, the future King George VI, was to write of the Battle of Jutland.

> At the commencement I was sitting on the top of a turret and had a very good view of the proceedings. I was up there during a lull, when a German ship started firing at us, and one salvo straddled us. We at once returned the fire. I was distinctly startled and jumped down the hole in the top like a shot rabbit! I didn't try the experiment again. The ship was in a fine state on the main deck. Inches of water sluicing about to prevent fires getting a hold on the deck. Most of the cabins were also flooded. The hands behaved splendidly, and all of them were in the best of spirits as their hearts desire had at last been granted, which was to be in action with the Germans... It was certainly a great experience to have been through.[2]

King George V was foremost a sailor, having seen active service with the Royal Navy from 1877 to 1892 but the war was to see few major engagements on the high seas and, although the king was not to forget the senior service and paid regular visits to the Grand Fleet, the slaughter on the Western Front naturally held his attention. Indeed, it troubled him not to live at the front like his allies the Tsar of Russia and the Kings of Belgium and Italy. His visits to the troops were generally confined to about a week but the king made the most of them and packed as much in as possible.

The first day of a visit to the Western Front in October 1915, saw the king visit an ammunition store, a general hospital, an Australian medical centre, and an Indian Convalescent Depot. Day two proved even more busy with an inspection of the Central Training Ground, a remount depot, a Canadian Base, a hospital for gas victims, and the Army Stores. On the third day there was a church parade, followed by lunch with the King and Queen of the Belgians. In the evening the king met with his generals. The next day he continued the diplomatic round with a visit from the president of the French Republic, which involved endless parades and medal presenting. The compliment was returned the day after when the king journeyed to the French lines, met the president and General Joffre, reviewed French colonial troops, and visited a communication trench.

Nothing was overlooked, from the kitchens and wash-houses of the Training Ground to the Ordnance Workshops of the Army Stores, where abandoned guns and boots found at the Front by the Salvage Corps were repaired and reissued. Nevertheless, things livened up somewhat when the king was with the French Army. Whilst visiting the trenches cannon fire could be heard overhead. At first the royal party thought it something of a show to make it more realistic but then the shots started to land a little too close for comfort!

Unfortunately, the perils of visiting the Front become only too clear when the king went to review the Royal Flying Corps at the end of his tour of inspection. It was normal for the king to travel along the ranks by car but on this occasion he was persuaded to ride on horseback, so that all on parade could see him. However, his mount was not used to a royal master and when the traditional three cheers for the king sounded, the horse reared and fell upon him. For the Prince of Wales, who was escorting his father, it was one of those moments that he would clearly remember for the rest of his life. 'I shall never forget the sight of the horse getting up and leaving my father still lying on the ground. For a few terrifying seconds I thought he was dead.' But then, to everyone's relief he opened his eyes, and in the words of his son, expressed 'indignant rage' amid the groans of pain.[3]

The king suffered a fractured pelvis and it was some days before he could be moved back to London by hospital train. However, before his departure King George received Sergeant Brooks from the Coldstream Guards aboard the train to award him the Victoria Cross. It had been the King's intention to decorate him on the very same parade ground where he had met his accident but it probably meant just as much, if not more, to Sergeant Brooks as he knelt at the King's hospital bed. The king could hardly raise himself from the pillow and the citation had to be read by an aide but he was determined to honour the man all the same.

The tragedy of war was not lost upon King George. Once when he attended a review of disabled ex-servicemen, that all too familiar stiff upper lip gave way as he watched men without sight, or without limbs attempt to parade before him. Upon inspection he turned to say a few words but they would not come. He could but salute and quickly turn away with tears in his eyes.

Earlier in the war the king had been involved in the question of a new medal for the Army to help bridge the gap between the Victoria Cross and less significant orders. The Secretary of State at the War Office, Lord Kitchener, established a committee to come up with the appropriate decoration, and the Military Cross was born but not without some problems. It was almost impossible to arrive at a ribbon that was not used either at home or abroad. In the end Lord Kitchener intervened in sheer exasperation and boldly declared, 'We'll have no nonsense... Plain[4] black and white, simple and dignified' but these were the colours of the Iron Cross! When it came to the time for the king to select a ribbon he remained locked away for half an hour with Lord Kitchener and a basket of ribbons, in the end plumping for a creation of Lady Ponsonby's, mauve on a white background.

To think that medals were the be-all and end-all to the king's war would be a mistake. He positively frowned on those who took to wearing stars on khaki, and in this respect the Prince of Wales was of the same opinion, particularly when it came to foreign orders and their presentation, which ran the risk of a firm embrace and a kiss on two cheeks. For the prince it had been an uphill struggle to get to the Front. When he eventually made it, he was attached to the staff of Sir John French, who commanded the British Expeditionary Force but it was a pen-pushing job surrounded by elderly generals of the Boer War. They liked their medals, whether in khaki or not, and they took him off to see Britain's allies, with the exchange of medals that came to characterise such visits. The Prince of Wales once wrote to King George V telling him of his depression with the continual rain. He was, however, in an office behind the lines, and although he desperately wanted to be in the thick of it, he knew how lucky he was to only have to contend with the rain hammering down on his tin roof. 'How thankful I am to think I am not moving forward tonight and am sitting back here in comfort, one does appreciate this comfort when one has been forward and seen what it's like in the lines now!! The nearest thing possible to hell whatever that is!!!'[5]

Fear for his safety was of obvious concern to both the palace and Whitehall but there was another risk that could not be ignored, that of capture. It was a point that the Prince of Wales had failed to appreciate when he made his now famous remark, 'What does it matter if I am killed, I have four brothers'. Lord Kitchener's response was unequivocal. 'If I were certain that you would be shot, I do not know if I should be right to restrain you. What I cannot permit is the chance, which exists until we have a settled line, of the enemy securing you as a prisoner.'[6] The nearest he ever came to participating in battle was from a distant trench where he acted as a spotter for a marksman, who had his sights trained on a breach in the German defences. Every time a head appeared the prince shouted 'fire', and although no one was hit, he knew he was pretty close because the Germans moved quickly enough.

Three of his brothers, the Princes Henry, George, and John were too young to enlist but as we have seen, Prince Albert did serve with the Royal Navy and participated in the Battle of Jutland, although a gastric illness ensured that this was his one glimpse of action on the high seas. Prolonged periods on sick leave did set a few malicious tongues wagging but he was soon to set the record straight when he joined the newly created Royal Air Force in 1918. A prince is used to more than one uniform and in a service made up of officers and men of the air services of both the Army and Royal Navy he did well, despite the need to adjust to new regulations and the different way of life experienced by all. Within a short time he had his own squadron at the RAF training school in St Leonard's-on-Sea. He was able to make France for the last month of the war to observe operations, although there was not the time for him to get his wings until after the conflict. Thereupon he became the first member of the royal family to learn to fly.

On the home front, the royal ladies were making a no less significant contribution towards the war effort, and there is a lovely story of the straight-laced Queen Mary visiting a London hospital. Passing through the maternity ward, the Queen's attention was drawn to a fair haired woman who in contrast had a baby with particularly dark hair. 'His father must have been very dark', remarked the queen, to which the mother replied, 'Sure Ma'am I don't know – he never took his hat off.'[7]

Hospital work was the wartime preoccupation of many a queen or princess, and none more so than for the king's cousin Princess Marie-Louise who ran a hospital in Bermondsey. There the princess would appear on the wards dressed as if she were going to a garden party at the palace, and dispense such homemade cures as white of raw egg in iced champagne, whisked to a stiff froth and served with oysters. In a less dramatic style Princess Louise, Duchess of Argyll, gave her full support to a Scottish hospital that provided servicemen with artificial limbs. It was only the second centre of its kind in the country, and the wooden limbs were made by a Clyde shipyard from willow trees – perhaps a worthy charity for a princess who was also an accomplished sculptor.

In four years, Princess Alexander of Teck was to spend only six weeks with her husband but she fully appreciated that her lot was far better than a great many service wives who were left with no income when their husbands enlisted. She therefore chaired the Sailors and Soldiers Families Association, and was involved in considerable fund raising to support the service families. Meanwhile, Princess Mary, the king's daughter, wished to show her appreciation to the troops. At the front the soldiers received just about enough from the government to buy some cigarettes and soap but little else. Under the circumstances, Princess Mary's Christmas boxes proved very popular. Every soldier received an embossed brass box with either tobacco and pipe, or for non-smokers, acid drops and a pencil case. The Indian troops received sugar candy and spice.

Feeding the troops was a demanding task, and back home factories worked very hard to keep up with the demand. Army biscuits were made in Preston, boots in Nottingham, cutlery in Sheffield, chocolate and cider in Norwich, tinned rations in Lowestoft, and jam in Histon. Indeed, the Home Front was very important to the war effort, and members of the royal family busied themselves with endless visits to the factories servicing the armed forces, including the munition centres. These could be found throughout the country from Dundee in the North to Bideford in the South-West. Many reflected the weaponry of modern warfare. For example, poison gas was produced in Runcorn, airships were built in Hawarden, barbed wire in Warrington, aeroplanes at Hendon, tanks in Lincoln, and submarine nets in London. Many of the weapons went abroad to other Entente countries. Nearly three billion bullets alone were exported to Belgium, France, Italy, Roumania, and Russia, along with rifles, grenades, mortar shells, machine guns, motor cycles, ambulances and aeroplanes.

There is no doubt that the monarchy responded well to the challenges of war but on the issue of its German ancestry it was extremely vulnerable. Two centuries may have passed since King George I arrived from Hanover without a word of English in his vocabulary but there were still people at court who spoke with German accents, and the war had ensured that anything remotely connected with the enemy had become totally alien to the British way of life; and this included the dachshund in the street. German parentage caused the removal of Prince Louis of Battenberg from the office of First Sea Lord. His sworn allegiance to the British Crown and his exemplary record in office could not save him in the face of a well orchestrated campaign of hate.

The king was powerless to help his first cousin but he refused to surrender reason to hysteria, and was astounded when the debate entered the saintly confines of Saint George's Chapel Windsor, and the Garter Banners of the German kaiser and such like had to be removed. Nevertheless, he could only mount a rearguard action as public opinion demanded change. The king was particularly stung by the reference in the *Daily Worker* to an 'alien and uninspiring court'. The king agreed that he might be uninspiring but was rather annoyed by being branded an alien. However, the newspaper was the mouthpiece for the British Communist Party and therefore prone to such radical views. Later, in 1917, the overthrow of the Tsar gave many a crowned head food for thought.

Having resigned himself to change, the king acted decisively and removed all German titles from court. The Royal House of Saxe-Coburg and Gotha disappeared and the Royal House of Windsor began its illustrious reign. But if it was a bitter pill for King George to swallow, it was even harder for others. Prince Alexander of Teck who became the Earl of Athlone considered the move to be petty camouflage. He was serving with the British Military Mission at the wartime headquarters of King Albert of the Belgians, a monarch whose country had suffered more than any other at the hands of the Germans but one who retained the royal name of Saxe-Coburg and Gotha. The former First Sea Lord, Prince Louis of Battenberg, who was staying with his son at the time, simply entered in the visitors' book, 'Arrived Prince Hyde.... departed Lord Jekyll'.

We therefore end the war as we started before the railings of Buckingham Palace. Peace had at last been declared and the king stood on the balcony before his loyal subjects. Amid the cheering a little boy perched high on his father's shoulders was heard to say 'Daddy, who's the funny man in the funny hat up there ? ' to which the father replied 't'ain't a funny man, t'ain't a funny hat, it is His Majesty the King'[8].

References:
1. *For My Grandchildren*, HRH Princess Alice, Countess of Athlone.
2 and 7. *Voices of the Great War*, Peter Vansittart.
3 and 5. *A King's Story*, HRH The Duke of Windsor.
4 and 6. *Recollections of Three Reigns*, Sir Frederick Ponsonby.
8. *My Memories of Six Reigns*, HH Princess Marie-Louise.

CHAPTER NINE. GREECE

Halt, Who Goes There, Friend or Foe?

Great Britain held the moral high ground when she entered the war in defence of Belgian neutrality, but there was nothing gallant in her subsequent treatment of neutral Greece. As with Germany and Belgium, Great Britain was to relegate the interests of a smaller nation in favour of military expediency, although British strategy lacked German brutality and its aim was to check German aggression. Nevertheless, the abuse of an historically friendly people played upon the national conscience and excuses were sought to justify the measures taken against Greece. They were to prove rather lame excuses, and in some instances downright lies, but the psychological stress of the war led people to see their worst enemies in their friends. Although it was the collective policy of the Entente Powers, and France was to be by far the greatest antagonist towards Greece, Great Britain did have the might to influence Entente policy, but she chose not to.

The pretext Great Britain used was the Serbo-Greek Treaty, and the failure of Greece to rally to the Serbian cause at the beginning of the war. A treaty existed between the signatories whereby if one were attacked by a third party, then the other would come to their defence. The treaty was concluded at the end of the Balkan Wars and the third party was generally assumed to mean Bulgaria. Serbia certainly did not offer assistance to Greece when in early 1914 she was in dispute with the Ottoman Empire over the possession of Greek islands, and when Austria-Hungary attacked Serbia, Greece saw no obligation to intervene, although she did provide military supplies to the Serbian Army. After Turkey entered the war on the side of Germany on 29 October 1914, the Entente Powers sought to take advantage of the deep-rooted rivalry between Athens and Constantinople to enlist Greek support. They nearly succeeded because the Greek high command did show an interest in the impending Dardanelles campaign and provided the Entente with their own plans for the invasion, but the Entente Powers chose to ignore their experience of Balkan warfare, and knowledge of the local terrain, which resulted in considerable carnage when the landings took place at Gallipoli on 25 April 1915.

Entente resistance to Greek participation in the Dardanelles stemmed from a condition set by Greece whereby the Entente Powers would respect her territorial integrity, and safeguard it at a future peace treaty. This condition was set because Greece knew very well that the Entente Powers were also courting Bulgaria and that Greek territory denied the Bulgarians during the Balkan Wars was being offered as an incentive. Serb territory was also under offer but with Serbia in alliance with the Entente Powers, and reliant upon their goodwill, she could do little to oppose the move. An independent and neutral Greece was a different matter. Nevertheless, there was a divergence of opinion in Greece that gave the Entente some hope because the prime minister, Eleutherios Venizelos, was willing to accept an unconditional entry into the war, whereas King Konstantinos I would only abandon neutrality under strict conditions that were not to the advantage of the Entente Powers. They therefore sought to support Venizelos at the expense of the king, who actually had widespread support in Greece for his stance.

Forgetting that King Konstantinos was Queen Alexandra's nephew and was on intimate terms with the British royal family, the Entente Powers paid close scrutiny to his German connections, and he was condemned before the world for being the kaiser's brother-in-law, and undergoing military training in the Prussian Guards' regiment which had led to the honorary rank of a German field marshal. This was carried out in the full knowledge that the king had from the very outset of war rejected a call from the kaiser to join forces with Germany. A British naval officer had discussed the original telegram on which the king had written 'nonsense' in response to the kaiser's plea. King Konstantinos bore no allegiance to Germany, although it would not be right to say that his military training did not influence his position because he knew the might of the German war machine and the limitations of his own military forces. 'We have not got what in Europe would be called a real army at all; it is rather like a militia, and with that it is not easy to fight against trained troops.'[1] This did not mean that neither he nor the Greek army lacked courage. In the First Balkan War they had successfully confronted the Turkish army, which had a religious zeal similar to the Japanese, whereby there was no fear of death, as to die for one's country was to guarantee paradise.

King Konstantinos was also tainted with German autocracy. Venizelos had resigned over Greek neutrality but was returned to office in the general election of June 1915. Although he had not overtly campaigned on a war ticket for fear of defeat, both he and the Entente ministers in Athens used his new mandate to bring the palace into line, but the king and the general staff would not move from the original position. Venizelos therefore accused the king of acting outside the constitution, and the situation was not helped when King Konstantinos fell ill with pneumonia and pleurisy. He was very ill from April to October. Two Austrian doctors of world authority, one a surgeon, the other a lung specialist, operated on the king but cocaine was used as an anaesthetic and this led to blood poisoning. For many weeks his life was in the balance and the enormous crowds that waited before the palace lent gravity to the situation, but the Entente simply accused the king of evading his responsibilities. Nevertheless, once out of immediate danger, but by no means recovered, the king did meet with Venizelos on a number of occasions but they could not overcome their differences and there was a further deterioration in his condition with the onset of influenza. Another operation was performed to reopen the wound and insert a pipe to drain excess fluid. It brought little sympathy from the Entente who unsuccessfully called for a regency with the obvious intention of manipulating the younger and less experienced crown prince.

The Greek constitution allowed the monarch some flexibility but King Konstantinos does not appear to have overstepped the mark, although the authoritarian myth persisted beyond his illness. It was known that the king believed that at time of war the politicians should leave the military operations to the generals, but this did not imply disrespect for democratic government despite the scurrilous campaign against him pursued by the politicians in the Entente capitals. Venizelos on the other hand breached the constitution when he invited Entente troops to Greece without the permission of parliament. The Serbian Treaty remained a useful propaganda weapon to the Entente and Greece had been forced to provide further reasons for not defending Serbia. One perfectly legitimate reason was that Serbia could not spare the 150,000 soldiers promised to Greece under the treaty. Venizelos therefore suggested to the king that the Entente Powers provide the force in place of Serbia, but King Konstantinos was sceptical as to whether or not the Entente could land sufficient forces in time to save Serbia and protect Greece from a backlash by the Central Powers. He therefore asked the prime minister to think again, but on 30 September 1915 he learnt that Entente troops were disembarking at Salonika. It led to another rift with the prime minister and Venizelos resigned for a second time.

The Central Powers did consolidate their position in Serbia before the Entente force was strong enough to move from Salonika. Germany and Bulgaria then reinforced their defences by taking possession of Greek fortresses near the Serbian border. The Greek soldiers abandoned the forts so as to avoid war with Germany, just as they had not opposed the Salonika landings for fear of war with Great Britain and France. The Entente Powers were, nevertheless, indignant that Greece had not opposed the enemy, and proceeded to exact revenge. One demand after another was made under the threat of naval bombardment. The Greek army was obliged to retire to the Peloponnesus beyond the reach of Entente forces, and pass war materials to the Entente. The Greek navy was forced to disarm its battleships and surrender its gunboats to the Entente. The merchant fleet was impounded. The Post Office and Telegraph services were commandeered, and even the king suffered the indignity of having his mail read. Finally, the Entente supported Venizelos when he declared an alternative government on the island of Corfu. The contempt that the Entente showed Greece knew no bounds, and the expression 'dirty Greeks' became common language.

The Entente Powers were able to intimidate Greece because after the second departure of Venizelos there was no effective government. Only the king exerted the authority to oppose the will of the Entente Powers, and they were implicated in a fire which very nearly killed him. The king's country retreat at Tatoi was surrounded by acres of pine forest which could easily catch fire at the height of summer. A serious fire broke out in the summer of 1916 which raged for 48 hours killing eighteen people and destroying two-thirds of the estate, including pavilions around the main house. The king narrowly escaped death but his ADC, who had been at his side, did not and was later identified by the rings on his fingers. Four men in a car had been seen acting suspiciously before the fire and it was widely believed that they were secret agents working for the Entente. There was no denying that the Entente had an extensive network of agents in Greece, but these agents were a pretty disreputable bunch, and it is likely that they were acting on their own initiative. Entente commanders on the ground certainly came to disregard their reports that Greece was a base for German submarines, even if these did inflame passions in the Entente capitals.

Following Roumania's declaration of war against the Central Powers on 27 August 1916, Greece once again attempted to negotiate entry to the Entente. Although the speedy defeat of Roumania was to justify Greek fears of belligerency, neutrality had failed to protect her territory and brought her to such a pitiful state that war now seemed the only way of restoring her fortunes. The Entente, however, had abandoned the king and rejected his advance out of hand. Venizelos was their man and to emphasise the point they presented the Athens government with a shopping list to equip the Venizelist army in Corfu. The list contained a demand for sixteen field batteries, sixteen mountain batteries, 40,000 rifles, 140 machine guns, considerable ammunition, and 50 motor vehicles. It proved one humiliation too many and the Athens government said no. The Entente responded with the usual gunboat diplomacy demanding release of the equipment by 1 December 1916, or troops would be landed in Athens to take the armaments. To their consternation they were obliged to follow through with their threat.

Pressure exerted by the Royal Army impacted upon the decision by the Athens government not to comply with the latest demand which the military considered unacceptable. Nevertheless, feelings ran high and King Konstantinos felt it necessary to visit the Athens garrison to ensure that when the Entente troops arrived, it was not his men who fired first. His enemies later used the visit as evidence that the king had inspired bloodshed, because when the Entente soldiers arrived someone fired a shot which sparked a day of fighting and left 93 dead and 280 people injured. Venizelos' agents were suspected of firing the first shot because the Royal Army was content merely to stand before Entente troops and block their access to strategic positions. Like the Royal Army, the Entente troops were under orders not to fire unless attacked. A number of shells fell in the palace gardens, one actually hit the palace near to the king's study where he was in urgent negotiations with the Entente ministers. A compromise agreement was reached whereby six artillery batteries were handed to the Entente, and with that the Entente ministers and troops withdrew from the capital.

Greece was not of course allowed to get away with openly defying the Entente Powers who introduced a blockade of ports which caused social deprivation. It was at this point that the Entente Powers insisted upon the transfer of the Royal Army to the Peloponnesus if Greece wanted to see the blockade lifted. As previously mentioned Greece complied with the demand, and even paraded the Royal Army in salute before the Entente flags but the blockade remained, and it was left to Queen Sophie's Patriotic League of Greek Women to fend off starvation with soup kitchens. The king and queen lived off carob-

beans, herbs, and black bread which was the daily diet of their subjects
king was to write to a friend 'I myself eat black bread; apparently it is im
sible to bake it well, and you find dirt in it'.[2] If the Entente aim was to in:
revolution they were to be sadly mistaken. The vast majority of Greek pe
would not renounce the king even if it promised them a good meal. Indeed,
day after Entente forces had been removed from Athens, the people took to
streets and purged the capital of Venizelist supporters.

The loyalty to King Konstantinos was still there when in June 1917,
Entente demanded his exile. The king chose to go rather than see his peo
suffer at Entente hands, but the Greeks thought otherwise, and besieged
palace, closely vetting everyone who went in and out. The king could o1
leave by deception, and as the attention of the crowd was drawn to the rear
the palace by the arrival of the royal motor cars, the royal family made
undignified dash from the front door. The plan very nearly failed when th
were spotted by the crowd and quickly surrounded. Forced into a tight huddl
the royal family slowly battled their way to the privacy of the royal gardens o
the opposite side of the road to the palace. Emotions were running high an
the police had to prevent a man shooting himself before them. 'Please let m
pass', said the king. 'It is for your own good. Let me do my duty'.[3] From Athen
King Konstantinos and Queen Sophie went to Tatoi, and from there to Oropos
where he set sail for Italy on 14 June 1917. Fishermen knelt and cried as the
yacht weighed anchor and sailed out to sea.

King Konstantinos was succeeded by his second son the 24-year-old
Prince Alexandros who wept throughout his hastily convened inauguration.
His elder brother, Crown Prince Giorgios, had also been rejected by the
Entente Powers because of his military education in Germany. This placed
Prince Alexandros in a very difficult position because the departure of King
Konstantinos heralded the return of Venizelos. He very quickly took Greece
into the Entente camp and put into the field an army that fought with some
distinction, but the price was very high, for he was to purge the military of
3,000 officers loyal to King Konstantinos, and similar action was taken against
parliament, the church and the judiciary. It did nothing to endear him to the
people. Similarly, it did little to reconcile him to the royal family, and before
long only King Alexandros remained in Greece. Court officials were also
replaced by those loyal to Venizelos. The new king had but one trusted
companion and that was Fritz his dog. He therefore fought to save the dog
when it was attacked by monkeys, but the king was bitten in the process. The
wounds became infected and after four weeks of intense pain he died on the
25 October 1920. His death caused the prime minister serious problems for
there was no obvious candidate to the throne other than King Konstantinos.
His only other son, Prince Pavlos would not accept the throne, and the issue
was still unresolved when Greece went to the polls on 14 November 1920, the
first general election since the Entente nations had returned Venizelos to
power. It resulted in the defeat of Venizelos who left the country under cover
of darkness.

The incoming government invited King Konstantinos back to Athens but he would not return unless it was the wish of the people and a plebiscite was arranged for 14 December 1920. In the meantime, Queen Mother Olga, the widow of King Giorgios I, became regent. Queen Olga was the only member of the royal family who was allowed back to Greece to be with King Alexandros in his illness, but did not arrive home until just after his death. Queen Olga was a Romanov and the outbreak of world war had found her trapped in Russia, where she remained until the revolution. This kept her apart from the bitter recriminations in Greece, although Venizelos did attempt to capitalise upon her popularity, when on the fourth anniversary of the capture of Salonika in September 1916, he had addressed an open telegram in which he remembered King Giorgios and the great achievements of his constitutional reign, then under threat. He therefore called upon the Queen Mother, an example of orthodox piety, to join in his prayers for the salvation of the country. Queen Olga could not bring herself to reply directly to Venizelos, and instead wired the Metropolitan of Salonika asking him to remind Venizelos that it was her son who had taken Salonika and that Greece would be better served if he remembered his oath of allegiance to King Konstantinos who was so disgracefully slandered.

King Konstantinos won the plebiscite by 1,013,734 votes to 10,383, but the victory was to be short lived. Although the world war was at an end, Greece was in armed conflict with Turkey over land in Asia Minor ceded to Venizelos by the Entente Powers. This had prompted a rebellion in Turkey, and a nationalist army led by Kemal Pasha was seeking to regain the territory in defiance of the Sultan who ruled at the behest of the Entente Powers. King Konstantinos was against the campaign in Asia Minor because Greece did not have the resources to maintain an Asiatic empire, and he knew that the Entente Powers were exhausted by war and in no position to provide effective support. He was also left in no doubt that he did not enjoy their support. At the time of the plebiscite, the Entente Powers had issued the following communiqué. 'Though they had no wish to interfere in the internal affairs of Greece, they felt bound to declare publicly that the restoration of the throne to a king whose disloyal attitude and conduct towards the Allies during the war had caused them great embarrassment and loss could only be regarded by them as a ratification by Greece of his hostile acts.'[4]

To withdraw from Asia Minor was far from easy. The fate of Greek prisoners who were murdered and in some cases skinned alive, did not bode well for the Greek communities that would be left behind. A diplomatic solution had to be found, and the king despatched his ministers to the Entente capitals, where they found hope in the first signs of disunity amongst the Allies. Great Britain was firmly committed to the sultanate, and had made favourable gains in Arabia, but France and Italy were not so loyal, and wanted an equal share of territory. Great Britain was therefore eager to broker a deal that would nip the Turkish rebellion in the bud and safeguard British interests. Discreet encouragement was given to the Greek campaign in Asia Minor, but

the initial success of the Royal Army against Kemal Pasha helped push France and Italy into an agreement with the rebel leader, and when they began to supply him with arms, the balance of power was to switch in Turkey's favour.

King Konstantinos was, however, allowed one last moment of glory when on 11 June 1921, a day after the birth of his nephew Prince Philippos, the future Duke of Edinburgh, he went to Asia Minor and received a rapturous welcome from his troops. A party of wounded soldiers aboard a hospital train were amongst the first to greet him. They were genuinely pleased to see him and, as he moved amongst them, so the soldiers who could walk got up and followed in his path their bandages trailing in the dust. The warmth of their reception was reflected throughout the front, culminating in a magnificent parade at Eski-Cheir. Twenty-four battle scarred standards were trooped before the king who later wrote of the parade. 'This took place near the battle-field, with troops that had only just returned, and when I saw the twenty-four standards, tattered and riddled with bullets, lowered in front of me for the salute, I felt a big lump in my throat. I tremble with emotion as I write this.'[5]

The Entente press did not waver in its opposition to the king, and portrayed the royal visit, indeed the war, as a carefully calculated plan by the king to consolidate his position at the expense of the Greek people. To the contrary, it was not widely known that Prime Minister Lloyd George had actually encouraged the Greek government to send the king to Asia Minor in the hope that his presence would inspire the military in battle. However, as Prince Nikolaos was to observe 'The internal inheritance bequeathed by Mr Venizelos was a Greece torn by internal strife and fierce hatreds'.[6] The army was no exception and when Turkey finally triumphed over Greece, a military coup on the island of Chios once again forced King Konstantinos from his throne. He abdicated on 27 September 1922. By then he was a dying man, a factor that further weakened his resistance to the coup, and he died in Italy on the 11 January 1923.

On this occasion, he was allowed to leave his eldest son behind, but the first reign of King Giorgios II was as unfortunate as that of his brother King Alexandros I. Kept as a virtual prisoner in his own palace, King Giorgios could not prevent the coup leaders from the summary execution of politicians and military leaders held responsible for the defeat. The former prime minister, Gounaris, was too ill to stand before his firing squad and was therefore strapped to a chair. The king's uncle, Prince Andreas, commanded the Twelfth Army in Asia Minor and he only escaped execution when King George V sent a British gunboat to rescue him. With him went his wife, daughters and young son Prince Philippos. Throughout the world war, King George V had been duty bound to support his government when confronted with the appeals of his first cousin King Konstantinos, going so far as to write:

> The Allied Powers have, from the outset, confined their demands
> to a benevolent neutrality. Unfortunately, this condition has not
> been observed. Not only have the proceedings of Your Majesty's

Government been open to grave objection, but the Allied Powers have received indubitable proof of action on the part of the Greek government, both damaging to their naval and military interests and of direct assistance to the enemy's forces.[7]

In private, however, he sympathised with King Konstantinos asking the prime minister Lloyd George 'Are we justified in interfering to this extent in the internal Government of a neutral and friendly country, even though we be one of the guarantors of its constitution? Are we acting up to our boasted position as the protector of smaller Powers?'

Surprisingly King Konstantinos never lost faith in Great Britain. 'If I only knew myself by what is written of me in the French and English newspapers, I should hate myself; but the British are the fairest minded people in the world, and when they are allowed to know the truth they will acquit me.'[8]

References:

1, 2 and 5. *A King's Private Letters*, Paola, Princess of Saxe-Weimar.
3, 4 and 6. *My Fifty Years*, HRH Prince Nicholas of Greece.
7 and 8. *King George V*, Harold Nicolson.

CHAPTER TEN. RUSSIA

Dynastic Rule

In contrast to King Konstantinos I, who was deprived of his throne for not declaring war, his cousin Tsar Nikolai II of Russia lost his crown by doing the very opposite and participating in the fight. Initially, albeit briefly, the war brought popular acclaim. Allusion to success was immediately made by focusing attention on the victory of 1812, when Emperor Napoleon I was defeated in his invasion of Russia. Tsar Aleksander I had won that victory after a pilgrimage to the ikon of the Virgin of Kazan, and so Tsar Nikolai II followed in his footsteps before travelling to Moscow and making a public appearance at the very spot from which Napoleon had watched the city burn. Meanwhile, the Bell of Ascension, which had been cast from the metal retrieved from the ashes, rang out in celebration.

The people warmed to the enactment of one of the greatest chapters in the annals of Russian military history with an enthusiasm that united gentry and peasantry alike. In the words of a bemused Mikhail Radzianko, the President of the Duma, 'The war has suddenly put an end to all our domestic strife. Throughout the Duma the one thought is of fighting Germany. The Russian people has not known such a wave of patriotism since 1812.'[1] Nikolai II had never been so popular, and when he made a balcony appearance at the Winter Palace in St Petersburg, the people crammed into the square below, fell to their knees and sang the national anthem 'God Save the Tsar'. It was a far cry from less happier days when demonstrators in front of the palace had been brought to their knees by a hail of bullets.

The positive response to the declaration of war reassured the tsar who disagreed with the general view that it would all be over by Christmas. He was preparing for a lengthy campaign that would not be won easily. The more serious minded of his ministers agreed, and it was for this reason that they opposed his wish to assume command of the army in the field. They argued that it would be wrong for him to put himself in a position where he could be personally accountable for military failure. By his own admission Tsar Nikolai was baffled by the question of supplies and provisions. He therefore appointed his uncle, the Grand Duke Nikolai Nikolaievich to be commander-in-chief and confined himself to frequent visits to the front. It was not, however, a situation he was content with. This is apparent from a letter the tsaritsa wrote to him at the time of his first tour of inspection:

> I am happy for you that you can at last manage to go, as I know how deeply you have been suffering all this time – your restless sleep had been proof of it – It was a topic I on purpose did not touch, knowing and perfectly understanding your feelings, at the same time realising that it is better you are not out at the head of the Army. The journey will be a tiny comfort.[2]

A special bond existed between Tsar Nikolai and his army, the origins of which went back to when he was a young officer in the Horse Guards, stationed at a garrison outside St Petersburg. It was the one occasion in his life when he could escape the inhibitions of court etiquette and participate in the mess room capers of his fellow compatriots. As a result, those days were to have a lasting effect, and although the imperial dignity would no longer survive being carried from the mess in a drunken stupor, it is evident from the following account that the tsar sent his wife that he could not have been happier than to return to regimental life:

> We lunched in two halls – one hundred and seventy men altogether. When we rose I spoke with every officer, which took an hour and a half but I did not mind that as it was most interesting to listen to their answers. At the end, I promoted them all, each to his next rank. The effect was tremendous.[3]

News arriving from the battlefields appeared to justify the decision to protect the tsar from any defeat. The invasion of East Prussia succeeded in relieving pressure on the western front but it met with an ignoble end. At Tannenberg, General Aleksander Samsonov committed suicide rather than join the 120,000 of his men taken prisoner, while General Paul Rennenkampf lost 10,000 men at the Battle of the Masurian Lakes. On the Galician Front, Russian successes could best be explained by a comparable show of mediocrity on the part of the Austro-Hungarian generals. The tsar was to make a victorious entry into Lemberg and sleep in a bed hitherto reserved for Kaiser Franz-Josef; but once the Germans helped consolidate the front it was a different matter, and throughout 1915 the Russians lost ground until even Poland was under the control of the Central Powers.

Curiously, the turn of events worked to the tsar's advantage. They presented him with a golden opportunity to come upon the scene as a knight in shining armour. The time was ripe for him to relieve Grand Duke Nikolai, and in September 1915, the tsar took up residence at Russian Army Headquarters. The dismissal of the grand duke was not the only change at the top. The Minister of War, General Vladimir Sukhomlinov was to be relieved of his post and imprisoned for the chronic munitions shortage which had plagued the war effort. He disliked Grand Duke Nikolai and is said to have withheld armaments out of sheer spite. Sukhomlinov therefore epitomised the rotten bureaucracy which was to claim first the grand duke, and then the tsar. It is revealing that only upon the intervention of the tsaritsa was a prohibition lifted on troops using the capital's tram system, even though the tsar had always considered it unjust.

Generally, the interference of Tsaritsa Alexandra Fedorovna was not so positive or welcome. Her presence could certainly be felt in the dismissal of the grand duke as commander-in-chief. She determined that her husband would play second fiddle to no one, and was therefore quick to plot the grand duke's humiliation. The situation was not helped by the demonstrations taking place in the now famous Red Square, in which the protesters demanded the abdication of the tsar, the internment of the tsaritsa, and the enthronement of Grand Duke Nikolai Nikolaievich. The tsar initially stood by his uncle in the wake of the tsaritsa's condemnation.

> I do not agree with you that Nikolasha ought to remain here (Army Headquarters) during my visit to Galicia. On the contrary, precisely because I am going in wartime to a conquered province, the Commander-in-Chief ought to accompany me. It is he who accompanies me, not I who am in his suite.[4]

Nevertheless, in the end the tsaritsa was to score a victory and the grand duke was packed off to command in the Caucasus in August 1915.

The tsaritsa had been born Princess Alix of Hesse-Darmstadt. The untimely death of her mother, Queen Victoria's third child Princess Alice, saw her brought up under the watchful eye of her English grandmother. Her upbringing was therefore at odds with her devotion to both orthodoxy and autocracy. In a message to the tsar she herself leaned more to a tsaritsa of the sixteenth century than one of the twentieth:

> How they all need to feel an iron will and hand – it has been a reign of gentleness and now must be the one of power and firmness – you are the lord and Master of Russia and God Almighty

placed you there and they shall bow down before your wisdom
and firmness, enough of kindness which they are not worthy of.[5]

Perhaps it bore relation to the life of virtual seclusion that she led at Tsarskoye Selo, surrounded by monuments to past glory. After all, it was with some justification that Tsaritsa Ekaterina II (1762–1796) wrote of her military successes. 'My garden at Tsarskoye Selo will soon look like a skittle alley; for at each brilliant stroke I get some monument erected.'[6] However, with the onset of war, Tsaritsa Alexandra did emerge to tend the wounded and during her daily visits to the hospital she undertook general surgical and sanitary duties. This was a side of her nature that few in the outside world came to appreciate, and one that was invariably misinterpreted. When she quashed an attempt by the Church to ban the Christmas tree because it originated in Germany, she was branded an enemy sympathiser, but as the tsaritsa was to comment. 'Why take away a pleasure from the wounded and the children because it originally came from Germany?'[7]

One achievement no one can deny her was the success of her marriage, and family life was an idyllic little world far removed from the harsh realities of the twentieth century. Only one shadow hung over the family home and that was the illness of the Tsarevich Alexis Nikolaievich. He was a haemophiliac and the slightest bruise or cut could lead to uncontrollable bleeding. It was therefore through a mother's love for her child that Grigory Rasputin came to manipulate the tsaritsa. He belonged to a religious sect called the Khlisty Staretz which did not form part of the established church. He came to prominence in 1912, when the tsarevich made an astounding recovery from what was given to be his death bed. His recovery came shortly after the tsaritsa received a cable from Rasputin in which he wrote that God had seen her tears and heard her prayers, so she was to grieve no more as her son would live. However, although Rasputin could apparently stop a bad case of bleeding he could not rid the tsarevich of his haemophilia and his services would be needed again. He therefore had a power base from which to wreak mayhem.

Rasputin was of dubious character with a liking for wine and women. The tsar was warned of his misdemeanours but chose to concentrate his mind on the war effort. However, the same ministers and generals who spoke of Rasputin were not quite so frank when it came to the stark realities of war. For instance whenever the tsar visited a regiment the troops were always smartened up and brought back behind the lines. The Russian army that lacked uniforms and equipment was never shown to Tsar Nikolai, and on one occasion when he visited Moscow, all the hospital trains were removed from the railway station regardless of the effect upon the wounded. However, the tsar did not lack interest in the common soldier. Before the war, he had refused to authorise the use of new equipment for the rank and file until he had personally put it through the rigours of an all day march.

At Army Headquarters, Tsar Nikolai cut a modest figure in his khaki uniform simply adorned with the Cross of St George and the epaulets of a colonel. The epaulets had been given to him by his father and were therefore of such sentimental value that he retained them upon his accession. A new arrival at headquarters would always receive a special welcome. To put him at ease the tsar would address him not by rank, or number, but by name, and then delve into that remarkable memory of his for some detail or other about the newcomer's regiment. The tutor to the tsarevich, Stanley Gibbs, recalled that despite of this he knew how to guard his dignity. 'One never dreamed of taking liberties; his presence was so quietly, naturally self possessed... His wonderful eyes of a most delicate blue looked you straight in the face with the kindest, tenderest expression.'[8]

The tsar's decision to install the Tsarevich Alexis at headquarters was a popular move. Like his father, he too possessed a charming personality and he immediately brought some light relief to the place. The British Attaché, Sir John Hanbury-Williams, captures one such moment:

> The Tsarevich is here and in good spirits. He dragged some of us off after lunch in the tent to a round fountain in the garden which has porpoise heads all around it, with two holes in each to represent eyes. The game was to plug up these holes with one's fingers, then turn on the fountain full split and suddenly let go. The result was that I nearly drowned the Emperor and his son, and they returned the compliment, and we all had to go back and change, laughing till we nearly cried, a childish amusement no doubt, but which did one good all the same.[9]

It has to be said that invariably the tsar's entourage came off the worse for his leisure pursuits. Walking was one of his favourite pastimes but the slippery roads took their toll. Within a matter of days one officer fell and bruised his nose and leg; another slipped and injured his ankle, while a third fell through some ice. It was therefore with some relief when the tsar retired to the hanging trapeze that was on board the imperial train.

The presence of Alexis Nikolaievich at his father's side was intended to strengthen morale in uncertain times. The tsar was under particular pressure to reconstruct the government in Petrograd, the new name for the German sounding St Petersburg. The state of the government was epitomised by Boris Sturmer who became President of the Council (prime minister) in June 1916. The French Ambassador could best describe him as being of 'third rate intellect, mean in spirit, low character and doubtful honesty.'[10] Rasputin was associated with his appointment. The tsar's correspondence to his wife reveals that he was not entirely blind to his meddling:

> Our friend's opinions of people are sometimes very strange, as you well know, therefore one must be careful, especially with appointments to high office.

Yet he always shied away from confrontation and would merely plead with his wife not to involve Rasputin.

> Only I beg you, do not drag our friend into this. The responsibility is with me, and therefore I wish to be free in my choice.[11]

This led to disquiet amongst the elite regiments closest to the monarchy. Their officers came from the aristocracy and were therefore best placed to follow events. However, the tsar failed to heed their warnings and only aggravated the situation by threatening to deprive them of their golden aiguillettes. He did, however, need their support now more than ever before. Casualties amongst the old guard, the traditional supporters of monarchy, were already running high and when the tsar visited the 1st Life Grenadier Ekaterinoslav Regiment, he could only find two colonels that he recognised.

In dealing with criticism the tsar was to show a distinction between the military and civilian populations. His language towards the society gossips was much stronger. Referring to the 'poisoned air of Petrograd' he was to comment. 'It isn't from the poor quarters but the drawing rooms that the worst smell comes! What a shame! What a disgrace! How can they be so devoid of conscience, patriotism and faith.'[12] It is unlikely he appreciated to what extent this included the imperial family. On a visit to his mother in the winter of 1916, he simply could not understand the coolness with which he was received by some of his relations, although he did notice that an ikon presented to the dowager tsaritsa was signed by all the family. Only his signature and that of his wife and children were missing.

The involvement of Grand Duke Dmitri Pavlovich in the murder of Rasputin certainly spoke of desperate times and was a damning indictment of the regime. The murder was masterminded by Prince Felix Yussoupov who came from one of the wealthiest and most noble families in Russia. It was to his palace in Petrograd that Rasputin was lured to his death. It was 17 December 1916, and in attendance were Prince Felix, Grand Duke Dmitri, and three other conspirators: the parliamentarian Purishkevich, an army officer called Sukhotin and a doctor called Lazovert. Once inside he was first poisoned, then shot, and his body dumped in the ice-bound Neva River. Before his death he had written to the tsar to say that should he be murdered by a Russian peasant, then the tsar would have no reason to fear his children and would reign for hundreds of years. However, should he ever die at the hands of a nobleman then the upper class would leave Russia and for twenty-five years there would be no nobles in the country. Furthermore, he went on to predict that if he were killed by a member of the imperial family, then the tsar's children and relations would survive him by only two years. He could not have spoken truer words.

On 15 March 1917, revolution forced the abdication of the tsar. With his departure from the throne peasants turned upon the landowners and seized their property. On 25 October 1917, the Bolsheviks took power and proceeded to murder members of the imperial family. The tsar and the tsar-itsa were shot alongside their children on 16 July 1918. It was a cruel death that the Soviet regime could never really justify. Aleksander Kerensky, who was to lead the provisional government following the overthrow of the monarchy, was to compare the tsar with the Bolsheviks. 'If he is compared with our modern bloodstained "friends of the people", it is clear that the former Tsar was a man by no means devoid of human feeling, whose nature was perverted by his surroundings and traditions.'[13]

Tsar Nikolai II was not, however, the last Emperor of Russia, for he had abdicated in favour of his brother Grand Duke Mikhail Alexandrovich whom the family acknowledged as Tsar Mikhail II. The two brothers had fallen out in recent years when Mikhail slipped abroad to secretly marry a divorcée by the name of Natalia Sheremetevsky. Tsar Nikolai had refused to recognise the union and decided that his brother should remain in exile. The outbreak of war brought about a reconciliation, and Mikhail returned home to command the Caucasian Cavalry Division in Galicia. He was soon mentioned in despatches and his brother decorated him with the prestigious Cross of St George. In a letter to his wife, dated 3 March 1915, the tsar wrote.

> Yesterday N. [Grand Duke Nikolai] brought me Ivanov's report about the splendid behaviour of Misha's [Grand Duke Mikhail's] division in the February fighting, when they were attacked in the Carpathians by two Austrian divisions. The Caucasians not only repelled the enemy, but actually attacked him, and were the first to enter Stanisavov, while Misha was the whole time in the line of fire.[14]

The Caucasian Cavalry Regiment was composed of ethnic minorities, and the success of his command may have indicated an ability to unite his multi-racial empire, but Tsar Mikhail II was not to be given the chance. The new provisional government asked to meet with him the day after his brother's abdication, but they were late for the audience, an unheard of occurrence in former times, which probably indicated their lukewarm support for him. Following lengthy deliberations between them, Mikhail authorised the last decree issued by the Romanovs, assigning his powers to the provisional government and he retired to his country estate, where the Bolsheviks eventually laid their hands upon him, transporting him to Perm and execution in isolated woodland. So ended the life of the last Tsar of all the Russias, the namesake of the very tsar who had founded the Romanov dynasty in 1613.

The fall of the Romanovs did not end the intrigue that was the hallmark of their last years. King Albert of the Belgians confided to his diary. 'What role have the English and French played in this tragedy? Their ambassadors have been very hasty in recognising the new government.' In London, politicians appeared to add credence to the king's suspicions by calling the first revolution a help to the Entente, whilst the press ran such headlines as 'Elimination of Tsaritsa kills hope for a separate peace in Russia'. In reality, the Entente Powers did not want the revolution, despite their fear for tsarist inefficiency, because they could not guarantee the commitment of a new government to the alliance.

The Entente were simply putting a brave face to a bad situation, and to endear themselves to the provisional government they very quickly disowned the Romanovs. King George V did send Tsar Nikolai II a message of sympathy but the provisional government took umbrage and it was never delivered to him. The British government therefore distanced itself from the old regime, and allowed the propagandists to attack tsarism until it was politically inappropriate for the king to honour his invitation for the tsar and his family to come to Great Britain. Entente endeavours failed to prevent the Bolshevik revolution. Lenin had ended his exile with a German rail ticket home, and he removed Russia from the war. The Treaty of Brest-Litovsk, signed on 3 March 1918, ended the fighting on the Eastern Front and allowed Germany to move her forces westwards applying further pressure to Great Britain and France.

References:
1 and 10. *An Ambassador's Memoirs*, Maurice Paleologue.
2, 5, and 7. *Letters of the Tsaritsa to the Tsar 1914-1916.*
3, 3, 4, 11, 12 and 14. *Letters of the Tsar to the Tsaritsa 1914-1917.*
6. *Catherine the Great*, John T. Alexander
8. *Tutor to the Tsarevich*, George Gibbs
9. *The Emperor Nicholas II, As I Knew Him*, Major General Sir John Hanbury-Williams.
13. *The Kerensky Memoirs*, Alexander Kerensky.

CHAPTER ELEVEN. ROUMANIA

Colonel of the 4th Rosiori Cavalry

The Russian Revolution prompted the fall of Roumania, fourteen months after she entered the war. The speed with which Roumania was defeated rekindled the controversy surrounding her entry into the war on the side of the Entente Powers. Her arrival on the battlefield had been delayed by serious internal divisions over which side to join. Roumania recognised the territorial gains that could be made at the expense of Austria-Hungary, but was held back by the traditional ties with Germany, which emanated from the Crown.

Prior to his accession in 1866, King Carol I of Roumania had been a Prince of Hohenzollern-Sigmaringen. Although he was to serve Roumania well, he was strongly influenced by his German background and he wanted to enter the war on the side of Germany, but his Roumanian-born subjects could see a golden opportunity to recapture the 'Greater Roumania' of a bygone age. This led to a deadlock between crown and people, because to achieve the

'Greater Roumania' would mean war with Austria-Hungary, and to fight Austria-Hungary would mean war with Germany. King Carol spoke of voluntary exile abroad, but the tension did not ease until his death on the 10 October 1914.

Being childless, King Carol was succeeded by his nephew who was also from the princely house of Hohenzollern-Sigmaringen. However, King Ferdinand had two saving graces. The first was that he was less of an autocrat than his uncle and he was soon to write to his brother in Germany: 'Although I am a member of the Hohenzollern family, I am the King of Roumania first and therefore I have to do what my subjects wish me to.'[1] The second was his marriage to the former Princess Marie of Edinburgh. A granddaughter of both Queen Victoria of Great Britain and Tsar Aleksander II of Russia, Queen Marie was firmly behind the Entente and she was to help lead her husband away from the Central Powers and into the arms of the Entente nations. The king did, however, move with extreme caution and it was not until the 27 August 1916 that he declared war on Austria-Hungary.

Queen Marie had a stronger personality than her husband and from the beginning she was to capture the public imagination. Maurice Paleologue, the French Ambassador to St Petersburg, was to make the following observation of the king and queen:

> By his calm and fearless energy, the King is keeping up the nation's courage and rallying everyone to the defence of the flag; gravely and without any sort of affectation, he is carrying out his professional duties splendidly as sovereign and leader... In the case of the Queen on the other hand, patriotism is taking the heroic form; there is a fiery and warmhearted ardour about her, an enthusiastic and chivalrous ardour, something of the sacred flame. So she has already become a figure of legend, for her proud and winning loveliness is the very incarnation of the soul of her people.'[2]

Two images exist of the queen during the war: the soldier queen upon her charger, resplendent in her uniform of the Colonel of the 4th Rosiori Cavalry Regiment, and the compassionate queen dressed in a simple Red Cross uniform. Both were to be needed in the face of the enemy and both were to make her a heroine of the day.

The queen was first apparent amongst the people of Bucharest as they suffered constant attack from the air. This was a totally alien form of warfare to the Roumanian people and the only early warning system they had were boy scouts running around the streets blowing whistles. The queen was to express the general sense of bewilderment when she witnessed one of the first raids. 'I saw something like a snow-white bird high up in the air, something that with outspread wings resembled the classical symbol of the Holy Ghost, and from that almost imperceptible speck of white in the shape of a dove, murder and disaster were hurled down upon innocent inhabitants peacefully walking in the streets !'³ Recollection of the carnage was to remain with the queen for the rest of her life. Being a young mother herself, one of the most harrowing scenes for the queen was that of a distraught mother with a child who had lost a leg in the bombing.

The king was faring little better at the front. Although he made initial advances into Transylvania the Central Powers were to counter-attack with a substantial force of Bulgars, Turks, and Germans. Led by two top German commanders, Field Marshal August von Mackensen and General Erich von Falkenhayn, they were quick to gain the upper hand. While Falkenhayn pushed the Roumanians out of Transylvania, Mackensen overcame the Danube defences within a day and joined his colleague in the march upon Bucharest. Unfortunately, not all of the Roumanian generals were of the same calibre as their German counterparts. One was to crack under the strain and forget where he had deployed his men. Another was to retreat in the face of enemy fire and for that he was marched onto the parade ground, publicly stripped of his rank, dressed in convict's clothes, and led off to five years hard labour. Bucharest was therefore in enemy hands by Christmas and the royal family and government were forced to flee to Jassy in the north of the country. Russian reinforcements could not help and all the British could do was send men in to destroy Roumania's rich oilfields to prevent them falling into enemy hands.

Shortly before the fall of Bucharest the king and queen lost their youngest son to typhoid fever. Prince Mircea was buried in the grounds of Cotroceni Palace. A little later when the queen left for Jassy, she was to leave the following note for whoever might occupy the palace. 'I do not know who will inhabit this house, a house that I have loved; the only prayer I ask is that they should not take away the flowers from the new little grave in the church.'⁴ During her son's illness, Queen Marie tore herself from his bedside to see her regiment off to war. The queen had become the Colonel of the 4th Rosiori Cavalry Regiment in 1897. It was to be the start of a very special relationship. Marie would participate in their riding lessons and every time they passed her residence they would announce their arrival with a special waltz and this would send their colonel scurrying out to review them. This close affinity was now to be extended to the entire army and Queen Marie was once to declare. 'O God, if only I were a man, with a man's rights and the spirit I have in my woman's body! I would fire them to desperate, glorious resistance.'⁵

The queen arrived in Jassy to utter chaos. The town was heavily over-populated and she was obliged to live on her train until a suitable house could be found for her. The housing shortage was a real problem. That winter was the coldest for a generation and with no shelter people were dropping dead in the streets. The ground was even too hard to bury them properly and disease was rife.

The king and queen's youngest daughter, Princess Ileana, would go into the streets with a thermos of tea and rum but she could only help the most needy. The queen concentrated on the hospitals. At one clearing station the wounded were white with what looked like dust but were in fact lice. Queen Marie soon put matters right and upon a second visit she could note with some satisfaction. 'It used to be one of the chief centres of infection, now it is perfection.' The queen was known to visit up to eight hospitals in a day.[6]

The winter months did at least see a lull in the fighting and this gave the authorities time to deal with the questions of homelessness, hunger and sickness. In this respect the Entente Powers were to come up trumps and British, Russian, and French medical teams poured into the country. Together they provided hospital treatment in the most inaccessible villages. Queen Marie would visit them all even when typhoid was raging. The doctors attempted to persuade her to take precautions and at least wear rubber gloves but she would have none of it. 'The soldiers all kiss my hand, and I really cannot ask them to kiss india rubber.'[7] Many of her visits were initially made in an open-top car which was no fun in the winter and in recognition of her services she was eventually presented with a hard-top Cadillac. Gone were the days when the queen would arrive at her destination with coats hanging down the side of her car for added protection against the wind and the rain.

The Russian Revolution came as a severe blow to Queen Marie. She was closely related to the imperial family and had a particular soft spot for her cousin Nicky. They had been very good to Roumania and train loads of supplies had been sent by Tsaritsa Alexandra Fedorovna, the Dowager Tsaritsa Marie Fedorovna, the Tsarevich Alexis and the queen's sister, Grand Duchess Kyrill. Now they were all dispossessed of their inheritance and living in peril of the mob. Nevertheless, the queen remained faithful to the old order. On a visit to one hospital she noticed that all the Russian soldiers had turned their St George medals around so that the Tsar's head was facing inwards. Smiling and looking them straight in the eye, she walked beside their beds turning their medals the correct way up.

It was a brave move because with the spread of Bolshevik propaganda the Russian troops within Roumania began to pose a more serious threat than the enemy, and none more so than to the safety of King Ferdinand and Queen Marie. The revolution came in the middle of a Roumanian offensive in which Russian support was crucial to success but the Russian soldiers initially dragged their heels and then went into full retreat. To counteract Bolshevik meddling within the Roumanian Army, King Ferdinand announced land reform for after the war and Queen Marie wrote articles of encouragement in newspapers that were distributed at the front. She also made a secret trip to the trenches and so close did she come to the enemy that an aide shouting in German to a trench nearby received a reply.

Although the king and queen were to retain the unity and support of the army, it was impossible to continue the fight without the Russians, and on 9 December 1917, Roumania agreed to an armistice. The mere thought of it sickened Queen Marie but for all her tears, and gallant little outbursts of defiance there was nothing she could do to alter the course of events. There was talk in Berlin of replacing King Ferdinand with Prince Joachim of Prussia but it came to nothing. When the kaiser made a triumphant visit to Roumania he laid a wreath at the tomb of loyal King Carol but he did not visit King Ferdinand and Queen Marie. He had already struck Ferdinand's name from the Hohenzollern family and the family acted as if Ferdinand was dead.

Nevertheless, the king and queen were confronted with a dynastic crisis. Their eldest son, the Crown Prince Carol, took advantage of the armistice to elope with his lover Ioana Lambrino. Aided and abetted by the occupation powers, he married her in Odessa on 31 August 1918. The constitution expressly forbade the heir to the throne to marry anyone other than a royal princess. Furthermore, in going to Odessa he was absent without leave from the Army. The prince was to return home but in parliament there were calls for him to abdicate his rights of succession and the monarchy visibly shook under the strain. The king overcame the problem by sentencing him to two and a half months imprisonment for desertion and promptly packed him off to a monastery. There the confused prince was persuaded to annul the marriage and thus overcome the constitutional difficulties.

Unfortunately, for the monarchy it was not to be the last occasion that Prince Carol was to put pleasure before duty, but in the short term happier days were in sight. The war ended on 11 November 1918, and Roumania received Bessarabia, Bucovina and Transylvania from the now defunct Austro-Hungarian Empire. This went some way to the creation of a 'Greater Roumania' but in many respects the queen was to lament the passing of the old order. Amid the euphoria at the abdication of Kaiser Wilhelm II she alone was to express regret:

> Kaiser Wilhelm and the Crown Prince have abdicated. It seems impossible. Proud cousin Bill! I cannot say I like it!' demurred the Queen. 'Kaiser Wilhelm tried to destroy us, but I did not want to see him destroyed. I wanted to see him beaten: yes, that I passionately desired because he wished to have this country wiped off the face of the earth. For us he represented a brutal, a merciless tyranny... But honestly I do not like to hear of his abdication. It hurts me somehow.[8]

These are remarkable sentiments when you consider what the Central Powers did to Roumania, but their behaviour vindicated the stance taken by King Ferdinand and Queen Marie, securing their positions in the hearts of the people. Unfortunately for Roumania, neither of them were alive to safeguard Roumania in the Second World War. Queen Marie outlived her husband by eleven years, and died on 19 July 1938, a great loss to Roumania.

References:

1. *The Last Great Romantic*, Hannah Pakula.
2. *An Ambassador's Memoirs*, Maurice Paleologue.
3, 4, 5, 6, 7 and 8. *The Story of My Life*, Queen Marie of Roumania.

CHAPTER TWELVE. GERMANY

The Beast of Berlin

There is evidence that just before the fighting began Kaiser Wilhelm II attempted to pull back from the fray; but to his enemies his military bravado of prewar years pronounced his guilt, and once swords had been drawn, the moral conduct of the Second Reich left much to be desired. At the Battle of Longwy in August 1914, Crown Prince Wilhelm was prepared to grant the French commander his freedom if he would undertake never to fight Germany again, an act of chivalry of the type that was soon to perish in the quest for ultimate victory.

Attitudes were further hardened by the propaganda campaign levelled against the German kaiser. An accurate representation of the campaign was a caricature that appeared in the British magazine *Punch* which expanded upon the myth that corpses were being used by the kaiser to make soap, and duly presented Wilhelm standing before a chemical plant telling a young recruit: 'And don't forget your Kaiser will find a use for you – alive or dead.'[1] It was this monster image that proved so effective and which prompted church congregations in America to scream for Kaiser Wilhelm to be boiled alive in oil. To the American press he was quite simply the Beast of Berlin.

The extent to which Entente propaganda vilified the kaiser was further illustrated by the French newspaper *Le Matin*. In a masterly piece of deception the newspaper took an innocent photograph of the kaiser in conversation with Crown Prince Wilhelm, and gave it far more sinister connotations by transforming it into a picture of them brawling. The original showed the prince smoking a cigar which he held across his chest away from his father's face. In the reproduced version, the cigar is missing which inferred that he was about to strike his father; and just to set the scene their faces were distorted to show anger. This was a photograph designed to show that even the crown prince hated his father.

Amid the cries of retribution came an almost lone voice of sympathy. The Scottish author John Buchan, in his wartime novel *Greenmantle* sought to portray the kaiser very much the victim of the monster he himself had created. The principal character in the novel is Sir Richard Hannay, a British secret agent, who gets to see the kaiser behind enemy lines. Stumm is a Prussian officer in the mould of Entente propaganda:

> The last I saw of him (the Kaiser) was a figure moving like a sleep-walker, with no spring in his step, amid his tall suite. I felt that I was looking on at a far bigger tragedy than any I had seen in action. Here was one that had loosed hell and the furies of hell had got hold of him. He was no common man, for in his presence I felt an attraction which was not merely the mastery of one used

Right: Kaiser Wilhelm II of Germany and King George V of Great Britain each wearing the uniform of the other's army – a photograph taken at the wedding of the Duke and Duchess of Brunswick in 1913. When the two countries went to war the following year, a caption was added: 'Times Change and We With Time.'

Below: A pre-war photograph of a visit by the King and Queen of Saxony to Kaiser Franz-Josef of Austria-Hungary. The kaiser stands before the royal visitors, while behind them can be seen Archduke Franz-Ferdinand (far left) in the plumed hat and next to him Archduke Karl. When Karl became emperor he attempted to negotiate peace with the Entente but the Germans got to hear about it and Austria-Hungary became a satellite state like Saxony.

Left: King Petar I of Serbia was 70 years of age when the First World War broke out, but that did not stop him from taking his rifle and joining his men in the trenches.

Right: King Albert of the Belgians with his daughter Princess Marie-Jose, the future Queen of Italy. Albert proved an able commander but he always looked like the civilian called to arms.

Above: Queen Elisabeth of the Belgians visits the ruins of Ypres.

Right: King Alfonso XIII of Spain. Through his example, Spain worked to help prisoners of war but failed to save Nurse Edith Cavell from the firing squad.

Left: The young Grand Duchess Marie-Adelaide of Luxembourg was forced by the Entente to abdicate when she failed to resist German occupation with her part-time army.

Left: The Grand Duchess Charlotte of Luxembourg at her wedding to Prince Felix of Bourbon-Parma.

Above: King George V of Great Britain visiting a munitions factory somewhere in England.

Right: Prince Albert as a midshipman aboard HMS *Collingwood*.

Above: The Prince of Wales with fellow recruits to the Grenadier Guards.

Left: King Konstantinos I of the Hellenes rides out in military fashion.

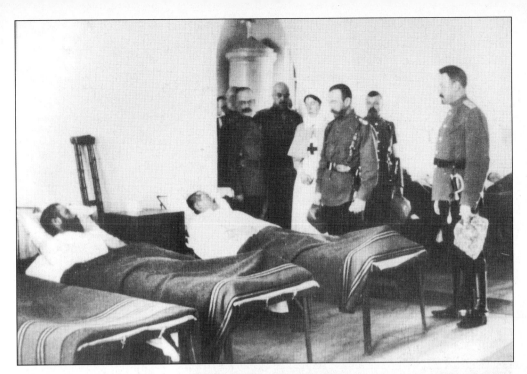

Above: Tsar Nikolai II of Russia visiting the sick. The nurse beside him is his sister, the Grand Duchess Olga.

Right: A photograph of the Tsarevich Alexis which was mass-produced and sold by *his* mother to raise money for the war effort.

Left: Queen Marie of Roumania, Colonel of the 4th Rosiori Cavalry.

Left: Kaiser Karl and Kaiserin Zita at their coronation in Budapest towards the end of 1916 – a familiar portrait but one that tells of Habsburg splendour. With his parents is Crown Prince Otto who is now a member of the European Parliament.

Above: Exile did not deter Kaiser Wilhelm II and his family from wearing their old imperial uniforms. Here he can be seen at the wedding in 1938 of his grandson, Prince Louis Ferdinand, to the Grand Duchess Kira of Russia. With the kaiser stand the groom's mother, Crown Princess Cecile (left), Princess Liegnitz, Wilhelm's second wife, and the Crown Prince Wilhelm.

Right: King Vittorio Emanuele III of Italy, a popular monarch in the First World War who fell from public esteem in the second.

Left: King Umberto II and Queen Marie-Jose of Italy. They are known as the 'May King and Queen' after the month in which they ruled Italy in 1946.

Below: The Norwegian royal family upon their return to Oslo in 1945. In this photograph are the three modern kings of Norway. From left to right: King Haakon VII, King Harald V and King Olav V.

Right: Count Folke Bernadotte of Sweden. The nephew of King Gustaf V who saved Jewish people from German concentration camps but was later killed in Palestine. (By kind permission of the Bernadotte Library, Stockholm.)

Right: King Christian X of Denmark standing between his two sons, Prince Knud to his left and the future King Frederik IX to his right. When the Danes were ordered by the Germans to surrender eight torpedo boats in the Second World War, they did so with their flags at half mast.

Left: King Leopold III of the Belgians (farthest from the camera) united on parade with his brother, Prince Charles. The Second World War was to divide them and, while Leopold was kept outside his kingdom, Charles was appointed prince regent.

Left: Queen Wilhelmina of the Netherlands at the time of her abdication in 1948. By then, the Queen had exchanged the tin hat, which she wore to escape Nazi paratroopers, for more regal attire.

Right: King George VI of Great Britain in jovial mood for this visit to the Royal Air Force. The war was actually to place the king under considerable strain and contributed to his untimely death in 1952.

Below: The Princess Elizabeth signs on at the Labour Exchange. As Queen Elizabeth II she was to preside over the 50th anniversary commemorations of VE and VJ Day in 1995.

Above: King George VI, Queen Elizabeth, and the Princesses Elizabeth and Margaret Rose attend Crathie Church on the Balmoral estate in Scotland. Their faith was of great strength in the war.

Below: Prince Paul of Yugoslavia with his family. Although a victim of circumstance, he only narrowly escaped being put on trial at Nuremberg.

Above and below: All boys like to play soldiers but, unlike King Petar II of Yugoslavia and King Mihai of Roumania, few grow up to be commander-in-chief.

Right: The Bulgarian royal family before King Boris III met a mysterious death in 1943. The little boy on his mother's knee is the exiled King Simeon II, who is not without his supporters in post-communist Bulgaria, as demonstrated by his warm welcome when he visited Sofia in May 1996.

Right: King Pavlos of the Hellenes in relaxed mood with his son, the future King Konstantinos II.

to command. That would not have impressed me, for I had never owned a master. But here was a human being who, unlike Stumm and his kind, had the power of laying himself alongside other men. This was the irony of it. Stumm would not have cared a tinker's cuss for all the massacres in history. But this man, the chief of a nation of Stumms, paid the price of war for the gifts that had made him successful in peace. He had imagination and nerves, and the one was white hot and the others were quivering. I would not have been in his shoes for the throne of the universe.[2]

Our perception of the kaiser is further clouded by his erratic temperament. In one breath he would call for no prisoners to be taken, and in another berate his officers for their poor treatment of the wounded. One moment he would be full of bloodcurdling stories about violet blue slopes 'blue with the coats of dead Frenchmen'[3], the next he would tour the fields after battle had been done covering the faces of those who had fallen. In reality the war was to play havoc with this highly strung man. At times it seemed positively to haunt him. He had a dream of his English and Russian relatives and all his ministers and generals marching past and mocking him. In the dream only the little Queen of Norway had been friendly to him.

This may well account for how he came to live in the shadow of his generals, particularly with the emergence of the Hindenburg-Ludendorff partnership, whose power base was such that they could displace the German Chancellor Theobold von Bethmann Hollweg. Kaiser Wilhelm was nearer the truth than most imagine when he said to Prince Max of Baden. 'The General Staff tells me nothing and never asks my advice. If people in Germany think I am the Supreme Commander they are grossly mistaken. I drink tea, saw wood and go for walks which please the gentlemen.'[4] To an aide he protested that he was only Hindenburg's adjutant, a remarkable statement from a man who had proclaimed himself the 'All-Highest'[5]. Field Marshal Hindenburg preferred to look upon their relationship in a different light. 'The Kaiser's great trust in us made a special royal approval unnecessary except in vital questions.'[6]

It was widely rumoured in Germany, that the kaiser was overlooked altogether when he attempted to stop the use of a poison gas successfully tested on goats wearing British gasmasks. It is difficult to imagine that he could have been ignored on such an emotive issue but his reluctance for the more controversial methods of war is recorded by Admiral Georg von Müller, who was attached to the kaiser's staff at General Headquarters. Admiral von Müller was to record in his diary a meeting with the kaiser on the subject of unrestricted submarine warfare :

His Majesty took the humane standpoint that the drowning of innocent passengers was an idea that appalled him. He also bore a responsibility before God for the manner of waging a war. On the other hand he must ask himself could he go against the counsel of his military advisers, and from humane considerations prolong the war at the cost of so many brave men who were defending their Fatherland?[7]

The authenticity of the account should not be doubted. Although a loyal servant of the crown, von Müller was no spell-bound courtier. By his own admission, and to his disappointment, the war had shown the kaiser in an altogether different light. Unrestricted submarine warfare was introduced with the blessing of the German people, and all manner of corporations sent messages of support to the kaiser, who was soon to answer his critics that in London 'they can't get potatoes for love or money'[8]. Yet when the war finally exhausted food stocks in Germany public opinion was quick to change.

The men and women in the street came to exist upon a daily diet of black bread, barley soup and vegetables. Restaurants attempted to relieve the monotony with stewed toadstools and porridge, whilst the authorities advertised alternative food such as crows, ravens, and daws but only after having first been soaked in camomile tea to remove their fishy taste. However, even such a rarity as smoked walrus could prove no substitute for the traditional fatty foods. In contrast to the suffering at home, when King Ferdinand of Bulgaria visited German Headquarters he was entertained to no less than five banquets, something that found Kaiser Wilhelm increasingly at odds with a people suffering from the deprivations at war. In fact, to the German people the kaiser became a remote figurehead. Throughout the war he lived near the Western Front and rarely journeyed to Berlin. The civilian population therefore began to think of life without him, and when the substitute foods began to run out they began to listen to the revolutionaries.

Contemptuous of protest, Kaiser Wilhelm II once declared that he held the final decree, and that was the revolver, but when workers' and soldiers' revolutionary councils began to appear at the end of October 1918, he could not rely on the armed forces to restore order. In part this was because the High Seas Fleet was instrumental in the breakout of revolution. The sailors heard rumours that the fleet was to be sent into action in a last bid attempt to win the war, and rather than face almost certain death, they turned on their officers and took control of the Naval Base at Kiel. In most major cities, a Marxist army called the Spartacus Union moved onto the streets. The Germans had played a significant part in bringing Lenin to power in Russia. It was they who had smuggled him back into Russia on the understanding that he would take the country out of the war enabling them to switch troops to the Western Front. The subsequent Treaty of Brest Litovsk, signed between Russia and Germany in March 1918, imposed humiliating terms upon the Bolshevik government. Lenin lost 1,300,000 miles of his new found empire, including Poland, Finland, and the Baltic states of Latvia, Lithuania, and Estonia. It was therefore with satisfaction that he saw the Marxist revolution unfold in Germany.

The German chancellor, Prince Max of Baden, was sufficiently shaken by the Marxist uprising to announce the kaiser's abdication. Having little to say in the matter, the kaiser crossed the Dutch border on the morning of 10 November 1918. Queen Wilhelmina was quick to grant him political asylum and that afternoon he was drinking an English cup of tea as the guest of Count Godard Bentinck at Amerongen. Shaken by events, he could only look on as the socialist leader, Friedrich Ebert, took power and declared Germany a republic. An armistice was signed and the war ended on 11 November 1918.

Five years to the day after Archduke Franz Ferdinand was assassinated, on 28 June 1919, Germany signed an humiliating peace treaty at Versailles. Ebert was to be derided for ratifying the treaty but with the use of flame-throwing mercenaries he saved Germany from Marxism, although his private army did in later years give Adolf Hitler the pretext for his storm-troopers.

Kaiser Wilhelm faced an uncertain future. The Treaty of Versailles allowed for him to be tried by the Entente Powers for crimes against international morality and there was at least one attempt by a group of American officers to kidnap him from the safety of Amerongen. However, they were acting without the authority of their superiors and all were to serve a prison sentence in America for their impromptu action. Nevertheless, they came very close to the kaiser. They managed to get inside Amerongen and it took Count Godard to explain to them the error of their ways whilst a detachment of Dutch troops was summoned to the house. Queen Wilhelmina of the Netherlands was very protective of the kaiser and this enabled him to spend the rest of his life in the Dutch countryside, where in 1920 he bought the manor house of Doorn and with the permission of the German government furnished it with items from his palace at Potsdam.

This ended the uncertainty of a return home. By allowing the kaiser to transfer his personal possessions to Doorn, President Ebert was making it abundantly clear that he was not welcome back in Germany. Certain events were to keep his hopes alive. When his wife, the Kaiserin Augusta Viktoria died in 1921, the government did not prevent her from being buried in Potsdam, nor impede the thousands of people who went to pay their last respects. Although the kaiser was not allowed to attend the funeral in Germany, his children were at liberty within the Republic. Furthermore, when Field Marshal Hindenburg became the state president in 1925, the kaiser must have hoped that a reassessment of his wartime leadership might lead to a reconciliation with his people. However, the severity of the Treaty of Versailles did not aid his cause.

The treaty forced Germany to pay war reparations for Entente property destroyed by German forces on land, sea and in the air. In the case of the high seas this involved the loss of merchant shipping to German submarines. The final bill came to a staggering 132 billion gold marks to be paid by instalments. The German economy therefore had little opportunity to recover from the war, and this clause of the treaty did nothing to enhance the living conditions of the German people. Hunger and deprivation remained. Further humiliation was inflicted with the loss of Alsace Lorraine and the port of Danzig, the demilitarisation of the Rhineland, the transfer of the Saar coalfields to the newly created League of Nations, and the loss of the Sudetenland to Czechoslovakia. The kaiser's much cherished colonial empire was also confiscated along with the German merchant navy. The military clauses forced the closure of the all war academies and cadet schools. The army was to be restricted to a small defensive force, with no offensive weapons such as tanks and aeroplanes. The navy was restricted to small warships and no submarines. Attempts were made to confiscate the High Seas Fleet but the Germans sent it to the bottom of the ocean before the Entente could take possession.

The German people deeply resented the treaty but the Weimar Republic, so named after the first national assembly there in 1919, had little option other than to sign the treaty. It did, however, win few friends for agreeing to Entente demands, and when a former corporal in the Bavarian Army came forward and publicly denounced the treaty he won considerable support throughout the country. His name was Adolf Hitler and he took the Nazi party to power in January 1933. Crown Prince Wilhelm was certainly won over, and when Eberhard Makowski, a leading storm trooper was shot and killed during a parade to celebrate Hitler's rise to power, the prince attended the funeral in the uniform of a Death's Head Hussar. It was not long before he too was seen in storm trooper uniform but his initial enthusiasm for the regime was to be displaced. Although Hitler became chancellor, and later, head of state through constitutional means, he quickly moved to dismantle all democratic institutions including the Reichstag which he burnt to the ground.

The storm troopers were instrumental in the repression of democracy. It was they who broke up opposition rallies, destroyed printing presses, and generally abused people who did not fit into the new order. Anti-semitism demonstrated the true nature of the regime but with his private army, and an effective propaganda machine, Hitler was to reign supreme. He was equally ruthless with his opponents in the Nazi party, and in what became known as the Night of the Long Knives he ordered the summary execution of Nazi leaders, the most notorious being Captain Rohm, the storm trooper chief of staff.

The loss of civil liberties was softened by a meteoric rise in living standards. Hitler put people back to work and put money back into their pockets. He built an extensive network of autobahns, the forerunner to the British motorway, and augmented towns and cities with a housing programme that won admiration abroad and brought the Duke and Duchess of Windsor to Germany in 1937. However, whilst German industry showed off to the world the 'peoples car', the VW Beetle, there was greater discretion shown with the tanks and aircraft that were also coming off the production lines in direct contravention of the Treaty of Versailles.

Initially Hitler was very discreet about his plans for the armed forces. A move towards conscription was pre-empted by the introduction of a course on defence sport. Training took place which involved the study of eagles in flight and through that the basics of gliding. Cross country works would in essence be lessons in marching and studies of the landscape would provide opportunities for battle drill. Hitler had a similar movement in mind for the formation of an air force, and this was called the Air Sport Federation. However, within two years his faithful storm troopers presented him with 27 fighter aircraft to mark his 46th birthday in 1935.

The rebuilding of his military machine, along with international apathy, allowed Hitler to move against the Treaty of Versailles, and he was soon to reclaim German territory under foreign control. He was also in a position to recover territory in Europe that had been denied to the German people in 1919. A union with Austria had won support with both these German-speaking nations but had been vetoed by the victorious Entente Powers. Therefore in 1938, fifth columnists brought Hitler to power in Austria and another old score was settled.

Kaiser Wilhelm II kept his views on the annexation of Austria to himself, preferring to concentrate on the arrangements for the marriage of his grandson Prince Louis Ferdinand to the Grand Duchess Kira of Russia. His final will and testament made his feelings known about the Nazi movement. If Hitler was in power when he died, then he was not to be buried in Berlin but at his beloved Doorn. He did, however, make one fundamental error before his death in 1941, and that was to send Adolf Hitler his congratulations on the fall of Paris in 1940. It only served to open old wounds and ensure that following the Second World War even Doorn did not remain a safe haven for the Hohenzollerns when it was requisitioned by the Dutch.

Hitler had now moved to the conquest of Europe, and the supremacy of power denied to Germany in the First World War. Amongst the countries that his troops were to invade and occupy were the kingdoms of Norway, Denmark, the Netherlands, Belgium, Greece, and Yugoslavia. The First World War had shed Europe of some pretty powerful monarchies, and the life expectancy of those remaining was now held in the balance.

References:
1. *Spreading Germs of Hate*, G. S. Viereck.
2. *Greenmantle*, John Buchan.
3, 4, 5 and 7. *The Kaiser and his Court*, Admiral Georg von Müller.
6. *Out of My Life*, Paul von Hindenburg .

CHAPTER THIRTEEN. AUSTRIA-HUNGARY

The Emperor's Last Waltz

Before we move to the Second World War, let us take one last look at the Habsburg Monarchy, because with the accession of a new emperor it was to the fore of peace moves, which is appropriate when it is remembered that it was Kaiser Franz Josef of Austria-Hungary, whose war with Serbia had set the world ablaze. Despite this, he did not suffer the international condemnation that was levelled against Kaiser Wilhelm II of Germany. Indeed, he was looked upon not so much as a warmongering despot but the victim of unscrupulous forces. Perhaps it was to his advantage that having signed the fateful declaration of war, he was to spend the last two years of his life in virtual seclusion. When he did finally emerge from the Hofburg Palace it was to his last resting place on the 30 November 1916. *The Times* wrote:

> The direct responsibility of Francis Joseph for this criminal policy cannot be ascertained. Age probably rendered him incapable of resisting pressure which in earlier years he might have had the strength to withstand. Rather than upon him, responsibility falls upon the German Emperor, the German military party, and their accomplices in Austria, and particularly in Hungary.[1]

A noticeable absentee from the funeral was Kaiser Wilhelm II. The official explanation was that the Austrian imperial family should be left alone in their grief but this was naturally received with some scepticism. The real reason was the threat of assassination but even this met with doubt, although it was not an entirely unreasonable supposition given that only the month before the Austrian Chancellor, Count Sturgkh, had died at the hand of an assassin, and it was the very excuse used by Franz Josef to keep Wilhelm away from the funeral of Archduke Franz Ferdinand back in 1914.

Kaiser Wilhelm did visit Vienna to attend the lying in state, and in the stillness of the Hofburg Chapel, he knelt in prayer beside Franz Josef's successor, Kaiser Karl I. However, the tranquillity of that moment, and the closeness of the sovereigns, was never really to be achieved again. Austria now had a young kaiser who had seen active service at the front and the misery of war at first hand. He was therefore determined to bring peace to his people, but his efforts to end the war brought him into conflict with his German ally. Throughout his short reign he made several moves to reach an understanding with the Entente, the most renowned of which has gone down in history as the Sixtus Affair. As the obituary for Franz Josef in *The Times* indicated, the Austro-Hungarian empire was looked upon sympathetically in both Paris and London, either as an important player in postwar Europe, or as a means of dividing the Central Powers. The French had already made peace overtures to Kaiser Franz Josef, and Kaiser Karl was quick to encourage further dialogue.

To assist him he enlisted the help of his brothers-in-law, the Princes Sixtus and Xavier of Bourbon Parma, who were serving with the Belgian Army. It was a classic example of dynastic diplomacy and one that was to be used throughout the war. France had used the Duc de Guise to woo his cousin King Ferdinand of Bulgaria. Germany used Count Toring to approach his brother-in-law King Albert of the Belgians, and the Grand Duke of Hesse to mediate with his brother-in-law, Tsar Nikolai II of Russia. Under the cover of darkness, and with the use of a side door at the Castle of Laxenburg in Austria, the Princes Sixtus and Xavier would meet Kaiser Karl and then journey to London and Paris. As they were Bourbon princes they had direct access to Buckingham Palace, and although members of the French royal family were barred from serving in the French Army, they also had access to the Elysée Palace. The Sixtus Affair was by far the most promising of all the peace initiatives, and saw Kaiser Karl commit himself in writing to the restoration of Serbian sovereignty, and the cession of Austro-Hungarian territory to Italy. He also went so far as to support demands for the German restoration of Belgian sovereignty, and the return to France of Alsace-Lorraine.

Alsace-Lorraine lay on the Franco-German border, and had been taken from France when Kaiser Wilhelm I defeated the Emperor Napoleon III in 1871. The issue had soured relations between the two countries ever since. Kaiser Karl had ancestral links with Alsace-Lorraine and had visited the province in prewar years. He knew that the hearts and minds of the Alsatian people were at one with France, and to compensate the Germans for the loss of the province he was prepared to give Germany outright control in Poland. However, this magnanimous gesture failed to secure peace, and there were many reasons for this.

Firstly, fortunes of war saw both sides take a step back whenever the fighting was in their favour. Secondly, to secure Italy as an ally, the Entente powers had offered her far more territory than Kaiser Karl could concede with honour, and Italy was not prepared to settle for anything less than she had been promised. Thirdly, Germany was committed to ultimate victory and would not listen to an Austrian peace plan. On a visit to German Headquarters, Kaiser Karl found it almost impossible to get Kaiser Wilhelm on his own, and had to resort to writing messages to him on menu cards.

Certainly, the Germans failed to take the matter seriously until a new government in Paris, that was less sympathetic to the Habsburg monarchy, published Kaiser Karl's correspondence on the Sixtus Affair. It sent shock waves through the German High Command and, at a hastily arranged conference Austria-Hungary was brow-beaten into mixing her regiments with those from Germany, thus making it impossible for Kaiser Karl to withdraw his army from the field and sue for a separate peace.

It did not, however, stop him from speaking out against the German High Command, and he refused to support the policy of unrestricted submarine warfare. His wife, the Kaiserin Zita was no less defiant, and there is a story that she upset Admiral von Holtzendorff, the head of a German naval delegation to Vienna, at a luncheon party at the Hofburg in 1917. The aim of unrestricted submarine warfare was also to target merchant shipping and cut off raw material supplies to Great Britain. The admiral would not accept the kaiserin's assertion that this would cause senseless suffering, and when he said that he worked best on an empty stomach she simply looked at the food before him and said: 'That should be easy enough, since admirals always manage to sit at a well spread table.'[2]

The transportation of Lenin to Russia was also opposed by the Austrian kaiser. To his mind once bolshevism took hold in Russia it would quickly spread to Germany and Austria-Hungary, and he could not afford to let that happen. The status quo was already under considerable strain from the ethnic minority groups that made up the Austro-Hungarian Empire. They wanted greater autonomy within the empire which the kaiser was prepared to give them but he did not have the time to create a federal empire whilst the war lasted. However, the more the ethnic groups contributed to the war effort, the more justified they felt in pressing home their demands for autonomy. Therefore when France and Italy officially recognised the emigré Czechoslovak National Council, and formed Czechoslovak legions of ex-prisoners of war to fight their former masters, the road to ruin was well established. When in desperation Kaiser Karl declared a federal empire in October 1918, the different nationalities could see a better future in an Entente victory.

The loss of the Empire brought down the Habsburg monarchy, and after releasing everyone from their allegiance to the crown, the kaiser retired with his family to the royal hunting lodge at Eckartsau. However, he refused to abdicate and the threat of armed revolutionaries eventually forced the family to move to Switzerland. Nevertheless, at 31 years of age he resisted premature retirement and made two abortive attempts to regain his Hungarian crown. To his misfortune, a former naval officer who had once sworn allegiance to the kaiser, and who now acted as his regent in Budapest, stood in his way. Admiral Horthy was determined to preserve his new found status and helped ensure that Kaiser Karl would not end his days in Hungary but on the Portuguese island of Madeira where he died on 1 April 1922.

Both restoration bids met with failure because Kaiser Karl would not risk bloodshed. In the first attempt he left Switzerland in a third class railway carriage disguised as a Portuguese labourer. Once in Hungary he secured limited support from the military and, given the element of surprise, he might have taken Budapest by force. Instead he went to the capital with one aide, and in an interview with Horthy he sought to regain power by persuasion. It was a brave yet naive move. He was alone in what turned out to be hostile territory, and when the regent refused to step aside as the kaiser expected, he was forced to leave the country under guard. He did, however, only leave Hungary when he received a written assurance from Horthy that his followers would not be persecuted. Entente pressure helped stiffen Horthy's resolve as there was a genuine threat to Hungary if Karl was restored to the throne.

He, nevertheless, was back in October 1921. This time he was accompanied by Kaiserin Zita, and they flew together in a hired aeroplane, their maiden flight. Once again they gathered loyal troops around them, and not wishing to make the same mistake as before, they went to Budapest with a trainload of troops. At one stage, Karl and Zita were seated on the locomotive footplate. However, Horthy had tightened security since the last royal visit, and to Karl's horror fighting broke out, resulting in the defeat of the royalist force. This time he did not get to see Horthy but the message was clear, and

Kaiser Karl was escorted from Hungary for a second time. Ironically, the people gave him a very warm welcome, but they were to have no say in the matter. Furthermore, on this occasion his supporters suffered retribution which deterred royalist activities in the future.

Despite his youth, Kaiser Karl was not a well man. During the First World War he had suffered a mild heart attack and, following the first restoration bid in Hungary, he had contracted lung problems which gave him a constant cough. After his premature death the Entente were left wondering whether they had really done enough for a monarch whose primary aim in the war had been to bring peace to Europe.

The fall of the monarchy therefore left a power vacuum that was to be filled by mediocre dictators such as Miklos Horthy in Budapest and Engelbert Dollfuss in Vienna. Both rulers were ultimately to lose power to Adolf Hitler. Whilst Horthy was to survive for 24 years Dollfuss, who had modelled his dictatorship on the Italian style, was assassinated within two years of coming to power, and the Austrian government was infiltrated by Nazi sympathisers. Pressure was brought to bear upon the authorities for a unification of the two German-speaking nations, and when Chancellor Kurt Schuschnigg tried to outwit the Germans with a plebiscite on Austrian independence, he was deposed by a Nazi coup d'etat in 1938. Thereafter, Austria was part of the Nazi war machine as Hitler embarked on the annexation of Czechoslovakia and the conquest of Europe.

The call by Chancellor Schuschnigg for a plebiscite, and the Nazi reaction to it, suggested that Hitler did not have the support of all the Austrian people; but the rapturous reception afforded Adolf Hitler when he visited Vienna did nothing to enhance the Austrian cause. Indeed, the Second World War was to haunt the country into the 1980s when controversy over President Waldheim's wartime activities brought diplomatic isolation. Events might have been quite different with a monarchy. Archduke Otto, the eldest son of Kaiser Karl was too young to be tainted by the First World War, or immersed in the bitter power struggle to follow. It is said that when Horthy was on his deathbed in 1957, he sought forgiveness of the Archduke Otto for his treatment of the kaiser.

Only one Habsburg retained a link with the new order, albeit a tentative one, and that was Princess Windischgratz, the only daughter of Crown Prince Rudolf. Following the revolution she divorced her husband and married Leopold Petznek, a member of the Revolutionary Council that had assumed power in 1918. Otherwise, the Habsburg causè in Austria was strangely enough left to the children of Archduke Franz-Ferdinand and the Duchess von Hohenberg. However, the decline of monarchy has not prevented Archduke Otto from making a positive contribution to European diplomacy, and as Doctor Otto von Habsburg he sits in the European Parliament.

References:
1. *Windsor and Habsburg*, John van der Kiste.
2. *Imperial Twilight*, Bertila Harding.

CHAPTER FOURTEEN

The Second World War

Germany invaded Poland on 1 September 1939. Three days later Great Britain and France declared war on Germany, but Poland fell on 27 September before they could mount a rescue operation. Nazi Germany had perfected a new strategy of war whereby tank divisions sped across the countryside, whilst aircraft launched a blanket attack from the air. It was known as the Blitzkrieg. It was with the same breathtaking speed that Hitler then went on to defeat Denmark, Norway, the Netherlands, Belgium and France in the April, May, and June of 1940. British and French troops did land in Norway to successfully challenge German forces in the north, but the Allies' efforts were undermined by the German advance through the Low Countries to France. This theatre of war now became the main priority and they were forced to send their troops en masse to Belgium and France. There they were swept back to the coast and eventually forced from the continent via Dunkirk.

With the fall of France, the war transferred from land to air and the Battle of Britain got under way. From August to October 1940, Great Britain was the target of day and night bombing raids. However, the Luftwaffe failed to break the British spirit. Italy also struck at British morale by joining Germany in an invasion of Egypt in the summer of 1940. Nevertheless, this was the only fighting to take place outside Europe in 1940. Benito Mussolini otherwise added to Europe's torment by an invasion of Greece in October 1940. The Greek Army put up unexpected resistance and it took German intervention to secure a Greek surrender on 21 April 1941. To secure this front the German army likewise occupied Yugoslavia at the same time. With Roumania and Bulgaria on the Axis side, this saw Hitler in control of the Balkans.

He moved further east with an invasion of the Soviet Union on 22 June 1941. Germany was supported in its Russian offensive by the Roumanian Army. The invasion brought to an end the German-Soviet cooperation of the first months of the war which had seen the Red Army invade and occupy East Poland and Finland. In other respects, the war in Europe really became a world war in 1941. Japan joined the Axis Powers with a surprise and devastating attack on United States forces at Pearl Harbor. This ignited the Far East with Japanese attacks on Thailand, British Malaya and Burma, the Dutch East Indies and the Philippines. Singapore likewise fell in the spring of 1942.

Great Britain was no longer alone in the fight against Nazi Germany. She now had the United States of America and the Soviet Union on side. America hit back at Japan with a significant victory on the high seas at the Battle of Midway. Meanwhile, the Soviet Union remained on the defensive until the Germans lost the Battle of Stalingrad in November 1942. The Allies were beginning to take the upper hand. The Royal Air Force certainly repaid Germany for the Battle of Britain with bombing raids on the Reich.

The surrender of Axis forces in the Middle East on 13 May 1943, led to the overthrow of Benito Mussolini and an Italian armistice that summer. However, Germany refused to give way in Italy, and held on in the north. The country was to remain divided and at war. One of the most dramatic and hard-fought battles in Italy was that for Monte Cassino in May 1944. Around the same time, Roumania also underwent a coup d'etat and like Italy changed sides. Soviet troops quickly occupied the country.

The next month, the Allies invaded Nazi-occupied Europe on 6 June 1944. Paris was liberated in August. By mid-November the Anglo-American force was at the German border. Hitler showed that his army was not yet to be beaten when he launched a strong counter-attack in the Ardennes. But the advance of the Red Army in the East, which came within 50 miles of Berlin by January 1945, placed him evermore on the defensive. In February, the British and Americans crossed the Rhine but it was the Soviet Army that first arrived in Berlin. To avoid the same death as Mussolini – execution and public display of his corpse – Adolf Hitler committed suicide in his bunker on 30 April. Germany formally surrendered to the Allies on 8 May 1945.

Japan carried on until August when the atomic bombs were dropped on Hiroshima and Nagasaki. In the meantime there had been continued bloodshed as the British fought the Japanese in Burma, and the Americans engaged them on one Pacific island after another.

CHAPTER FIFTEEN. ITALY

Second Roman Empire

Italian participation in the First World War had not been without its problems and following a serious defeat at the Battle of Caporetto on 24 October 1917, the Entente had been obliged to send in reinforcements to bolster the Isonzo Front. Over 200,000 Italians were either killed or taken prisoner at Caporetto. Yet the Italian defection to the Entente was an enormous blow to Austro-German morale, and it stretched the Central Powers' resources still further with the opening of another combat front. The Royal Italian Army also restored its reputation at the Battle of Vittorio Veneto which helped knock Austria-Hungary from the war, and gave Italy Trieste and the Trentino.

The end of the war coincided with the King of Italy's birthday on 11 November 1918. *The Sunday Times* therefore felt justified in extolling the virtues of Britain's Italian ally. Under the headline 'An Auspicious Birthday' the newspaper wrote an article on the eve of his birthday which began:

It is a pleasant convention for congratulations to be publicly offered on the birthdays of sovereigns; but it will be more than a mere convention in the case of the forty-ninth birthday of the gallant ally to this country, King Victor Emmanuel of Italy to be celebrated tomorrow – it will be the spontaneous outburst of cordiality from this country to one who has fought the good fight, not by deputy but in his own person, and who has deserved well of his own country, and of the Entente as a whole.

It ended:

It will be the earnest hope of all friends of Italy that King Victor Emmanuel will live to see his country advance far and rapid on that road to the new and splendid future upon which she has started under the historic banner of Savoy.[1]

The king had been brought up in the mould of the nineteenth century soldier king. Much of his youth was directed by a military tutor and playtime meant digging trenches and building castles in the palace gardens, whilst holidays abroad meant tours of famous battlefields. When the First World War came, and Italy joined the Entente, Vittorio Emanuele spent the entire war at the front amongst his soldiers. He became a legendary hero very much like King Albert of the Belgians, and there are stories galore of his exploits but it is difficult to ascertain fact from fiction given the hero worship he received from the peasant soldier. There is, however one account which speaks of the bond between the king and his army but does not over-glorify the monarch and therefore rings true. An artillery lieutenant wrote of the king to his family at home:

Yesterday was the happiest and most historic day of my life, for I had the good fortune to approach and speak to the King. I saw too, with what simplicity he sat on the ground amongst us, eating his lunch and sharing his salami and cheese with the soldiers. He graciously gave me a handful of cherries, and praised the good marksmanship of my battery.[2]

The king was well respected throughout the ranks and their support in the post war age of fascism was something Mussolini could not overlook.

It was during a wartime visit to a hospital near Udine that the two men first met, the king as commander-in-chief and Mussolini a sergeant in the Bersaglieri, and later it was this inequality of rank that was to guide both men as they sought to control the armed forces; the king reluctant to see a former sergeant at the helm, Il Duce determined to be on an equal footing with the king. Imagine therefore the clash that ensued when Mussolini assumed a military rank hitherto reserved for the sovereign. It was the only time throughout the fascist era that the king was known to threaten abdication and it was only the start of things to come.

Italy did go on to achieve momentous things but it was not the splendid future that *The Sunday Times* had quite envisaged. For it was Italy that introduced fascism to the world, and then embarked upon a colonial expansion, a second Roman Empire, that helped to ensure the First World War was anything but the war to end all wars. The conquest of Abyssinia in 1936 put Italy on course for another world conflict and Armageddon.

To understand what Abyssinia meant to the Italian people it is necessary only to look back to the British Empire and the affection shown here for India. In support of Mussolini's legionaries Italy appeared united as never before, and rejoiced in victory. The excitement in the streets even penetrated the Quirinal Palace. The king was normally a sound sleeper but that night he could only look at a map of Africa and marvel at the success of the Italian Army. He was now the Emperor of Abyssinia. The League of Nations took another view and imposed economic sanctions upon Italy but in a symbolic act of defiance, 250,000 women assembled at the Tomb of the Unknown Warrior to donate their gold to the state. The first in the queue was Queen Elena with her wedding ring. The Abyssinians also registered a protest vote when in 1937 they attempted to blow up the viceroy at an almsgiving ceremony to celebrate the birth of the king's grandson, the Prince of Naples. The viceroy was a royal cousin, the Duke of Aosta and although he escaped with his life, many figures in the colonial government did not. For three days and three nights the Italians exacted a bloody revenge that did not bode well for this latest chapter in the history of the House of Savoy.

Success and greed prompted Mussolini, who styled himself Il Duce, to go further and Albania was the next to fall; but it is true to say that he did not have the same level of support from the Italian people, and certainly not from the king. Expansion in Europe was a dangerous game. It was the Balkans that had ignited the First World War and now Mussolini was treading the same path. More importantly fascist Germany was up to the same game, and it was only a matter of time before things came to a head. 'Why risk the venture in order to grab four rocks?'[3] the king asked of Foreign Minister Ciano, prompting Mussolini to remark: 'If Hitler had to deal with a nincompoop of a king he would not have been able to take Austria and Czechoslovakia.'[4]

Nevertheless, when the Albanians journeyed to Rome to swear fidelity to their new king, they appeared more awe-inspired by the giant bronze statue of Il Duce than the small figure that sat upon his throne to the side of it. Size seemed to matter to the Italians, something that probably gave the five-foot-high king his inferiority complex. Much was made of Mussolini's office, a vast chamber, empty of all furniture other than his writing table and chair, situated at the opposite end of the room to the door and designed that very way to humble the most august of visitors. The principle seems to have worked many years before when Queen Victoria of Great Britain visited King Umberto I. The Queen recalled that she had to be pushed in her wheelchair along the chamber. 'The distance being very great, which made me very shy.'[5]

The relationship between the king and Il Duce was not helped by the former's distrust of Germany. Vittorio Emanuele was passionately anti-German and did not hesitate to brand the Germans as 'rascals and beggars'[6] to Mussolini's face. In fact he went so far as to call Hitler a 'psycho-physio-logical degenerate under the influence of narcotics.'[7] It was said that the palace, through the Princess of Piedmont, tipped off her brother, King Leopold III of the Belgians, about the forthcoming German invasion. In contrast, the fascist militia acted angrily towards a newspaper that published a personal plea from Queen Wilhelmina of the Netherlands to the Italian king upon the German invasion of the lowlands. The paper was literally ripped from the newsstands and burned in the streets, its readers tossed unceremoniously into the Trevi Fountain.

Mussolini did have his own reservations about German capabilities. In a jibe aimed just as much at the success of the new VW Beetle as anything else, he maintained: 'The Germans are a military people but not a warrior people. Give the Germans a great deal of sausage, butter, beer, and a cheap car and they will never want to risk their skins.'[8] It took German military successes in Europe to change his mind, and no doubt the situation was helped by Hitler's gift of two armoured railway cars, complete with sixteen anti-aircraft guns 'to protect a life which is precious not only to the Italian people but also to the German nation.'[9]

With German supremacy firmly on the cards, the king also overcame his earlier reservations about entering the war on the German side. In the words of Count Ciano: 'Now that the sword is about to be unsheathed, the king, like all members of the House of Savoy, is preparing to be a soldier, and only a soldier.'[10] This prompted another quip from Il Duce: 'Princes ought to be enlisted as civilians.' At the time the sentiment was all the more heartfelt as he haggled with the king for command of the armed forces. Vittorio Emanuele won but by way of compromise. He stayed the commander-in-chief but delegated the military conduct of the war to Mussolini.

The introduction of the Nazi or Roman salute, was vehemently opposed by the king, as was the goose or Roman step. Mussolini refused to acknowl-edge it as a German import arguing that the goose featured in ancient history as having saved Rome from the Gauls. The king later admitted that it looked good on the parade ground and raised no further objections but as usual Mussolini had the last word, if on this occasion it was under his breath. 'My dear solemn idiot, it was precisely with you that I had to argue most in order to introduce it.'[12]

To excel on the parade ground is one thing but the success of an army rests with its performance in battle. Il Duce was the master of set-piece parades but totally incompetent when it came to field operations, and under his leadership the Italian Army failed to live up to expectations. Military action against France ended in farce even though Germany had already brought the republic to the brink of defeat; and the Greek Army, that no one really rated at the time, practically brought Mussolini to his knees in a clash between the descendants of Caesar and those of Alexander the Great. All in all it spelt an end to the modern-day legions set aside for an invasion of Britain two thou-sand years after their forefathers had landed there.

The newly proclaimed, and much prized, empire also disintegrated under the strain. Abyssinia was returned to its rightful heirs and the Duke of Aosta later died of tuberculosis, a British prisoner of war. Albania was beginning to flex its independent muscles which involved a higher concentration of troops than was otherwise appropriate in time of war. When the king made a wartime visit to Tirana he was shot at, and when he gave a reception, the guests made off with the silver knives and forks. Efforts were made to revive Italian imperialism but without success. The royal visit to Albania persuaded the queen's nephew, Prince Michael Petrovich, not to accept an Italian sponsored restoration of the Montenegran throne and although the king's nephew, the Duke of Spoleto, did become King Tomislav II of an independent Croatia he did not attempt to set foot in his new kingdom. This was probably just as well as the chief minister was Ante Pavelic who had played a part in the assassination of King Aleksander I of Yugoslavia, and he was considered a loyal subject.

Mussolini did his best to harden attitudes towards the war, going so far as to sound false air raid alarms in Rome and to use anti-aircraft batteries for greater realism. However, when the war eventually arrived with genuine air raids the people reacted angrily. The king faced a hostile crowd when he toured the damaged areas, and his mood was not helped when he visited a military airfield to find it deserted. The commander called it 'preventative decentralisation'.[13] Yet, it finally caused the king to stop and think about Il Duce's future, and the Allied invasion of Sicily spurred him into action.

Encouraged by a revolt of the fascist Grand Council that transferred constitutional authority away from Mussolini and back to the crown, the king dismissed the dictator in dramatic fashion on 25 July 1943. Peeved by the Grand Council, Mussolini had gone to see the king for support unaware that behind practically every bush in the royal park lurked an officer of the carabinieri. He did not therefore meet with words of encouragement, rather a string of anti-fascist jokes and rhymes that left him dumbstruck, and with that the once-mighty dictator was whisked away to his mountain-top prison in the back of an ambulance.

Many were to ask why King Vittorio Emanuele III had not acted sooner. Later King Umberto II stated that he believed his father overestimated Il Duce's hold on the Italian people and grossly underestimated their loyalty to the older institutions such as the monarchy, and he was probably right. Mussolini recognised this, he retained the crown, and in the end it was the crown that prevailed, even if it did only survive fascism by a few short years. There is, however, something else to consider and that was the king's respect for Il Duce. Although they were to constantly quarrel over different things, the king recognised that Mussolini had initially done much for Italy. As an American journalist was to write:

> Mussolini had given Italy a tremendous prestige before the war
> and every Italian gained more of a national consciousness from

it. Within one year (of war) Mussolini wiped that prestige away. With it vanished the adoration he once received.[14]

Regardless of when the king should or should not have acted, the news was well received by the people and the king was toasted from one province to the next but the euphoria was to be short lived.

The new government headed by the conqueror of Abyssinia Marshal Badoglio, secured peace very much on Allied terms which excluded military aid for Rome. Before his overthrow Il Duce had allowed the Germans to penetrate the capital, and liaison officers were attached to all the ministries of state. Without Allied help the king's position in Rome was untenable, and he was forced to flee the capital, moving south towards the Allies but it was a controversial move, and one quite frankly for which he was not to be forgiven. The brutality of the German occupation only increased the bitterness of the Roman people.

A German demand made of General Carlos Calvi di Bergolo illustrated the suffering of the Roman people. The general was the commandant of Rome and the husband of the king and queen's eldest daughter Princess Yolanda. He was ordered to provide a list of 6,000 leading citizens who were to be held hostage against terrorism. Calvi di Bergolo merely gave his own name and that of his deputy Colonel Giuseppe Montezzemolo. Both were arrested and the colonel's body was later found in a quarry outside Rome. He had been executed along with 334 other people. All had been shot in the back of the head as they knelt on the ground.

A few days after the king had fled from Rome Adolf Hitler rescued Benito Mussolini from imprisonment on 12 September 1943. The Badoglio government kept the fallen dictator in a hastily requisitioned hotel at the top of an enormous mountain called Gran Sasso in central Italy. The makeshift prison was said to be impregnable. A well-guarded cable car provided sole access from the ground. The high altitude and rugged mountain summit ruled out a parachute raid, and the little field behind the hotel was considered too small to land an aircraft. Yet the Germans managed to land a number of gliders in the field and overcome the guard. A small light aircraft followed the gliders and it was in this aeroplane that Mussolini left his mountain prison. There was genuine concern that the aircraft would not have sufficient ground in which to gather speed for take off. When it did leave the edge of the mountain the aircraft went into a nose-dive. Everyone thought that Mussolini was about to die as it took some minutes for the pilot to pull the plane up again.

The rescue of Mussolini helped divide the kingdom. Until his death at the hands of Italian partisans in 1945, Il Duce held sway over the so called Salo Republic in the north of the country. To the south the Allies controlled Sicily and the other liberated territories, whilst the king was left with the four provinces of Bari, Lecce, Taranto and Brindisi. Just as Mussolini owed power to Nazi Germany, so the fate of King Vittorio Emanuele came to rest with the big three, Great Britain, America and the Soviet Union. This was not without its humiliations and the Italian king was told to leave Naples when King George VI went there to visit Allied troops.

He was not the only one to feel embarrassed by his departure. The crew of a British patrol boat failed to recognise the king and queen of Italy when the royal couple were arrested on an early morning fishing trip off shore from where King George was staying. Queen Elena was particularly loud in her indignation and the British monarch got to hear of the incident, although it did not result in an invitation to breakfast. But the queen was anxious to keep up appearances and she gave the sailors an enormous visiting card to pass on to King George. Harold Macmillan was on the British staff and he got to see the card. To his mind it was a card of 'Alice in Wonderland proportions' and it must have been a strange world that King Vittorio Emanuele and Queen Elena then found themselves in.

Life was preferable to that in the German concentration camp that was the prison and last resting place of their third daughter Princess Mafalda. She disappeared after Italy went over to the Allies. At the end of the war it was discovered that she had been taken hostage by the Germans and sent to the concentration camp of Buchenwald. There she was given the name of Frau Abeda and housed in Shed 15 for sensitive prisoners. The shed was segregated from other inmates by a high fence and situated next to SS guard quarters. The barracks were often targeted by Allied bombers and Shed 15 was hit during an air raid on 24 August 1944. Princess Mafalda was rescued from the rubble with burns and a crushed arm. She lay in hospital for four days without proper medical treatment. Not until the onset of gangrene did the doctors operate but it came too late to save the princess. It is thought that treatment was deliberately withheld to hasten her death, which happened around the same time that her father was ejected from Naples.

The Allies were at one in their determination to remove the king but divided as to the monarchy's future. Great Britain, with a tradition of monarchy, considered the Italian crown to be the best guarantor of stable postwar government. America, being younger than many of the dynasties that ruled in Europe, and having found her way in the world without recourse to princes, was in two minds, whilst needless to say the Soviet Union was no friend of monarchy. The war had first to be won, and so a decision was put off until the fighting was over but domestic discontent with the king prompted the Allies to seek his abdication. They failed but did get agreement to a transfer of executive power upon the liberation of Rome to his son and heir, Umberto, Prince of Piedmont, who acted as Lieutenant General of the Realm.

Rome was duly liberated on 4 June 1944, and four days later the King formally handed over power to his son but not without first having attempted a comeback. This time he failed as the Allies were in no mood for further compromise. In fact British officials spoke of enforced exile in Kenya, no doubt with reference to the former prince regent of Yugoslavia who had been sent there to dwell upon his alleged support for Germany. In the end, it was still to be a matter of exile but in a country of his choice, Egypt rather than Kenya.

King Vittorio Emanuele III abdicated on 9 May 1946 but this was too late to prevent his son sharing the same indignity and a life of exile in Portugal.

The odds were certainly not in Prince Umberto's favour. Such was the sensitivity surrounding the monarchy that he could not even accompany the Allied troops when they entered Rome and had to make do with a brief consolation visit afterwards. Yet he was to recover much lost ground, and by the time a referendum on the monarchy was forced upon him on 2 June 1946, he had won Rome back to the cause.

Under Umberto the Quirinal Palace became a centre for the welfare of the people and this helped to improve the king's standing. A guest house in the palace gardens was transformed into a hospital for children who had been disabled in the air raids. King Umberto and Queen Marie-Jose would make regular visits to the hospital where they met with hugs and kisses from the children. An outdoor dispensary was also opened in the palace grounds and hundreds of people made use of this free service. The king and queen were often amongst the crowds sharing their problems and adding comfort were they could.

Although King Umberto II was to lose to the country at large the margin was much smaller than expected: 12,700,000 votes to 10,700,000. It meant that he was destined to make no other name for himself other than that of the last king of Italy. Before Umberto left there was one last big gathering at the Quirinal. Three thousand officers and men of the Royal Cavalry appeared in the palace courtyard to say goodbye. The military tradition of the House of Savoy was at an end. Meanwhile the monarchy paid its last respects to the Army. From his new home in Egypt, King Vittorio Emanuele III visited the Italian cemetery at El Alamein and walked amongst the graves to honour the war dead.

References:

1. *Newspapers of the First World War,* Ian Williams.
2. *Victor Emmanuel III, King of Italy*, Reverend A. Robertson.
5. *Beloved and Darling Child*, Agatha Ramm.
9 and 14. *Italy from Within*, Richard G. Massock.
13. *The Fall of the House of Savoy*, Robert Katz.
All other quotations come from *Ciano's Diary 1939-1943*, Malcolm Muggeridge.

CHAPTER SIXTEEN. ALBANIA

Son of the Mountain Eagle

When King Zog went to see his newborn son he took with him a pistol and placing the baby's hands against the gun he called upon him to be strong and courageous like his ancestors. It was an ancient custom appropriate to a baby descended from the Lords of the Mathi who first stepped into Albanian history in 1450 when Sultan Murad III of Turkey placed a price on their heads for highway robbery. It was also a custom equally relevant to 5 April 1939 and, as if to demonstrate exactly why, the Royal Italian Air Force disrupted an impressive military parade in honour of Crown Prince Leka by dropping leaflets calling for the overthrow of the king. Two days later, Queen Geraldine and her baby were taken across the Greek border on a stretcher closely followed by King Zog. Benito Mussolini had shown that in common with Adolf Hitler he too could walk into other countries and take control. It was not, however, the first time Italy had intervened in Albania, and there is still controversy over the role of the Italian minister to Tirana in the downfall of Prince Wilhelm of Wied, who briefly occupied the princely throne before the First World War.

Albania had been a much coveted prize during the Balkan Wars and this attracted the attention of the European Powers. Italy was particularly interested as ownership of Albania gave control over the Otranto Channel which connected the Adriatic Sea with the Mediterranean. Through an international control commission Albania was given a German ruler. Prince Wilhelm of Wied was a neutral candidate acceptable to all the European powers, and this is the only explanation that can be given for his arrival in Albania on 7 March 1914, because in other respects he lacked the qualities to enforce order on an otherwise lawless land. He was a captain in the German Army and this junior command did not equip him to overcome outside meddling, particularly from Greece who laid claim to southern Albania and was exercising its own form of ethnic cleansing, and Turkey who objected to a non-muslim head of state. The endless vendettas between clans did not help. The vendettas would start with the slaughter of an opponent's dog, and would end with a man's dead body in the street, where it could lie for days because anyone touching the body would become an enemy of the murderer and perpetuate the killing. Unrest was therefore widespread.

The prince had a force of Dutch gendarmerie to maintain law and order but they were rather heavy-handed with the Albanian people. Matters came to a head when Wilhelm's chief minister Essad Pasha took exception to Dutch reaction to a peasant demonstration in Tirana, and demanded the resignation of the officer in charge. The gendarmerie sought to neutralise him with the confiscation of Albanian artillery in Tirana. Initially, Prince Wilhelm supported his minister, but foreign diplomats changed his mind. Essad Pasha handed in his resignation, prompting Wilhelm to change his mind for a third time. The Interior Minister was sent to dismiss the Dutch officer, but he wanted something in writing from the prince. By the time the minister had returned to the palace, the foreign diplomats had been at work again to the detriment of Essad Pasha who was arrested that night on charges of treason and very quickly bundled out of the country.

This prompted a rebellion amongst Essad Pasha's supporters who were joined by others when the Dutch gendarmerie turned their machine-guns on a delegation of provincial town elders who had nothing to do with the rebellion but were erroneously mistaken for warlords. The policemen were very quickly taken hostage by the rebels and arrayed before the citadel at Durazzo where Prince Wilhelm had taken refuge. There he courageously sat out a three-month siege until the outbreak of the First World War and the desertion of his European backers forced him to leave Albania on 5 September 1914. So ended a reign which was not dissimilar to the modern day troubles in Bosnia, with the international community struggling to restore order, peacekeeping forces taken hostage and ethnic cleansing to hand. Following the war Essad Pasha went on to proclaim himself king of territory he controlled in central Albanian but he was assassinated in 1920.

The Italian minister was rumoured to be behind Essad Pasha and his plans for a coup d'etat, but if that were the case, Italy did not profit from espionage. Austria-Hungary was to occupy Albania for the duration of the First World War. Although Italy was to gain a foothold in Albania after the war, she was forced out by Ahmed Bey Zogu who had raised an Albanian Legion for the Austro-Hungarian Army, and was now one of the best armed tribal leaders in the country. The support of United States President Wilson and his belief in self-determination did much to help Zogu secure control, but he was no democrat and his rise to power was not without bloodshed. Ironically, when he achieved high office he sought to consolidate his position through Italian support, signing a treaty of friendship with Italy in 1926, and a more formal alliance in 1927. Although the treaties restricted Albanian autonomy, they did provide Zogu with the finance he needed to modernise his country. When he came to power Tirana, the capital of Albania, was in reality a small town with run-down wooden houses, open sewers and muddy streets. Whilst he built new houses, hospitals, schools, and roads, his people felt good about themselves and their ruler. Fifty-five assassination attempts might contradict this theory but in the main it worked.

To encourage what is today known as the 'feel good factor', Zogu made Albania a kingdom, and on 31 August 1928, he became King Zog I Skanderbeg III. The last part to his title was to link him to the fifteenth century national hero Giorgio Skanderbeg, who had won widespread recognition for his struggle against the Ottoman Empire.

Albania, like most of the Balkans, had once belonged to Turkey, and the sultan had taken hostages from amongst the landed gentry in response to an unsuccessful attempt to break with Constantinople at the turn of the century. Ahmed Zogu was one of the hostages who at the age of five had been taken before Sultan Abdul Hamid II. He was, however, to display a rebellious streak, and when he refused to become the adjutant to an Ottoman prince, he had been banished from court and forbidden to return to his homeland. The Young Turks' revolution provided him with his ticket home, and he even tricked the new Ottoman rulers into arming his tribe on the pretext that they would fight for Turkish interests in the Balkans. His aim, however, was to achieve Albanian independence.

During the First World War, he had gone on to deceive the Austrians in exactly the same way and for the same reason. They even made him an

Austro-Hungarian colonel, although they did become wise to his game, if a little too late to stop the arms, and when he was summoned to Vienna to pay homage to the newly installed Kaiser Karl, the authorities took the precaution of detaining him in Austria for the remainder of the war. It was in Vienna that one of the most spectacular attempts was later made on his life. Zog took the precaution to leave buildings by the side door, and this was the case when he went to the opera one night, but his chauffeur rather carelessly put on the interior light of the car, and this made him a perfect target for the gunman waiting for him in the street. As the car drove away from the opera house, gunshots were fired killing an aide and wounding the king who jumped out of the car and returned fire with his companion, his golden gun.

There were few signs of the rebel when he became king. To see Zog in his magnificent white uniform, tall and slender with aristocratic hands and of timid voice, few would have associated him with the rough and tumble of his rise to power. From a colonel in the Austrian army, he went on to become Albanian interior minister, prime minister, president, and monarch, all by the time he was 33 years of age. With the monarchy came a queen mother who supervised the royal kitchen to prevent King Zog suffering food poisoning, and a bevy of princesses, royal sisters, one of whom was married to the grandson of the last Sultan of Turkey, and all of whom headed a Women's Guard to protect their brother. A favourite nephew, Prince Tati, was designated the heir to the throne. Zog also brought to prominence his godfather called Krosi who unsettled the diplomatic corps by wearing guns in the pockets of his morning suit and was known as the 'Scabby One'.

An Italian marriage had been mooted but King Zog was afraid that once the knot had been tied he would be disposed of to make way for the legitimate succession of the Royal House of Savoy. He knew that close reliance on Italy was not without its risks. It was Italian contractors who flooded into the country to undertake the building projects financed by Rome and this allowed Mussolini to infiltrate Albanian society. A land reclamation scheme at Durazzo also allowed him to get within the fortifications that had protected Prince Wilhelm. King Zog therefore tried to counterbalance these developments by engaging British advisers to run the gendarmerie. The first inspector general of police was a Colonel Stirling who had fought with Lawrence of Arabia and boasted some rather colourful Hashemite decorations at official parades. His presence infuriated the Italians but it was not until 1938 that they could force the king remove the British officers from the gendarmerie. It also did not go unnoticed in fascist circles that Jewish intellectuals, fugitives of Nazi tyranny, had been well received in Albania. However, to Zog it was not a matter of political ideology but the perfect opportunity to enhance Albanian culture.

King Zog was to marry the Hungarian Countess Geraldine Apponyi and have his own son. The Italians were to use the king's devotion to his family for their own political ends. As the Italian invasion of Albania approached in 1939, Count Ciano was to write 'Zog loves his wife and indeed his whole family very much. I believe that he will prefer to ensure a quiet future for his dear ones. And, frankly, I cannot imagine Geraldine running around fighting through the mountains of Unthi or of Mirdizu in her ninth month of pregnancy'[1] and this from the man who had been the best man at the wedding! With an invasion close to hand, an Italian diplomat called upon the king to avoid a fight. 'I hope your Majesty will find the happiest solution. Sometimes one catches the lion through his cub'; to which King Zog replied: 'And sometimes the lion falls together with the cub, defending both himself and his offspring.'[2]

In February 1939, Italy took the decision to invade Albania at Easter. and while she built her invasion force diplomatic pressure was brought to bear on King Zog to comply without a fight. Meanwhile, Count Ciano attempted to destabilise the king through increased espionage and his agents were told to 'darken the waters like an octopus.'[3] The months that followed were very tense days for Albania. King Zog was locked in an almost constant round of audiences with his ministers, military advisers and diplomats. Nevertheless, the king was an old hand at dealing with Italy. He always delayed replying to Italian requests for the very reason that once one request had been met another would be forthcoming. The king also resorted to constitutional government when it suited him and answers would be delayed whilst he consulted with his ministers. Everyone knew that something was afoot with Italy, and when the Italian colony was evacuated at the beginning of April, their worst fears were justified. Italy wanted to rule Albania and leave King Zog to govern the palace gardens. However, as a monarch who enjoyed power he refused to be Mussolini's puppet, and on 7 April 1939 the Italian army marched into Albania. Shortly afterwards King Zog crossed the Greek border.

The king's safety within the palace grounds had already been brought into question when on one of his daily walks around the garden he had spotted the glint of a rifle in the window of a building overlooking the palace. The would-be assassin was caught and confessed to some form of fascist involvement. The king had a fear of assassination, of dying like a dog, and interestingly enough, it was after an attempt on his life by a powerful clan known as the Sacred Union that Zog had briefly left Albania for Yugoslavia in 1924, the one interruption to his otherwise meteoric rise to power. Zog was then prime minister and he was shot whilst entering the national assembly to deliver a speech. Despite the gunshot wounds he addressed parliament and there is no doubt that Zog possessed courage. Nevertheless, the speed of his departure in 1939 surprised some, and perhaps the Italians were right to calculate on family loyalty. Italian success in stirring up animosity between the Albanian tribes with a few well-chosen bribes may also have had a bearing on developments. The different clans certainly did not resist the crown being transferred to the King of Italy.

Two thousand officials escorted the king and queen into exile and with so many of his influential supporters out of Albania there were no effective counter-demonstrations of support at home. Italy was very nervous about the king mounting an attack from Greece, and considerable pressure was exerted on Athens to move the king on. Eventually France came to the rescue with an offer of sanctuary and the royal party set off across Europe to their new home. Europe was now an hazardous place to travel and a safe route was devised that took them through Turkey, Roumania, Poland, Lithuania, Latvia, Estonia, Sweden and Belgium. The tour was a personal triumph for the king and queen who were given a rousing welcome at each stage of their journey. Considerable sympathy was shown for the queen who had been forced to leave Albania within hours of giving birth to Crown Prince Leka. It was only by fortune that the baby survived the journey – at one stop the king and queen had been swept from the railway station by the welcoming party only to realise that the crown prince had been left behind on the train.

Benito Mussolini had chased the royal family from Greece and Adolf Hitler was to chase them from France. The invasion of France within a year of their arrival, saw King Zog and Queen Geraldine on the road again. This time they were accompanied by thousands of French refugees in their race to the coast. The king and queen had something of a head start because they were travelling in a powerful Mercedes car given to them as a wedding present by Adolf Hitler. It was bright red and identical to one owned by Hitler. This either protected them from Luftwaffe pilots who were wary of machine-gunning the dictator's car, or made them an obvious target to those who knew otherwise. Eventually they crossed the Channel to Great Britain where they spent the war years, living at such places as the Ritz and Sunningdale Park.

Once in Britain, the queen sold the car as it bore too close an association to Hitler but the cheque for £800.00 bounced, and the police were called in. They found the car in Scotland but the thief had sold the car on and King Zog was obliged to pay £800.00 to get the car back. It was not their only brush with the underworld. When they went on a shopping trip to Harrods, the king lost his wallet to a pick-pocket. However, by an amazing stroke of luck the king saw someone else pick-pocketing the man who had stolen his wallet and he was able to get his money back. The wallet contained £1000.00 and seemed to confirm the rumours that King Zog had left Albania with the national coffers, but the king was actually a wealthy landowner in his own right, and long before the invasion had amassed a considerable fortune through the sale or rent of land to Italian contractors. Confusion certainly existed over the long-term dispute with communist Albania regarding funds held by the Bank of England that were frozen in retaliation for the sinking of two British warships off the Albanian coast in 1946.

Neither love nor money would give him back his country. In common with most of Eastern Europe, Albania disappeared behind the iron curtain and King Zog was not to see his homeland again.

References:
1 and 3. *Ciano's Diary 1939-1943*, Malcolm Muggeridge.
2. *Geraldine of the Albanians*, Gwen Robyns.

CHAPTER SEVENTEEN. NORWAY

'All for Norway'

Every year Norway sends Great Britain an enormous Christmas tree to stand in Trafalgar Square. It is to thank the British people for their help during the Second World War, a period in time when the world was not at peace and there was little goodwill between mankind.

The battle for Norway was as much a naval campaign as a land force operation and it is therefore not entirely inappropriate that the tree should stand alongside Nelson's Column. An international code exists whereby a nation must allow the shipping of other countries the right of 'innocent passage' through its territorial waters. However, to safeguard the security of a nation, foreign warships can be excluded from certain areas of coastline. In the case of Norway the areas concerned are the Oslofjord, Horten, Kristiansand, Bergen, and Trondheimsfjord. After the outbreak of war in 1939, German shipping increasingly sought the protection of the Norwegian coastline, but in February 1940, a supply ship for the cruiser *Graf Spee* penetrated the restricted zone around Bergen. The name of the ship was the *Altmark* and it carried 300 British prisoners of war. Norwegian patrol boats intercepted the *Altmark*, but when their requests to search the ship were turned down, they seemed powerless to intervene. The Royal Navy therefore sent the destroyer HMS *Cossack* into Norwegian waters and by force of arms removed the prisoners.

It is widely acknowledged that the incident prompted the German invasion of Norway on 9 April 1940. German warships had been sighted off the Norwegian coast in the very early hours of the morning, and before long the coastline was a blaze of activity. The first Norwegian vessel to challenge the German armada at the entrance of the Oslofjord was a small whaling boat that had been requisitioned by the navy and given a deck gun. The German ships replied by shelling the boat. The Norwegian captain was crippled in the attack and he rolled overboard rather than face capture. The use of a whaling boat emphasised the inadequacies of the Royal Norwegian Navy but the Germans were not to have it all their own way. Further down the Oslofjord the Oscarsborg fortress engaged the armada with outdated cannons but deadly accuracy and the cruiser *Blücher* was sunk. The remaining German ships turned around and headed back down the fjord where they landed motorised troops who took the fortress from the rear, and proceeded to Oslo by road. At the Horten Naval Base, the Norwegian ship *Olav Trygvason* sank two German minesweepers, and severely damaged a destroyer and the cruiser *Emden*. At Narvik the German navy destroyed two turn-of-the-century Norwegian vessels, the *Norge* and *Eidsvold*, but over the next three days the British navy sank all the German ships at Narvik.

Everywhere along the Norwegian coast the Germans were losing valuable warships and this saw them resort to deception which included masquerading as Allied shipping. The fortress of Kristiansand successfully repulsed one naval assault by sinking the cruiser *Karlsruhe*. The Germans therefore tricked the commander into surrender by wiring him, in Norwegian code, to expect French warships to help in his defence. When the German warships re-appeared he allowed them to sail past the fortress unhindered. Similar tactics were employed at Bergen. When a Norwegian patrol boat challenged unidentified warships, an officer on the bridge of one of the ships replied in perfect English that they were a British squadron to help the Norwegians fight the Germans, but as Great Britain had no more right of passage to Bergen than Germany, the fortress opened fire and crippled the cruiser *Königsberg*. Having got into Norway by telling the Norwegians they were the allies there to help them, the Germans then proceeded to tell them that they were there to protect Norway from the British and French. It was a lie that the German commanders even passed down to their own men, and having gone there as friends they were to be nice to the Norwegian girls.

Despite the bravado of the Norwegian navy the coastline was soon in enemy hands and German troops took up the fight ashore. That did not, however, remove the German shipping from the scene and throughout the 60-day war further naval vessels were lost. The battle cruisers *Scharnhorst* and *Gneisenau* were to suffer damage and many of their supply ships were sent to the bottom. The British sank two in the Vestfjorden. Another was captured off Bodø with a valuable cargo of war material, including a printing press to help with German propaganda in Norway. A polish submarine sent another vessel to the bottom of the Malangenfjord. The *Aegir* and *Draug* of the Norwegian navy destroyed further German shipping as it attempted to use Norwegian ports. The Germans started the campaign with a force that numbered ten battle cruisers, fourteen destroyers, 28 submarines, 21 torpedo boats, eight minesweepers, and a countless supply of service ships. They ended it with seven warships: three cruisers and four destroyers. The rest had either been destroyed, or withdrawn for repair. The Allies had their share of fatalities. During the evacuation of southern Norway the Luftwaffe sank the destroyers *Afridi* and *Bison*. The British also lost their aircraft carrier HMS *Glorious* off North Norway.

At 4.30am, Doctor Brauer the German minister in Norway, had demanded that the Norwegian government end all resistance and surrender strategic military installations to the occupation forces. He also wanted control of all internal and external communications which would have rendered Norway little more than a German province and isolated her from the outside world. In rejecting the ultimatum the government simply quoted from one of Adolf Hitler's speeches in which he ridiculed a nation that accepted violation without resistance. With that they packed their bags and moved to Hamar, a city 100 miles inland from Oslo, with easy access to other parts of the country, and an escape route to Sweden if the worst should happen. They departed by train, and with them rode the royal family, members of parliament, leading military officers and foreign legation staff. The official seals of state and the national gold reserve were also accommodated. The royal family consisted of King Haakon VII, Crown Prince Olav, Crown Princess Martha, and their children ten-year-old Princess Ragnhild, eight-year-old Princess Astrid and three-year-old Prince Harald. Everyone was particularly impressed by the royal children who remained calm throughout the journey even if, through the innocence of childhood, they were excited by the fireworks around them. They were, however, displaying an attribute of royalty, and one that was to hold their grandfather in good stead in the days ahead.

It was a perfectly executed evacuation but the government of Johan Nygaardsvold was full of self doubt and recrimination. It had always pursued an anti-militarist policy and now when confronted with invasion the armed forces did not have the infrastructure nor weaponry to rise to the situation. Once at Hamar the prime minister therefore tendered his resignation but the king would not hear of a change of government at such a critical time, and in consultation with the Storting he moved to strengthen the cabinet by including politicians from other parties. In fact he kept his nerve as others around him began to waver, something that was not lost upon the Germans, and when the king stiffened cabinet resistance to German demands for a notorious Norwegian Nazi to become prime minister, they sought to capture him dead or alive. As the Germans advanced on Hamar, King Haakon moved to Elverum, and from there to a tiny hamlet called Nybergsund where the Luftwaffe finally caught up with him. Initially the royal party took cover under the bridge at Nybergsund but the bombing became so intense they had to run for cover under nearby trees, and as they ran they were machine-gunned by the German planes. It was to be the same story wherever the king went and many towns and villages were reduced to ashes for sheltering him.

Nevertheless, following Nybergsund every effort was made to keep the king's movements a secret, and on one occasion he was forced to travel in the back of a goods train so as to avoid detection. It was very gruelling for a man in his late 60s but not once did the king complain. Crown Princess Martha had by now been evacuated to her native Sweden along with her children, but Crown Prince Olav remained at his father's side, a close companion throughout those difficult days. The crown prince was also his trusted advisor, and the two would always be locked in in-depth discussion before an important decision was made – not because the king was indecisive but because Prince Olav was the next in line to the throne, and if something should happen to King Haakon it was important that the prince did not inherit decisions with which he did not agree. The crown prince also helped brighten the king's day even if by accident. At one hiding place the tension was briefly lifted by the expression on the prince's face when he accidentally poured salt and not sugar into his coffee. When he fell asleep across the table, King Haakon simply smiled and said 'Young people are fortunate. They can always sleep'[1].

A suggestion by the minister of defence that the crown prince become commander-in-chief of the army was soon discounted by the government. It was probably recognised that not even the crown prince could prevent a

German victory. The invasion had thrown the Norwegian Army into total chaos. It was largely a volunteer force and the speed of the invasion had prevented thousands of men from being called to arms. Many had reported to their mobilisation centres only to find them in German hands, others had fled into the mountains where they joined forces with soldiers in a similar position to form small fighting forces dotted here and there. It took some time for General Headquarters to find out the location of such groups, and time was something they did not have. Without tanks, artillery, and with only limited air support, the army could do little more than engage in defensive action. Everything hinged upon the British, French and Polish forces that arrived in Norway on 18 April but they were as equally ill-equipped as the Norwegians and by the beginning of May they felt compelled to evacuate southern Norway.

Norwegian General Headquarters had no alternative but to follow suit. They were running dangerously low on ammunition and the bullets used by the Allies did not even fit the rifles used by the Norwegians. King Haakon therefore boarded a British warship, HMS *Glasgow*, and sailed for Tromsø in the north. There the Allied campaign met with more success. The north of Norway was not as accessible as the south and the rugged mountain terrain provided an ideal location for guerrilla warfare. The Allies were also far more determined in their defence of the north because of the port of Narvik and the traffic that passed through it from the iron ore fields of Sweden. This more than anything, was the cause of Anglo-German interest in Norway. The iron ore was a valuable commodity to either war effort, and it would be advantageous for one side to deprive the other of access to this market. Germany had not been the only one to compile a blueprint on the occupation of north Norway. It was very much the case, though, that Germany got there first.

Control of Narvik was therefore hotly disputed and provided the spectacle of German alpine troops fighting the French Foreign Legion. When the allies retook the city the people of Narvik showed their gratitude by making a new standard for the Foreign Legion from the party frock of one of its inhabitants. However, the Allies withdrew from Narvik before the mayor had time to brush up on his French and present them with the flag. The battle for France was underway, and the Allied forces were redeployed accordingly. King Haakon and his government were once again faced with the agonising decision of following the Allies in retreat, but this time around it meant exile overseas. The Norwegian commander-in-chief, General Otto Ruge, is said to have attempted negotiation for the freedom of the northernmost part of Norway. The general was close to the king and it was assumed that he acted with his blessing, but this is most unlikely given King Haakon's actions following the invasion. In fact his departure for England aboard HMS *Devonshire* was an example of his commitment to continue the struggle for a free and independent Norway. It was 7 June 1940, and it was to be another five years to the day before he was to see his country again.

The absence of the king deprived the Germans of the legal authority they so badly wanted for their new order in Norway. So a constitutional battle began in which the Germans sought to use the Storting in the dethronement of King Haakon. At the time of the invasion only three members of the Storting had been missing from the crucial debates at Hamar and Elverum, but it had not been practical for the entire Storting subsequently to move around the country with the king and the government, so the deputies had given them authority to conduct the war as they saw fit, and gone their separate ways. As a result, only three members of the Storting went into exile on 7 June. The German authorities therefore convened the Storting at Eidsvold, and bullied the deputies into a repudiation of the king and the Nygaardsvold Government. It was at Eidsvold that the Constitutional Assembly of 1814 had declared the kingdom of Norway a 'free independent, indivisible and unalienable realm',[2] and it was therefore not by chance that the Germans had ordered the Storting to Eidsvold to validate their regime.

The insult was not lost upon King Haakon who hit back in a radio broadcast from London on 18 July 1940. His position was unequivocal. The Constitutional Assembly of 1814 did not recognise the mandate of a deputy who came from an area of Norway under foreign occupation. The constitution allowed for the king to wage war abroad and he had the consent of the Storting. In others words, he had seen fit to carry on the fight outside Norway. He also doubted if it was the free will of the people that he abdicate, and he was right. The war had awakened close feelings between the king and his people. Talking of his arrival in Norway in 1905, King Haakon was to comment: 'My new country became unspeakably dear to me and I felt drawn by personal bonds to the Norwegian people. My motto 'All for Norway' has always been, and still is, the deciding factor in all my work'.[3] Meanwhile, Theodor Broch, the Mayor of Narvik was to write of the king: 'Ever since, thirty five years before, he had been elected to the throne of Norway, we had thought of him as something to be taken for granted. He was a living part of our constitution. Perhaps we had not even been conscious of our real affection for this kindly and simple man. His motto – All for Norway – was engraved on our money. We had seen it so often that we no longer associated anything specific with it. Now that he was in mortal danger, we began to appreciate his lifelong contribution.'[4]

Rumours were rife that Nazi officials were thinking of putting Prince Harald on the throne. At three years of age he could easily be manipulated but Crown Princess Martha rather dashed their hopes when she accepted an invitation from President Roosevelt to live in the United States. There was, however, one Norwegian who was anxious to serve Germany and that was Major Vidkin Quisling. He had gained notoriety as a military attaché at the Norwegian legation in Petrograd following the Bolshevik revolution. Entranced by the success of the revolution, he returned to Norway to raise a red army of his own, and when that failed, he sought to rally the workers through the Agrarian Party. He clearly wanted power, and he did briefly achieve ministerial rank in 1931 as defence minister, but the Norwegians failed to take him seriously. One reason was the famous red pepper attack, when he claimed that the Bolsheviks set upon him one night and sought to extract military secrets from him by throwing red pepper in his face.

Disenchanted by the Agrarian Party, Quisling moved further to the right, forming his own fascist party, the Nasjonal Samling, which translated into the National Unity Party. His movement attracted just over one percent of the electorate and was not represented inside the Storting. Although he failed to charm the Norwegian people, he did manage to win favour with Adolf Hitler, so much so that when Germany invaded Norway King Haakon was told to accept Quisling as his prime minister. The king refused and promptly left with the legitimate government for the mountains. Judges, bishops, diplomats, civil servants, trade union members and teachers all took the king's lead, but by far the most damaging rebuttal was the defection of so-called members of his cabinet, officials whom he counted among his supporters, who were not asked about joining his government, and who fled to the front to serve their king and not Major Quisling. Hitler thought Quisling to have more influence in Norway than transpired to be the case, and he quickly sent in Reichskommissar Josef Terboven to bring the Norwegians to heel. Through Terboven, Hitler extracted from the Storting a semblance of legitimacy for his new order in Norway, and then suppressed all democratic institutions, and freedom of speech. Few could therefore obstruct the appointment of Vidkin Quisling as minister-president in 1942.

His name was to become synonymous with treachery and collaborators elsewhere in Europe were to be dubbed 'Quislings'. The rapid fall of Norway had also given the impression abroad that the country was made up of Quislings, a charge the Norwegians sought to dispel through active resistance at home and abroad.

By far the greatest asset Norway brought to the war effort was her merchant fleet. It was the fourth largest in the world, and in stark comparison to the somewhat dated warships of the navy, it consisted of 1,400 fairly modern vessels. By the end of the war nearly half of them had been lost to enemy action, along with 3,000 Norwegian seamen. The fight had therefore returned to the sea.

It was very much a time for reassessment. The *Altmark* affair, and the abortive expeditionary force to Norway had done little to endear the British to the Norwegian people. When the German invasion force arrived, the British minister in Oslo was even accused of lighting a beacon for enemy planes as he hurriedly burnt sensitive files in the grounds of the legation. People could see the funny side of events when upon his flight from Oslo the authorities provide him with overnight accommodation in a mental hospital. However, the war years were to see a strong bond develop between Norway and Great Britain. King Haakon, Crown Prince Olav, and the Nygaardsvold Government settled near to London so as to be at the heart of Allied operations, but the majority of refugees went to Scotland, which is of course that much nearer to Norway. There Norwegian soldiers used the similar terrain to practice for the liberation of their homeland, whilst Norwegian school children were taught without Nazi-inspired education reforms, and Norwegian and Scottish seamen happily fished the same waters without a hint of a cod war. They also ran secret sorties to and from Norway. So frequent did they become that they were known as the Shetland Bus. It is not therefore without significance that since the war Norwegian monarchs have chosen Edinburgh for their state visits to Britain.

Some Norwegian refugees returned to Norway as secret agents. Their greatest feat was a daring raid on the Norsk Hydro plant at Vermork. Norway was the only country in Europe to produce heavy water on a large scale. The Germans wanted the use of this water to test the production of atomic power, heavy water having two atoms of deuterium rather than the two atoms of hydrogen in normal water. This gives heavy water a higher freezing point, and greater density and weight. The Germans needed it to slow down fast neutrons to fission uranium 235 and trigger a chain reaction. Agents therefore went into Norway to destroy the storage tanks inside the factory. This they achieved with the minimum of difficulty thanks to the noise generated by the plant, but the Germans soon resumed production, and it became obvious that bigger explosives were needed to bring the plant to a standstill. The American Air Force therefore bombed the plant with 10,000 times the weight of the explosives used by the Norwegian agents. This halted production for the remainder of the war but failed to destroy the entire stock of heavy water, which the Germans planned to remove from the country. The Norwegian agents were therefore redeployed to identify the route of transportation, and find the most vulnerable point of attack. The ferry across Lake Tinnsjo proved to be that point. The agents planted their explosives, timing them to go off when the ferry was in the middle of the lake, sending the heavy water tanks to the bottom of the deepest part of the lake.

A poem was published to commemorate King Haakon's 70th birthday on 3 August 1942. In three short verses it spoke of the hope the king gave a tormented people.

> 'My all for Norway,' Truly
> You kept the pledge you vowed,
> Even when with cries unruly
> Our rebel tongues were loud.
> Unmoved, though we might name you
> In rude, uncourtly speech,
> No single class could claim you,
> The king of all and each.
>
> Such calm and upright bearing
> Befits a kingly throne;
> In your bright honour sharing
> We make your fame our own.
> Even that black day that greeted
> Our broken sword and shield,
> And saw our hosts defeated,
> Still found you in the field.

> The paltry treason spurning
> Of dastard hireling bands,
> In hopes of your returning
> Your realm united stands.
> Though now disarmed and feeble,
> Uncowed we still remain;
> Here waits your land, your people,
> To greet you home again![5]

King Haakon went home on 7 June 1945, five years to the day after he left Norway, and devoted the remaining twelve years of his life to the reconstruction of the country. Many towns had been destroyed at the time of the invasion, and when the Germans left they adopted a 'scorched earth' policy in parts of Norway. The king had much to do and see. The Norwegians therefore chose to cast aside their characteristic dislike of ostentation and indulge the king with a royal yacht, a mark of their respect and appreciation. The king could then use the fjords to tour the country in comfort and style. The yacht, which the king named the *Norge*, has a royal suite, eight guest cabins, five saloons, and a very impressive galley. It is still in service today, and with the imminent decommissioning of *Britannia*, it will be one of only two royal yachts left to European monarchy, the other being owned by King Haakon's great niece Queen Margrethe II of Denmark.

References:

1, 2 and 3. *I Saw it Happen in Norway*, C. J. Hambro.
4. *The Mountains Wait*, Theodor Broch.
5. *Haakon VII of Norway*, Tim Greve.

CHAPTER EIGHTEEN. SWEDEN

Scout's Honour

The best known Swede in contemporary history is probably Raoul Wallenburg, the diplomat who saved Jews from Nazi oppression and fell foul of Soviet tyranny. His disappearance behind Soviet lines at the end of the war, and the alleged sightings of him in labour camps subsequently have kept his story alive. Yet there is someone else, a fellow compatriot, whose humanitarian work deserves equal merit, and whose life was brought to an abrupt end in the service of others. His name was Count Folke Bernadotte, and he was a nephew of King Gustaf V of Sweden.

The count was little known to the outside world before he discreetly appeared upon the international scene in the closing stages of the war. Prior to that he been a leading light in the Boy Scout movement, a commitment that had not been restricted to one night a week at the local hall but a full time job that took Bernadotte to every scout pack in Sweden, and in some cases beyond. He firmly believed that scouting was not just about tying knots and lighting camp fires but moral education. Taking this into consideration the full extent of his mission is appreciated, especially as it took place in the dark days of the 1930s and the rise of Adolf Hitler.

The core values of scouting were to enable Count Bernadotte to meet the challenges of that era and to provide the impetus for an international career devoted to the wellbeing of others. The opportunity arose when he became vice president of the Swedish Red Cross in 1943. Sweden was at peace but the world was at war. Nevertheless, the kingdom was not sheltered from the turmoil beyond its borders. Fellow Scandinavian countries lay victims of Nazi aggression. The threat of invasion was there, as was the suffering of their neighbours. An uneasy calm existed in Sweden, a sense of helplessness relieved only by men of vision such as Folke Bernadotte.

He was quick to make his mark and upon his appointment made provision not only for the home front but for work at an international level, and in this direction he set two clear objectives: humanitarian help to the civilian population and the exchange of prisoners of war. Initial successes in the second of these categories enhanced his standing with both the Allied and Axis powers, and when it became clear that Germany was to lose the war, he was able to go to Berlin and negotiate the release of civilians in Nazi concentration camps. This was an uncomfortable journey that in the words of his biographer Ralph Hewins took him to 'the gates of hell'.

In the German capital he experienced his first blitz and the word 'hell' once again appears but this time in Folke Bernadotte's account of that evening. Berlin did indeed depict the innermost bowels of the earth: 'A raging inferno that in the light of day provided a barren landscape, even the sky was black with soot.' He was to conclude; 'That fiery night in Berlin thoroughly impressed upon me the appalling realities of war.' But more awaited him when he became the first Red Cross official to visit a concentration camp. The row upon row of human skeletons that greeted him told of another hell.

To get inside a concentration camp was all the more remarkable considering the unsavoury characters Bernadotte came up against. Murderers like Obergrüppenführer Ernst Kaltenbrunner who controlled the camps, Professor Karl Gebhardt who ran the German Red Cross but experimented on the inmates of Auschwitz, and finally the Gestapo chief Heinrich Himmler. Perhaps the imminent premature demise of the thousand year Reich was causing many a Nazi thug to fear for his own fate. Bernadotte had earlier said to his staff 'We must not talk politics or get into quarrels with the Germans. We must even, if necessary, flatter and cajole them – however much it may stick in our throats. The object is human life and to mitigate human suffering and any means to this end is legitimate.'

Himmler was one of the most complicated people Bernadotte had ever met. He was a commander-in-chief who, in his plain SS uniform, looked nothing more than a minor official one would pass in a street without a second glance; a man with a sense of humour that was contrasted to the cold, forbidding presence of his subordinates; a man who probably broke every rule of the Geneva Convention, yet praised the days when battles were interrupted to tend to the wounded and bury the dead. He was a contradiction in terms that Folke Bernadotte was able to exploit as everything Himmler stood for crumbled away, and that included Hitler in his concrete bunker. Said Himmler of Bernadotte 'I'm surprised you're only a major,' to which the count responded 'I don't think it's any more surprising than the fact that you're a commander-in-chief.'

The Scandinavians who had been transported to concentration camps in Germany, and this included the best part of the Danish police force, were Bernadotte's first priority. At the initial meeting with Himmler he had secured permission for the Red Cross to bring together all Scandinavian prisoners in one camp near to the Danish border. This would enable them to be moved across the border at a moment's notice should the Germans contemplate their slaughter when the end came. Neuengamme was to be the camp, and it was this camp that Bernadotte first entered.

There were to be four meetings in total, and at the second Bernadotte went on to obtain permission for the removal to Sweden of all Scandinavian women in captivity, all Norwegian students, all Danish policemen and all those who were seriously ill. At the third and fourth meetings he secured the evacuation to Sweden of all Scandinavians, regardless of sex, and state of health. Women of other nationalities, including those of the Jewish faith also went. As a direct result of his negotiations with Himmler, 20,573 people found their way to the safety of Sweden in the last days of war.

The Germans had not intended the number to be this high but wheresoever possible the Swedes took advantage of the situation to help as many people as they could. Whilst the Neuengamme commandant was liaising with Himmler in Berlin 800 sick inmates were sent to Sweden even though only 150 of them fitted the criteria set by the Germans for evacuation.

The operation was not without its difficulties. At the top there was Himmler who wavered on such matters as compensation. The Allied publicity given to Belsen upon its liberation was another factor. Then there was Kaltenbrunner, who tried to resist his master's orders; and the individual camp commandants who placed petty obstacles in the way of the Red Cross convoys. The prisoners also displayed initial reservations as in the past the Germans had been known to use buses in Red Cross colours to transport inmates to their deaths.

Bernadotte had a first class team at his disposal consisting of 250 staff, 36 buses and twelve lorries, that for three months did nothing but criss-cross the German countryside in a bid to save lives – a peace mission in a war zone. Once three buses were attacked from the air within 48 hours of each other, killing 36 Red Cross officials and patients.

At the end of the war, Count Folke Bernadotte was honoured by many countries, Denmark, Norway, Finland, the Netherlands, the United States,

France and Poland to name but a few. However, not content to rest upon his laurels he continued his humanitarian work. In 1948 he accepted the post of United Nations Mediator in Palestine, only to be assassinated five months later attempting to resolve a problem that has only recently shown signs of a settlement. The crime was all the greater given that he helped Jews escape the Nazi concentration camps.

Despite everything he had not forgotten the scout association. His last service to the movement had been to get scouting up and running again in Germany, and to help bury once and for all the Hitler Youth movement. In turn, the scout movement did not forget him and his funeral cortège was escorted through the streets of Stockholm by cub scouts eager to pay their last respects.

References:
Quotations are taken from *Count Folke Bernadotte* by Ralph Hewins.

CHAPTER NINETEEN. DENMARK AND BELGIUM

A King's Ransom

Denmark was attacked on the same day as Norway, 9 April 1940. Copenhagen was seized by 600 German soldiers who for three days had lain hidden aboard coaling vessels at anchor in the harbour. They met with minimal resistance and it took just three hours to secure the capital. The only serious fighting took place before the Amalienborg Palace, the official residence of King Christian X of Denmark. The Royal Life Guards therefore added honour to an otherwise ignominious defeat. Equally, they demonstrated that the monarchy had been the one institution to prompt a stand, and by implication, the only institution to lead the country to freedom.

King Christian was an elderly man who had ruled Denmark since 1912. The invasion was therefore to deal him a heavy blow. The German commander was one of the first people to see him after the invasion and noticed that although he conducted himself with the greatest dignity there was no disguising the shock to the system he had just received, and his whole body trembled throughout the audience. Yet within his frail body there still existed a will of iron. His granddaughter, Queen Margrethe II, has admitted that the royal family lived in awe of him. The Germans therefore stood little chance. They wanted the Danes to believe they had come as friends to protect them from Great Britain but King Christian would have none of it and from the very first day of occupation he made it abundantly clear that he was only cooperating under duress.

He came to represent a passive resistance to German authority that in many respects was to be as effective as the saboteur with his dynamite. He achieved it in a number of ways but there was one in particular for which he will always be remembered and that is his daily ride through the streets of Copenhagen. He undertook these rides before the war but with the arrival of the Germans they acquired a greater significance. On horseback, and without a lifeguard or servant in sight, he would ride through the streets smiling and saluting to passers-by as he went. It was an act of solidarity that won the approval of the Danes. He demonstrated a moral authority that was to inspire many stories of his wartime activities. Some were true and some were not but, whether fact or fiction, they testified to the remarkable courage of the king, and through his example, the Danish people.

Observers were quick to note that on his daily rides the king did not acknowledge the German soldiers who stopped to salute him and this inspired a similar attitude in others, whereby as far as possible the Germans were ignored. This was successful at a grass roots level but when it came to German officialdom life was not quite so simple. The Anti-Comintern Pact is an example of where the Danish and German governments were hopelessly at odds. The pact was signed by the Axis Powers to check the rise of communism, and was to be the forerunner of the Tripartite Pact of September 1940. The very nature of the pact went against the Danish tradition of parliamentary democracy which included communist representation. The Germans, however, insisted on the Danes adopting anti-communist legislation, and this led to the first real backlash against Germany on the streets of Copenhagen. Clearly there was a point when Denmark could cooperate no further without surrendering the very principles upon which the country existed.

The Danes were just as forthright in their opposition to anti-Jewish legislation. No one discriminated against the Jews, nor collaborated in the overall policy of their extermination. Instead, they succeeded in evacuating the vast majority of Danish Jews across the water to the safety of neutral Sweden. This was a cat and mouse trip that had to be taken at the dead of night to avoid land and sea patrols; very much a matter of life and death, not just for the Jews but the Danes who helped them. It is widely believed that the king let his views be known on the subject by wearing the Star of David upon his sleeve. However, this particular story is but a legend, although it still pays tribute to Denmark, the only country generally acknowledged to have success-fully impeded the mass murder of the Jewish people by the Third Reich.

King Christian was once again placed at the centre of events when it came to the inevitable break with the German authorities in the summer of 1943. Martial law was imposed and that meant direct rule from Berlin. With some pride, the Danes would say that it was the king's terse response to the birthday greetings he received from Adolf Hitler that prompted the crack down. It was rumoured that the German leader expected something more than the simple 'thank you' he got back, and to someone of his disturbed mind such insignificant detail could be of great importance. Yet there was more to it than that. Denmark was awakening from the nightmare. Gone were the days when the Danes would sabotage new road and rail links with Germany by merely pouring sand into the engines of the construction tractors and lorries.

Machine guns and dynamite had arrived upon the scene and Denmark was getting out of control.

The Danish police were unable to keep control of the ever growing number of street demonstrations. It was difficult for them to move against crowds chanting King Christian's name. The police force was therefore disbanded and those officers who were not quick enough to go underground were packed off to concentration camps in Germany. Their release was later arranged by Count Folke Bernadotte.

The British made life a little more awkward for the Germans with regular bombing raids over Denmark. The most famous raid was on Shellhus, Gestapo Headquarters, in Copenhagen. It was a difficult target situated in a built-up area near to a school. Danish prisoners were also housed at the top of the building so as to deter an Allied air attack. On the 21 March 1945, eighteen Mosquito aeroplanes made a low level attack with the aim of hitting the lower part of the building. Shellhus was set ablaze and many prisoners escaped in the confusion, but the fourth mosquito ran into an approach building near to the school. The building was set alight and the following aircraft mistook this for the target. The school was next door and 86 children were killed.

Great Britain became the centre for Danish freedom fighters. A Danish Council was formed in London to coordinate activity and Danes were allowed to enlist in the Royal East Kent Regiment of which King Christian was the colonel-in-chief. Merchant shipping at sea for the invasion defied orders to return to Danish ports and instead regrouped under the Union Jack. These ships were later permitted to fly the Danish flag on the foremast in recognition of their sterling work.

To re-assert their authority, the Germans introduced a number of measures one of which was to place the king under house arrest. In truth the palace walls were already his prison following a riding accident that had crippled him the previous Autumn. It was a miserable climax to the war and a worrying time for the royal family. As a child, Queen Margrethe II could sense the tension and her wartime recollections do capture the intimidation and fear that went with German rule. There was the visit to the seaside ruined by German aircraft buzzing people on the beach. The afternoon filled with anxiety when her father failed to return home on time, and the constant telephone messages that her mother sent via the Swedish Legation to her other grand-father in Stockholm, the future King Gustaf VI Adolf. 'Tell him that at such an hour we were all still safe.'[1] This final recollection probably best describes the uncertainty facing the royal family in the last years of the war.

It is not by chance that Denmark should be the oldest kingdom in Europe. Endurance is all about resilience and the twentieth century was to be no exception. The Danish monarchy was therefore to survive the Second World War and the present queen can remember awakening one day to an altogether happier world where laughter could once again be heard in the streets. The Germans had gone and on 5 May 1945, she went with her grand-mother, Queen Alexandrine, to see the Lifeguards return to sentry duty and the Royal Standard restored to its rightful place above the palace. During the occupation, Queen Margrethe was brought up to recognise only the flags of Denmark, Sweden and Great Britain. A flag is after all a powerful symbol that can command allegiance and represent a nation's independence, history and culture. The swastika had been given no credence whatsoever and relegated to a group of flags known simply as 'other flags'.

Imagine therefore the significance of the Anglo-French communiqué issued to King Leopold III of the Belgians when he forewarned the Allies of surrender. 'The French and British Governments agree that their armies should save the honour of the flag in dissociating themselves from the Belgian Army.'[2] It was a direct affront to the integrity of the king who had commanded Belgian forces in the field, and totally at odds with the Allies' treatment of King Christian. At face value it is difficult to understand why this should be, especially when Denmark surrendered within a matter of hours, whilst Belgium fought for eighteen days following the German invasion of the Low Countries on 10 May 1940. Furthermore, whereas the reputation of King Albert of the Belgians was used to destroy his son, King Leopold, no one confronted King Christian with the dramatic escape from Norway of his brother, King Haakon VII.

To suggest King Christian X was a fifth columnist is quite ridiculous but it was a charge readily levelled against King Leopold III. One of the more bizarre stories to gain credence was of his death in the very same car crash that killed his wife Queen Astrid in 1935, and his replacement by a look-alike German agent. To explain the motive behind such allegations one needs to look at the strategic position of Belgium, a country that has endured more than its fair share of battles in European history. In a repeat performance of the First World War, France and Great Britain had rushed to defend Belgium against the latest challenge from Adolf Hitler. Both countries recognised that Belgian independence was essential to their own security. When Belgium failed to match her record from the previous war, it was from Paris and London that the main assault upon King Leopold was made. The Allies discontent with the Belgian surrender of 28 May 1940, became public knowledge when the French prime minister, Paul Reynaud, went on the air and personally attacked the king. This was a remarkable radio broadcast that many would say was intended to divert attention away from his own shortcomings and the less than healthy state of the French army. Certainly the allegations he made against King Leopold have since been disproved and could have been discounted at the time. The most damaging charge was that he failed to give notice of the surrender but the French must have known of the weakness of the Belgian position because overall command of the allied operations had been given to France, and the king had spoken to his allies of possible capitulation on 26/27 May.

Indeed, when it became obvious that the Belgians were beaten, King Leopold did everything to assist with the evacuation of Anglo-French forces. Their route to the coast was clearly marked out by Belgian forces with roadside arrows resembling aircraft in flight. Bridges were blown and floodgates opened before the advancing Germans and 2,000 trucks were placed across the railway line running between the opposing armies. In all the Allies were given three valuable days to evacuate their forces.

Dunkirk was to give substance to M. Reynaud's accusations, especially in Great Britain. The majority of people knew someone in Belgium and northern France. Public opinion, and pressure from the French persuaded the British prime minister, Winston Churchill, to support his French counterpart on this issue but no one was told that Dunkirk had already been planned before the Belgian surrender and was intended as the evacuation point for all three armies.

A problem for the king was that once a prisoner of war he could do nothing to capture public imagination abroad. Confined as he was to the Palace of Laeken, the only occasion he was allowed to venture out was on a much publicised visit to Hitler, and to his enemies that was proof of his German credentials. The fact that he had declined a social visit at the start of his captivity and was only making this one on humanitarian grounds to obtain food and medicine for the Belgian people was neither here nor there. Furthermore, his German captors were left in no doubt of the king's attitude towards them. When the German commander, General von Reichenau, first went to the palace the king looked at him with such hostility as to bring him to an immediate standstill and the same experience was to befall other German officers.

The king had no intention of collaborating with the Germans and was quick to enact Article 82 of the constitution which declared him 'unable to reign'. (This is a controversial clause used in 1992 by King Baudouin to disassociate himself from legislation permitting abortion). However, both parliament and government went into exile and voices were raised as to why King Leopold had not simplified matters by joining them. Some questioned whether the king as a constitutional monarch should have declined the advice of his ministers to leave the country. The answer lay of course in the constitution itself which automatically gave the king supreme command of the armed forces upon violation of Belgian territory. Whilst the government debated such constitutional niceties the king directed military operations. This is an important point when comparing the king to other monarchs who sought refuge abroad and bore only titular command of their armies.

Much was made of Hitler's 'gift' to King Leopold of the palace at Laeken but in common with members of the Belgian, and for that matter the Dutch armed forces, he was simply returning to his home following demobilisation. A panel of jurists was asked by the king to rule upon his decision to surrender and they concluded that the decision was a military action empowered to him under the constitution, and that he was within his rights to remain in Belgium. Some politicians still disagreed. One was to comment. 'He was not a general... his main preoccupation has been not to cause loss of life or the destruction of towns.'[3]

One of the reasons behind the decision to surrender had been the million or so refugees caught between the armies but it was hypocritical for the political establishment to attack the king on such an issue when the government-in-exile had endorsed M. Reynaud's broadcast for fear of what might happen to the Belgian refugees who had crossed the border into France. Furthermore, there was no escaping the fact that they had a king who genuinely cared for his people and throughout his imprisonment he did what he could to help them. He gave generously to charity and worked very hard to get medicine, food and clothes from the American Red Cross. He also vigorously protested to the German authorities about the concentration camps in Belgium, and urged clemency for some 800 people facing the death sentence. This included his Jewish subjects and when the Germans insisted that he did not try to help them, arrangements were made for his mother to take up the challenge on his behalf.

Queen Elisabeth was to show the same support for her son as she had given her husband in the 1914-18 war. Yet her loyalty to King Leopold was to be used against him, and the critics came up with the notion that her German parentage, had a bearing on the king's decision to surrender and remain in Belgium. Imagine therefore what they made of his sister's life in Italy as the wife of Crown Prince Umberto. It was an unpleasant trait of the whole campaign to use members of the royal family as pawns in the attack upon the king, and matters reached a crescendo when on 11 September 1941 the king married Mademoiselle Liliane Baels, who was created the Princess de Réthy. To the king's adversaries the marriage was unforgivable at a time of national hardship, and the princess was to become a much maligned figure. It was widely rumoured that the king had previously denied his brother, Prince Charles, the right to marry a commoner, and that Leopold's second marriage had forced them apart. Whether or not this was the case, it was a useful weapon in the wrong hands especially when Charles became Prince Regent.

The memory of King Albert and his success in the First World War was to be constantly used against King Leopold. In Paris, they even went as far as draping King Albert's monument in black. However, King Leopold did not entirely give up the armed struggle and to the resistance he became known as 'Le Patron', a source of financial aid and encouragement. The Grenadier Guards, demobilised by the Germans, were quietly reorganised as part of the resistance movement which was known as the Secret Army. A Commandant Fichefet secretly met with the king on a weekly basis to advise him of developments and King Leopold paid for the grenadiers to be re-armed with guns and ammunition on the black market. He also ensured that the Secret Army passed on to the Allies as much information as possible about German defences. After the war, Winston Churchill admitted that 80 percent of intelligence from occupied Europe came from Belgium.

The last will and testament of ten resistance fighters executed by the Germans told of the support for the king within the Secret Army:

We have always considered the king as our leader.
We shall die considering him as such and saluting him
respectfully.

We ask that he shall continue to hold the destinies of Belgium in
    his hands. We will help him from above.
We understand and share both his personal sufferings and those
    which are caused by the sufferings of his people.
We do not pass judgment on his marriage. For us he is the King.
We confide to him the fate of our families.

From prison. 21st January 1942.[4]

Plans were afoot for the Secret Army to rescue King Leopold but the
Germans got to hear of them and heavily fortified Laeken with extra guards,
barbed wire and look-out towers. It might also be supposed that the
Germans had an idea that the king was in contact with the resistance. There
was enough activity around King Leopold to arouse their suspicions. It was
not without coincidence that twenty members of the royal household were
to die in German custody. It may certainly have influenced the German decision to remove the king from Belgium following the Allied landings in
Normandy.

Whatever lay behind the decision to transfer the king to Germany, it
was to have a disastrous effect on the peace and stability of postwar Belgium.
The country was liberated in September 1944 but the Allies did not reach the
king until the following May. As a result the politicians were the first to arrive
home, allowing them time to manifest considerable resentment towards the
monarch. They did so in blatant contradiction of two people close to wartime
events in Belgium.

The first was General von Falkenhausen who was interrogated by the
Allies following his capture on the liberation of Belgium. On 10 September
1945, his interrogators included a Belgian civilian who wanted the general to
confirm that it was at the request of King Leopold III that he was deported to
Germany and on the eve of his departure the king had opened champagne in
celebration. Falkenhausen denied this. The king was angered at the deporta-
tion and had presented him with a strongly worded note of protest to Hitler.
In the past the general had been reprimanded for the violent tone of Leopold's
protests on other issues, and fearing the consequences of this latest note he
insisted that the king reword it. The Belgian interrogator said that was a lie
because he had the evidence of a palace servant who took the king the champagne. When the general challenged him to produce the servant he was told.
The servant is dead and that the king was a good play actor... I replied that it
was a disgusting lie.'[5]

    The second was Joseph G. Davis, a former United States ambassador
to Belgium who said of King Leopold III:

History will perhaps say that he made an error of judgement...
But be that as it may, I am sure that the verdict of history will be
that in his hour of trial the honour and personal nobility of

Leopold of Belgium was unscathed and without stain and bore the stamp of greatness. To my mind it is completely impossible that it should be otherwise.[6]

References:

1. *Queen in Denmark*, Anne Wolden-Raethinge.
2. *The Prisoner at Laeken*, Emile Cammaerts.
3, 4, 5 and 6. *Leopold III*, James Page.

CHAPTER TWENTY. THE NETHERLANDS

'I Shall Maintain'

The Netherlands was the first country to be subject to a massive airborne attack and the speed with which it was effected was quite breathtaking. The waterways that criss-crossed the countryside were no barrier to an army that descended from the skies. In the spring of 1940, the Dutch awaited two major royal events, the birthday of Crown Princess Juliana at the end of April, and the christening of the infant Princess Irene in May. The birthday celebrations went ahead with a ceremonial drive through the Hague but Amsterdam was to miss the pageantry of a royal christening. The Germans had arrived and it was around the font at Buckingham Palace in London that the royal family gathered. Defeat was very quick.

Queen Wilhelmina was at her palace, the Huis ten Bosch, on the outskirts of the Hague when the paratroopers began to descend on 9 May 1940. She was therefore moved into town for greater safety but even at the Noordeinde Palace she was pinned down in her air raid shelter by either German aircraft or sniper fire from the Dutch Nazi party's headquarters overlooking the palace. Her son-in-law Prince Bernhard did his best to defend the family, shooting back at the snipers and aircraft with his machine-gun but the odds were against them and exile beckoned.

Crown Princess Juliana, Prince Bernhard and their daughters were the first to go and they escaped to the docks in an armoured van belonging to the Netherlands Bank. The crown jewels went with them in a cardboard box. A British destroyer awaited the royal party but upon their arrival a German aeroplane came across them. It dropped a magnetic mine at the harbour entrance to prevent the destroyer leaving but the mine's parachute failed to open and it exploded upon hitting the water leaving it clear for the ship to move off. The Queen took no chances when she followed them on 13 May, and throughout the channel crossing she wore a regulation steel helmet perched on top of her hat.

They were traumatic days and none more so than for a queen who was 60 years old; but Wilhelmina would not be intimidated. She was far from happy to be leaving the country and even when forced to take refuge on the

British destroyer, the Queen did her utmost to persuade the captain to sail around the Dutch coast so that she might join the Army. The request was politely declined, and she had no other choice but to cross to England. Once in Harwich, it also took the prompt despatch of the royal train from London to deter a return home on a Dutch merchant ship. This fighting spirit made Queen Wilhelmina a formidable opponent of Nazi Germany.

Almost immediately upon her arrival in London, the queen made a radio broadcast to the Netherlands. Nazi sympathisers at home were eager to portray the queen and the government which followed her into exile as deserters and there was no doubting that the Dutch people were shocked by the sudden turn of events. She gave the following reasons for their departure: the navy, and remnants of the army were still free. So too was the empire, as yet unmolested by the Japanese.

> To keep alive the voice and symbol of Holland as an inspiration and rallying point for our army, our navy, our countless subjects in the empire and, indeed, for the Dutch men and women all over the world who will give their all for the resurrection of their beloved country.
>
> To keep aloft the banner, unseen yet ever present for those who have lost their voice but neither hope nor vision.
>
> To speak for Holland to the world, not of the justice of its cause which needs no advocacy in the eyes of honest men, not of the unspeakable horrors and infamous stratagems imposed on its brave army and innocent population – but of the values, ideals, of christian civilisation, that Holland is defending at the side of the allies against the onslaught of barbarism.

The Queen ended with a promise. 'I remain true to the motto of Orange, of Holland, of all that immense part of the world that is fighting for that which is infinitely more precious than life – I shall maintain'.[1]

Queen Wilhelmina had explained why it was her duty to go abroad but she was also to talk of the personal anguish at leaving the country:

> I will not at this time of universal suffering speak of the bitter heart-searchings which this decision has cost one who barely a year ago was stirred to her depths by the generous devotion of a warm-hearted people when it celebrated the jubilee of its Queen – of the woman who for forty years has tried to serve her nation. She tried to serve it on that day of fateful decision and will endeavour to serve it to her last breath.[2]

In return the people renewed their loyalty to the House of Orange. The Germans took revenge by prohibiting Queen Wilhelmina's picture in private homes or public places. Orange flags, ribbons and other royalist emblems were also banned. This included the carnations that Prince Bernhard always wore. Streets named after members of the royal family were changed to honour the Nazi overlords. New born babies could not bear royal names, and further measures were required when the parents switched to names like Winston, after Winston Churchill, or Franklin, after Franklin D. Roosevelt. Of course the Dutch got around the rules in their own discreet way and on royal birthdays they would wash their orange blouses, or red, white and blue linen, and hang them on the washing line in the garden.

It was only the start of things to come and over the years Queen Wilhelmina would make regular broadcasts addressing the issues of the day. Royal displeasure would come like a thunderbolt from the skies. The shame of Dutch Nazis and the inhuman treatment of Dutch Jews were the theme of just two such broadcasts. At the same time, her words of encouragement gave a much needed boost to ordinary Dutch people and some broadcasts were dedicated to the underground press, railway workers or ordinary mothers and wives. Above all her fighting spirit, and talk of liberation did give the country the hope it so badly needed.

The broadcasts inspired many of her countrymen also to cross the channel and take up the armed struggle against the enemy. They became know as Engelandvaarders, or Englandfarers to the English tongue, and provided the Queen with first hand knowledge of conditions and public opinion inside the country. Indeed, Queen Wilhelmina made a point of seeing every new arrival regardless of his or her position in life. More often than not it was a difficult encounter for both parties. Wilhelmina had been queen since she was ten years of age, a legendary figure to the many Engelandvaarders who had known no other sovereign.

Tradition laid down that one should not do this and not do that when before the queen, never say no to the queen even if the answer is no, never offer physical assistance even if the queen tripped before your very eyes, never smoke within a hundred yards of her and so on, the list seemed endless. The queen for her part had led a cosseted life and before the war had rarely taken afternoon tea with anyone outside court circles. However, the war gave her the opportunity to make amends and she firmly grasped it but her new democratic disposition was not without its problems as her niece Princess Alice, Countess of Athlone, was to testify. When Queen Wilhelmina visited the Athlones in Canada, she insisted on carrying her own suitcases from the plane only to find she had no hands free to welcome the dignitaries awaiting her on the tarmac.

In London, the queen, like many an Engelandvaarder, felt a sense of frustration at not being in the thick of it. The only reminder of the armed struggle was the war that raged over the skies of England. Princess Juliana and her daughters had moved to the safety of Canada but the queen and Prince Bernhard stayed to face the endless bombing raids and both were to have lucky escapes. Queen Wilhelmina had only just got out of bed to put away some jewellery she had previously forgotten to take off when a bomb fell upon her house and brought a beam down across the bed. Prince Bernhard was just about to leave a friend's house when a bomb struck and demolished the staircase upon which he was about to set foot. Had he not been called back into the room for something he could have been killed. As it was he was on the third floor and could not get out until a fireman came to the window with the words 'Put out the lights... Don't you know the 'ouse 'as been 'it by a bomb?'[3]

The first anniversary of the German invasion was commemorated in the charred ruins of the Dutch church in Austin Friars, and if the setting was not bleak enough, the outlook was no brighter. Within another year the Japanese had occupied the Dutch East Indies. Radio Bandung made a final broadcast with the words. 'We are now closing down. Farewell until better times. Long live the Queen.'[4] The surrender ceremony was caught on newsreel and shown in Japan. Whilst senior Japanese officials dictated terms, younger Japanese officers were seen behind the Dutch representatives slapping them, pulling their hair, or twisting their ears if they so much as dared to speak out of turn or object to the proceedings. Upon signing the document of surrender, the senior Dutch officer was dragged from the room by his hair and forced to pose on the veranda for an official photograph.

The Dutch East Indies had not gone quietly. The Dutch Royal Air Force had caused much damage to Japanese shipping, and it was reported that in 1942 Dutch aircraft hit 32 ships when they attacked a Japanese convoy off Borneo. However, it was a two-way process and what remained of the Dutch navy was also lost in the East, which was a blow to the Allies. They needed all the vessels that they could lay their hands on and good use was to be made of Dutch merchant shipping in the convoys that travelled to and from Murmansk. Even the Dutch fishing fleets helped relieve the food shortages.

Merchant seamen were not the only Dutch to journey to the Soviet Union, although the others went there with the Germans. A 'Netherlands Legion' was raised by Nazi sympathisers from within occupied Holland. A 'Netherlands East Company' was also formed to encourage the migration of Dutch farmers to the Ukraine. The short shrift given the legion by the Red Army indicated the fate that awaited the farmers, and those who did venture there were used as farm labourers rather than the farming magnates promised under the scheme.

In contrast, Queen Wilhelmina went westwards on a visit to America in the summer of 1942. The queen had never flown before, and like most people on their maiden flight, she marvelled at the sight of the sun setting above the clouds. The President placed a flying boat at the her disposal and every effort was made to make the flight as comfortable and safe as possible. However, the queen was not amused when bad weather delayed her departure by two days and was quite adamant with the United States pilots. 'If you refuse to take me up in this weather I'll get some of my own Dutch boys. We're used to a little rain in Holland.'[5] But the need for such precautions was apparent upon her return to London when she found that the Duke of Kent had just been killed in an air crash.

Apart from the false start, and a very tall lectern, the visit was an unqualified success. The queen's address to both houses of Congress earned her a standing ovation but it was almost impossible to see her above the lectern. (Fifty years on, and America has yet to adjust to a monarch who is less than six foot in height. When Queen Elizabeth II made her most recent visit to Washington she too was hidden behind a lectern.) Notwithstanding such technical hitches, the president made a lasting impression on Queen Wilhelmina, and once back in England she would sit up until three in the morning to hear one of his fireside chats on the radio.

What the president made of the queen is not recorded but Churchill was said to be scared stiff of her, although he was quite relaxed with his Dutch counterpart Professor Gerbrandy, who he nicknamed Cherry Brandy. When they first met, Gerbrandy mistakenly said goodbye rather than hello, to which Churchill responded somewhat tongue in cheek. 'Sir, I wish that all political meetings were as short and to the point.'[6]

Dutch interests on the American continent were usually represented by Crown Princess Juliana who lived in Canada. There were many Dutch immigrants in America and Canada to keep her busy and in addition to the public relations side of her duties there was the practical work involved with running the Dutch Red Cross. The organisation was then needed more than ever, and to set an example the Crown Princess was one of the first to give blood through the blood donor scheme. In addition to her official functions, Princess Juliana had a young family to bring up and in 1943 a third daughter was born. She was christened Margriet after the marguerite flower which Queen Wilhelmina had adopted as a symbol of resistance. The queen explained the choice of name on Radio Orange.

> In choosing this name it is the parents' intention to establish a life-long tie between our severely tried people in the occupied parts of the empire and the new born child.
>
> Who does not remember the marguerites that bloom in meadow and field in the month of May, and that every year overlay the memory of all the suffering and sorrow of those terrible days of May 1940 with their whiteness, whispering to us of a better future.
>
> May it soon be granted to Margriet to live in her fatherland among her people and like her flowering namesakes of the fields, may she represent our living and constantly renewed homage to all those who made the great sacrifice, which will prove to be the seed from which will spring a truly free and great fatherland and empire.[7]

Prince Bernhard was in Ottawa for his daughter's birth but his high spirits were rather dampened when he caught mumps from Princess Beatrix. This just about summed up the misery of his exile. In London, the War Ministry looked upon him as a German prince by birth, and not a Dutch prince by marriage. Even King George VI could not move them to give him a job. Queen Wilhelmina had no such reservations as to where her son-in-law's loyalties lay, and so she forced him upon the British by making Bernhard the liaison officer for Dutch forces. Furthermore, whereas King George VI failed to get him into British Intelligence, the queen put him to work in Dutch intelligence which established an effective secret service for clandestine operations at home.

This put the prince in touch with the resistance forces inside Holland. They were doing a superb job given that the open countryside did not offer the traditional landscape for guerrilla warfare. The price was high. By mid-1943 over 2,000 people had been executed for alleged resistance. His contact with the underground movement made Prince Bernhard an ideal choice to lead a new army consisting of regular army units and the resistance fighters back home. His moment came on 3 September 1944, when the queen appointed him Commander-in-Chief of the Interior Forces, and he participated in Allied operations under General Eisenhower. This meant that liberation was on hand, and Bernhard was to be the first member of the royal family to go home.

Liberation came in stages. Maastricht, whose name has since become synonymous with European unity, was the first large Dutch town to be liberated. The concept of a European super-state had been aired in the war. Those in favour of such a development argued through the press that Europe would only remain weak whilst the different countries there continued to quarrel over their historic rights to territory. As in the Balkans, all had owned the same land at some stage or another and it was now time to put the differences aside and move forward together. Europe was also exhausted by two world wars in twenty years, and it would be the super-states like America that would hold power in the future. Unity would place Europe on a par with America. However, in a letter to *The Times* newspaper the Dutch Foreign Minister, Dr E. N. van Kleffens defended the sovereignty of the smaller nations like the Netherlands. After all he was fighting for Dutch independence.

Prince Bernhard found that the Netherlands was still a hostile place. Nazi units continued to roam the countryside, and it became prudent for the prince to remove his gold-braided epaulets and don a false moustache before venturing out beyond army quarters. It was certainly no place for the queen, and Wilhelmina was obliged to sit out another winter in London. It was a painful time. At home the people had no food to eat, or fuel to burn, and the weather was particularly atrocious. Aide-de-camp Erik Hazelhoff, caught the queen's torment in his memoirs *Soldier of Orange*.

> The queen was sitting in a small armchair, wrapped in some sort of blanket. For the first time in my experience she didn't rise to greet me. An aura of great agitation emanated from her. 'Have you heard? They're dropping dead in the streets.' It came so unexpectedly, I stared at her bewildered. 'The people', she

explained with a gesture of impatience. 'The people are dropping dead in the streets.'

I hardly knew what she was talking about and could be of no help. Furthermore, I was so shocked by her horror and grief that I thanked God when our meeting ended. This time something made me pause at the door and bow in her direction but she had already forgotten about me. She sat staring out of the window into the grey afternoon, huddled in her blanket like a wounded bird.[8]

It was a long winter for both queen and country but the queen's return home in the spring of 1945 at last gave cause for celebration. However, when the American outriders escorting the royal cavalcade switched on their sirens they were soon told to turn them off. 'I'm not a fire engine'[9] protested the queen. Yet her arrival did attract all the excitement of a fire engine with its sirens blazing, and the people were soon on the streets to welcome her home. The queen savoured those first few days on Dutch soil. At Eede she crossed the border on foot to an enthusiastic welcome. In Sluiskil she took the marguerite from her lapel and laid it on a bridge in tribute to the resistance fighters who had been executed there by the Germans. At Hulst she had lunch with the local resistance leaders and their wives, consisting of bread, coffee and apples from the burgomaster's garden. In Breda she went to church and met the Polish General Maczek who had helped in the liberation. The royal party also journeyed to Westkapelle aboard an amphibious craft. The area had been flooded by bombing raids on the surrounding dykes and the queen was confronted by a vast expanse of water, with church steeples and roof tops just visible above the water. Shortly afterwards she visited the coal mines at Heerlen and encouraged the miners in the production of coal.

Not once had Queen Wilhelmina doubted that justice would be done and that the Netherlands would one day be liberated. The road to victory had been long and hard but the queen had been motivated by an inner faith, the strength of which was to be demonstrated upon her return home. Fearful of German booby traps or mines, a member of the queen's staff had once tried to prevent her walking across an area of garden that had yet to be given the all clear. The queen simply looked at him in utter astonishment and said. 'Oh come now Captain, do you really believe I'll suddenly blow up? Boom just like that? '[10] Such was her belief in final victory and the triumph of good over evil.

There is a verse of the Dutch national anthem, the Wilhelmus, which is rarely sung today but which was very apt to Queen Wilhelmina, and the Netherlands, at the end of the war:

> Steadfast my heart remaineth,
>   In my adversity.
> My princely courage straineth,
>   All nerves to live and be.

I've praised the Lord my master,
With fervid heart and tense,
To save me from disaster,
And prove my innocence.

References:

1 and 2. *Queen Wilhelmina*, Philip Paneth.

3. *HRH Prince Bernhard of the Netherlands*, Alden Hatch.

4 and 7. *Lonely But Not Alone*, HRH Princess Wilhelmina of the Netherlands.

5, 6, 8. and 10. *Soldier of Orange*, Erik Hazelhoff.

9. *The Hunger Winter*, Henri van der Zee.

CHAPTER TWENTY-ONE. FRANCE

Princely Recruits to the Foreign Legion

Hitler finally avenged the humiliation of Versailles with the fall of France on 22 June 1940. To reinforce the landmark he ordered the French armistice to be concluded in the same railway carriage used by the Entente for the German surrender in 1918. Hitler attended the ceremony and was particularly pleased to receive the French surrender from Marshal Pétain, the victor of Verdun. Indeed, his pleasure was such that he was caught on newsreel stamping his foot with joy. This spontaneous gesture brought him ridicule because the Americans tampered with the film to make it look as if he was doing a silly dance, and duly distributed it around the cinemas of the free world.

The railway carriage once belonged to the Emperor Napoleon III. His widow, the Empress Eugénie, had recognised the weakness of the new European order established in 1918. She considered the United States policy of self-determination a danger, the League of Nations a folly, and the creation of new countries like Czechoslovakia a risk. In due time she was proved correct and the armistice found Prince Louis Napoleon, the current Bonapartist pretender, training with the Foreign Legion in North Africa.

The Law of Exile forbade the prince from setting foot in France which included French North Africa. However, he was conscious of his military heritage, and under the false name of M. Blanchard he enlisted with the Legion, an organisation which men usually joined to forget their past! At six foot three inches in height he was a person who stood out in a crowd, and it was not long before his true identity was known. Fortunately for him, the prime minister was otherwise preoccupied with more pressing affairs of state and Prince Louis-Napoleon was allowed to stay on, perhaps in the knowledge that the armistice was looming and with demobilisation he would return to his home in Switzerland.

The injustice of German rule persuaded him to return to France and join the French resistance movement. This led to his capture by the Gestapo and he spent four months in prison. Whilst there the Germans sought his collaboration but the prince refused all incentives to change sides. He was therefore released from prison under German surveillance. He very quickly went underground again and eventually joined the Free French Forces. He was wounded in action and later decorated with the Légion d'Honneur, a military decoration first instituted by the Emperor Napoleon I.

Hitler greatly admired the military genius of the Emperor Napoleon I and on a sight-seeing tour of Paris which included a visit to the Emperor's blood-coloured marble tomb at the Dome Les Invalides, he came up with the idea of transferring the remains of the emperor's son from Vienna to Paris. The boy is known by a number of titles, from the King of Rome, to the Duke of Reichstadt, to the Emperor Napoleon II. Upon the defeat of his father, the prince had gone to Vienna with his Habsburg mother, the Empress Marie Louise, and it was there that he had died in 1832 at the age of 21.

Eager to carry out his plan, Hitler gave orders for the remains to be taken to Paris in December 1940 and reinterred with all the trappings of a state funeral. The idea was to win the Parisians to his cause but the gesture failed to impress them, and in mid-winter the ordinary man in the street called out for coal rather than ashes. Their hostility made it advisable for the cortège to complete the last leg of its journey through the torchlit streets of Paris at the dead of night. This only added to the eerie atmosphere surrounding the whole affair.

A greater awareness of French history would have told Hitler of the futility of the gesture. One hundred years before in 1840, King Louis Philippe had attempted to win Bonapartist support by bringing the body of Emperor Napoleon I back to France. Yet the event only served to undermine his monarchy and pave the way for the Second Empire under the Emperor Napoleon III.

A former president of the French chamber of deputies, Edouard Herriot, once said that everything good and solid about France was accomplished not by the republics, nor by the empires, but by the Bourbon kings. With this ringing endorsement of his heritage, the Comte de Paris, and Bourbon pretender to the throne, likewise tricked his way into the Foreign Legion at the outset of war. There he did not use the style of King Henri VI as was afforded him by his supporters, but that of Private Orliac. To his mind the head of the royal house of France could only hold two military ranks, that of commander-in-chief, or private second class.

In common with Prince Louis-Napoleon he was demobilised before he saw action but chose not to join the Free French. The Comte de Paris was prepared to fight for one country but with defeat came disunity. France was divided into two camps. Under the terms of the armistice, Germany occupied two-thirds of the nation, whilst the remaining territory fell under the nominal control of Marshal Philippe Pétain. His government sat at the spa town of Vichy and his territory became known as Vichy France. There were also Frenchmen who could not accept the armistice, most notably General Charles de Gaulle, and they chose to continue the fight from abroad. They were called Free Frenchmen.

No love was lost between the Free French and Vichy collaborators and control of the North African empire was hotly disputed. The divisions were reflected by the colonial command in Algeria. The two sides were therefore set for a clash in North Africa. The Comte de Paris was anxious to avoid a bloody encounter between Frenchmen and he attempted to broker a deal from his home in Morocco. He won few friends by attempting to represent all Frenchmen regardless of political creed. Negotiations with the Vichy government quickly broke down. Henri found the meeting to be 'painful and revolting', adding that the Vichy representatives were cowards who would not take matters at face value. His bargaining power in Vichy France declined when a monarchist by the name of Bonnier de la Chapelle assassinated Admiral Darlan, a leading Vichy supporter in Algeria. The murder was not, however, carried out with the knowledge or support of the Comte de Paris.

As for the Free French, General de Gaulle once remarked that had Henri joined him he would have secured a Bourbon restoration at the end of the war. However, his was a lonely voice that spoke in favour of the Comte de Paris. To treat with the collaborators, however well intentioned, did not go down well with General Giraud who was the French high commissioner in Algeria, and when the comte went to see him Giraud used the Law of Exile to remove him from his office and for that matter from Algeria.

His peace efforts had ended in farce but ironically during the postwar years he was seen as the pretender with the most chance of restoration. His friendship with de Gaulle certainly helped his prospects, as did the repeal of the Law of Exile in 1950. Henri also waged an energetic campaign in contrast to his predecessors who swore by the divine right of kings and sat back waiting for the French people to see the error of their ways. Instead Henri went out to them with his message of elected monarchy, a half-way measure which did not capture the public imagination. This prompted the Comte de Paris to think that perhaps Prince Louis-Napoleon had the right idea about living quietly in a Paris suburb. A restoration of kingdom, and empire seem very remote but Bourbon and Bonapartes still feature in the annuals of French history.

CHAPTER TWENTY-TWO. GREAT BRITAIN

Duty First

One of the most enduring images of King George VI is that of his wartime visits to the East End of London in the wake of the German bombers. A reporter from *The Daily Herald* witnessed the death and destruction that awaited the king and the amazing way in which he raised the spirits of the people around him.

It was 9 September 1940, and the king stood before a crater the size of four London buses. Twenty houses had once stood on that spot, and as the king looked across the road he saw a line of terraced houses without any back walls. Inside the rooms lay broken furniture with pictures hanging precariously at an angle on the walls. Behind him stood a further row of houses with every window broken and every curtain torn. To emphasise the human tragedy before him, the king stood with a wedding photograph at his feet, the bride holding a horseshoe for good luck. Demolition workers had pulled eight people from the debris, three of whom had died. A dog had also been found alive and a search was underway for his master.

King George commented on how incredible it was that so few people had been killed given the size of the explosion. He asked the demolition workers about the type of bombs that the Germans were using and was told that they appeared to be a larger type than used before. He also chatted at length with the victims for whom he had a simple and heartfelt message: 'You are very brave'. He was warmly cheered by the people, including one woman who had lost three children.

Queen Elizabeth was also a much valued visitor to the East End. Winston Churchill said of her that 'Many an aching heart found some solace in her gracious smile.'[1] One day she came across an elderly lady in tears. When she asked what was wrong she was told that the lady's pet dog had hidden under the rubble and was too frightened to come out.[2] Perhaps I can get him out' said the queen; 'I'm rather good with dogs' and with that she knelt down amid the rubble and proceeded to coax the pet out of the hole. Before long it was back in the arms of its owner behaving as if it did not have a care in the world. It was difficult, however, for the king and queen not to be deeply affected by what they saw and heard. The queen wrote to her mother-in-law Queen Mary. 'I feel quite exhausted after seeing and hearing so much sadness, sorrow, heroism and magnificent spirit. The destruction is so awful, and the people so wonderful – they deserve a better world.'[3]

The king and queen were not immune from the hardships that faced other people. The Guards regiments are close to the monarchy and they knew many of the officers and men who died when a V-1 flying bomb fell upon Wellington Barracks during a church parade. The Guards Chapel received a direct hit, and of the 200 people at the service, over 120 were killed. Buckingham Palace, which is just down the road from the barracks, was to be bombed throughout the war. The extent of the structural damage was not appreciated until well after the war, and when the Princess Elizabeth married in 1947, there were some hastily arranged repairs to the balcony. In the majority of instances the king and queen were not at home but on one occasion they were inside the palace when two bombs landed only yards from the royal apartments. Both were clearly shocked by the raid and in his diary the king admitted that for the next few days he felt uneasy about sitting in his room, and was for ever glancing out of the window. Yet it helped him face those who had suffered at the hands of the Luftwaffe. 'I feel that our tours of bombed areas in London are helping the people who have lost their relations and homes and we have both found a new bond with them, as Buckingham Palace has been bombed as well as their homes, and nobody is immune from it.'[4]

Nevertheless, Buckingham Palace remained the principal residence of the sovereign. Indeed, the king decided upon weekly investitures and thousands of people passed through the palace gates to receive their decorations. Civilians would be awarded the George Cross, or George Medal. They were honours created by the king in direct response to what he saw on his tours of bomb-damaged Britain. War heroes, such as those who had fought in the famous Battle of the River Plate, or those who had taken part in the Dambusters raids, would also gather for their military decorations. The interest shown by the royal family in their exploits was only too apparent when a fighter pilot returned to the palace for his fourth wartime decoration. To his utter surprise the king said in reference to the Princess Elizabeth, 'My daughter will be very thrilled when I tell her I have seen you again today. She knows all about your victories and reads every word she can about you.'[5]

Despite the stiff upper lip response to the attacks on Buckingham Palace they did highlight the vulnerability of the king and queen to enemy action. A group of officers from the Guards regiments and Household Cavalry were formed to act as personal bodyguards and became known as the Coates Mission after their commander Colonel J. S. Coates. However, a visitor to Windsor Castle asked the king what would happen if German parachutists landed on the lawn. King George confidently pressed a button in the wall to sound the alarm but nothing happened and it was left to an equerry to locate the rather red-faced bodyguards and spur them into action. Nevertheless, the king and queen were ready for any lapse in security as both had learnt how to fire a revolver. Fortunately they were not required to defend themselves and the only unauthorised person to enter the palace grounds was an army deserter who found his way into the queen's bathroom at Windsor Castle. He had been very upset by the death of his family in a bombing raid and, inspired by the media coverage of the royal tours to the East End of London, he had turned to the queen for consolation. Although initially frightened by the unexpected encounter, Queen Elizabeth was able to calm him down long enough for her to ring for help and on this occasion the guards did answer the call.

Security was also an issue when the king made overseas visits to the armed forces. Although he was to visit the British Expeditionary Force in France at the outset of war, it was not until 1943 when the Allies started to win key battles, that it was considered safe enough for him to make further tours of inspection. However, in the remaining two years of the war, he was to make up for lost time and visit British forces in France, North Africa, Italy, Malta and the Low Countries. For obvious reasons no advance publicity was given to the visits and the reaction of the servicemen to the sudden arrival of the king was something to be seen. When he appeared on a beach in Algiers half naked men ran from the sea and greeted him with 'God Save the King' and 'For He's a Jolly Good Fellow.'

Concern for his safety certainly prevented the king witnessing the D-Day landings on the Normandy coast. The prime minister, Winston Churchill, had suggested to the king that they might both watch the proceedings from one of the battleships taking part in the invasion and the king had been greatly excited by the proposal. However, his advisers were appalled to think what might happen if both the king and the prime minister were killed in action. He could not therefore travel to Normandy until ten days after the Allied landings, and then only under the protection of a flotilla of minesweepers and a double line of supply ships that stretched the entire channel. Once there he toured the different beachheads in an amphibious truck and then went further inland to visit General Montgomery at his headquarters. Within hours he was safely back on ship but as HMS *Arethusa* made her way home there was a security alert as the ship's radar picked up an aircraft that had penetrated allied air defences. It turned out not to be a direct threat to the ship but one of Hitler's new flying bombs heading for London. In the next few months such bombs were to keep the king very busy with tours on the stricken areas as they descended upon London by day and night.

Having been convinced by his advisers that it was rather foolhardy to watch the invasion, the king had become worried for the safety of the prime minister but he had a terrible problem persuading Winston Churchill to follow suit and abandon the scheme. Only the night before the invasion did he eventually win the prime minister around after he threatened to drive to the coast and personally prevent him from boarding his ship. The king greatly admired the prime minister and could not contemplate fighting the war without him. It was an altogether different story from when Winston Churchill entered Number 10 Downing Street in 1940. As a known supporter of the exiled King Edward VIII he was guaranteed a less than enthusiastic welcome at the palace but through the calamities of war both men came to see great virtues in each other and before long the customary formalities of an audience would be replaced with a quiet lunch for two. This reflected a strong friendship and enabled them to talk about secret information without anyone else present. Politics took a back seat for the duration of the war and Churchill headed a government of national unity in which the opposition leader, Clement Attlee, was deputy prime minister.

The invasion of Normandy, or D-Day as it is known, was undertaken in conjunction with American forces and the man in overall charge of operations was General Dwight Eisenhower. Had he not led Allied forces and gone on to become the President of The United States of America, his one claim to fame might have been that he actually brought the king of England to his knees. The general had asked to see the grounds of Windsor Castle but only if his visit did not in any way inconvenience the king and queen. King George therefore offered to stay out of sight so as not to embarrass the general. However, the sun was to lure the royal family outside and in the tranquillity of their garden, the king quite forgot about the visit. Suddenly he heard the sound of voices and remembered his earlier undertaking to remain indoors. There was nothing for it but for the royal family to beat a hasty retreat on their hands and knees through the nearest door in the castle walls.

American troops and supplies had poured into Great Britain in the months leading to the invasion and it was not long before some people were referring to an American invasion of Britain. However, it was only a short time previously that the king had been worried for his West Indian subjects after the government agreed to allow America to build air and sea bases in the West Indies in exchange for 50 destroyers from the First World War. The king wrote to his private secretary. 'The Americans have got to understand that in leasing the bases the question of sovereignty does not come in. These islands are part of the British Colonial Empire, and I am not going to see my West Indian subjects handed over to the U.S. authorities.'[6] This took place prior to Pearl Harbor and any hesitation the king might have had was gone by the time he and the queen played host to Mrs Roosevelt at Buckingham Palace in 1942.

America was by then alongside Britain fighting the Axis Powers, Japan included, and the First Lady was in Britain to inspect American forces and to study the role of women in the war effort. In her reports home she was to provide a rare glimpse of life within the four walls of the palace. To all intents and purposes it differed little from that of the man in the street. Blown out windows had been replaced by mica in small wooden frames. It was winter and the palace was very cold with only one small electric heater in each room, along with one light bulb regardless of the size of the apartments. At the dinner table she sat down to reconstituted eggs and pies, followed by puddings made of root vegetables. Only one thing told her that she was at the Court of St James and that was the gold plates upon which the wartime diet was served. Although the king and queen did not visit the United States during the war, they were often to be found touring American bases in Great Britain. On one such tour to an American air base in 1944, they were accompanied by the Princess Elizabeth who named a Flying Fortress bomber the *Rose of York*, and was presented with a large bouquet of white roses.

The Princess came of age during the war and assumed an ever increasing number of public engagements. This very much fitted the image of the 'family firm', a concept of monarchy that was to be developed by King George VI, and immortalised by Queen Elizabeth, when at the beginning of the war she said of the proposal to evacuate her daughters to Canada 'The Princesses could not go without me, I could not leave without the King, and of course the King will never leave.' The Princess Elizabeth was sixteen on 21 April 1942, and in common with other people of her age had registered under the National Registration Act for service in the auxiliary forces, or the munitions factories. The government then debated in cabinet whether or not the princess, as heiress to the throne, should concentrate on her royal duties, or see war service of a different kind. The cabinet took the view that preparation for the throne was a national service in its own right, and the princess should not therefore be asked to serve elsewhere. A public statement was made to this effect but the princess had other ideas and it was later announced that she had joined the Auxiliary Territorial Service, and was at a driving training centre somewhere in the south of England.

The Princess Elizabeth joined the ATS as an honorary second subaltern but her father had only recently appointed her as Colonel of the Grenadier Guards so there was some confusion as to how the Princess should be addressed. It was therefore decided that those within the ATS of equal or senior rank should call her Princess, whilst junior ranks should address her as Ma'am. Meanwhile, the Princess Elizabeth overcame the problem with the Guards by reviewing them in civilian clothes and not in her subaltern's uniform. It was not the first time that a member of the royal family had to adjust their military rank in time of war. The Dukes of Gloucester and Kent had accepted a lower rank to one they normally held in peace time so that they could see active service. The king's nephews the Honourable George and Gerald Lascelles also joined units of the armed services and saw active service. In 1944 the elder was captured and eventually imprisoned in Colditz prisoner of war camp.

Although the king's sister, the Princess Royal, was Controller Commandant of the ATS, it was the less glamorous of the auxiliary services. The princess was actually based at No 1 Mechanical Transport Training Centre in Camberley, and to pass the driving course she had to drive a range of vehicles from staff cars to field ambulances, and sixteen-hundredweight lorries had to be mastered. Training to be a mechanic was also mandatory and the Princess Elizabeth was required to dismantle and reassemble engines like anyone else. It was therefore a strange choice for a future queen to make but she clearly benefited from the experience. One of the greatest advantages was that it brought her into contact with women of different backgrounds. The princess also came to understand the preparation required for a royal visit. After the king and queen had visited the base to see for themselves the nature of their daughter's work, the Princess Elizabeth was to comment 'I'd no idea before how much preparation has to be made in advance of a royal visit. Next time I go anywhere on an official occasion, I'll know something about what has been done beforehand !'[7]

The Cabinet decision that the Princess Elizabeth should concentrate on her training for the throne was nonetheless correct. The king did not enjoy good health and the tension of the war years did not help. In fact it caused him to smoke more and this contributed to the cancer that was to kill him prematurely in 1952. King George VI was nevertheless a good tutor, and through his example to duty, Queen Elizabeth II has proved an admirable monarch. The king has left his mark and his impact on Great Britain should not be underestimated.

References:

1. *Silver Wedding*, Louis Wulff.
2 and 3. *The Queen Mother, 75 Glorious Years*, Angus Hall.
4 and 6. *King George VI*, Denis Judd
5 and 7. *Queen of Tomorrow*, Louis Wulff.

CHAPTER TWENTY-THREE. YUGOSLAVIA

Guardians of the Realm

A Croat separatist movement called the Ustase was to emerge in the 1930s in a bid to recapture Croatian independence and experience the tenth century kingdom of King Tomislav I. However, this romantic illusion was from the start to be distorted by blood and violence. The Ustase was to represent fascist thuggery at its worst and with the support of Mussolini it also came to pose a serious threat to Yugoslav unity. One of its first victims was King Aleksander whom the Ustase assassinated in 1934 whilst he was on a visit to Marseilles in France. With a cry of 'vive le roi' the terrorist had leapt on to the running board of the king's car, and with his Italian revolver, shot dead the sovereign at point blank range. Yugoslavia took the assassination before the League of Nations but could not persuade the major powers to take action against Italy. They were therefore forced into futile negotiations with Italy for the suppression of terrorist activities and the internment of Ustase ringleaders; a reminder perhaps of the assassination of Archduke Franz-Ferdinand and the demands made upon Serbia by Austria-Hungary.

The task of reconciliation fell to Prince Paul of Yugoslavia who was to act as regent for the eleven-year-old King Petar II. He met the Croats half way by giving them control over their own domestic affairs whilst retaining the defence and foreign policy portfolios for the Yugoslav parliament. There was, however, no accommodation of terrorist demands and he was to be no less reviled by the Ustase terrorists than the late King Aleksander I. Yet he was in a stronger position than the king because Adolf Hitler was courting Yugoslavia and he had some control over Benito Mussolini; but Hitler was not the type of friend that Prince Paul wanted. On a visit to Berchtesgaden on 4 March 1941, he told Hitler and Foreign Minister Ribbentrop that he would not remain in power for six months if he entered into an alliance with the man who helped murder his king. Ribbentrop replied that his grasp on power actually rested with his signing the Tripartite Pact, to which Hitler added that he could no longer prevent an Italian invasion if the pact was not signed.

A decision on joining the Tripartite Pact, and thus allying Yugoslavia to the Axis Powers, was now urgent. Benito Mussolini had invaded Greece the previous year and Yugoslavia was seen as a vital communication link between German and Italian forces. This placed Prince Paul in an almost impossible position. It was essential that he prevent an Axis invasion. This would almost certainly see the country divided between Germany, Italy and Bulgaria. Yet it was equally important that he maintain unity amongst the ethnic peoples of Yugoslavia. However, the prospect of a German treaty was dividing the country. The Serbs retained their Anglo-French sympathies from the First World War, whilst the Croats and Slovenes who sat between Germany and Serbia, saw the Tripartite Pact as the only safeguard against an invasion of their lands. Their resolve to fight was open to question as was the possibility of separate treaties with the Axis.

The Tripartite Pact also caused Prince Paul something of a personal dilemma. His wife, Princess Olga, was a Greek princess and his sister-in-law, Princess Marina, was the Duchess of Kent. His sympathies therefore lay with the allies, and in particular Great Britain where he had been educated and where he proposed to live in retirement. Hitler realised where Prince Paul's true allegiance lay and said to Count Ciano, the Italian foreign minister, 'Yugoslavia will only remain neutral as long as it is dangerous for her to go over openly to the side of the Western democracies. The very moment things go bad for Germany and Italy she will at once openly join the other side in the hope of giving the course of events a final twist to the disadvantage of the Axis.'[1] Behind the scenes Prince Paul certainly did his best to keep the British informed of developments within the Axis camp, and when the Italians cracked Britain's secret code and were able to read Foreign Office telegrams, it was the British Ambassador to Belgrade who first heard the news.

Fortunately for Hitler, Great Britain was only providing the prince with moral support. Whitehall seemed totally oblivious to Yugoslav vulnerability. The British Ambassador would write home of the geographical importance of Yugoslavia to the Axis Powers and their economic hold over the Balkans, but no effective aid was ever forthcoming, and when the Foreign Office finally came to realise Prince Paul's predicament, Great Britain was hard pressed to produce arms for her own troops let alone for Yugoslavia. The British Ambassador could only quote to Prince Paul from the Bible and the Second Book to the Corinthians 'Do not unite yourselves with unbelievers; they are no fit mates for you... Come away and leave them, separate yourselves, says the Lord; touch nothing unclean.' Prince Paul was not very impressed with this response and was in a state of despair when Churchill declared that smaller nations such as Yugoslavia should not tie the hands of greater powers who were fighting for the rights and freedoms of the smaller countries.

The United States of America was of similar opinion to Great Britain. Their minister in Belgrade expressed the opinion that nations who did not resist aggression were not worthy of independence, and certainly could not count on American support at the end of the war. The Soviet Union showed greater understanding and sent a representative to Yugoslavia to discuss military cooperation but he merely ascertained the strengths and weaknesses of the Yugoslav army and disappeared back across the border without another word. Until then, Yugoslavia had not recognised the Soviet Union. Many White Russians had sought sanctuary in Yugoslavia and had been represented at the Yugoslav court by a tsarist minister. To them such treachery was only to be expected of the Soviets, and Princess Olga was to recall in her diary. 'I had the ordeal of receiving the Soviet Minister and wife at eleven ! I wore a cross round my neck which I held all the time.'[2]

Prince Paul was further deterred from taking an independent stance by the poor state of the Yugoslav armed forces. Their inadequacies were even apparent to the young king who was given a ride in a 1924 Renault tank. The demonstration involved the vehicle descending a slope, crossing a stream, and climbing a steep bank. With a very loud bang the tank ambled forward and slowly overcame the first two hurdles, but when it came to climbing the bank opposite, it lost its tracking and on a second attempt caught fire. King Petar was to lament that this accurately reflected the condition of the Tank Corps which were no match against the German Mark IV tanks. It also said something of the military command which was made up of elderly generals who had greater faith in the ox than modern technology. When the king told one general that he thought there should be more motorised troops, he was told that 'our bullocks may have been slower but they never ran out of petrol.'[3]

Yugoslav unity depended on peace but she lived in close proximity to the Axis Powers, and was unable to safeguard her independence without economic or military aid from the Western Powers. She was also unable to withstand the assault of a modern army. Prince Paul therefore had little option but to bow to pressure from Berlin and sign the Tripartite Pact. He did not, however, commit Yugoslavia to fight alongside the Axis Powers but merely to allow the access of their troops through Yugoslav territory: a significant victory in the dealings of a 'small nation' with Nazi Germany. All the more so when Hitler agreed to the publication of such terms following the signing of the pact on 25 March 1941. The people had to know the exact terms of the treaty if he was to survive in power. Nothing, however, would reconcile the Serbs to any form of treaty with the Axis, and whilst the people took to the streets by day, rebel army officers seized power by night.

It took a mere four hours to dislodge the regency, with only one fatality. A policeman was killed for refusing to hand over the radio station, a solitary act of defiance not reflected elsewhere. Indeed the police headquarters, like most other government buildings was almost handed to the rebels on a gold platter. The prince regent was en route to Croatia at the time of the coup, and although he was to return to the capital to formally abdicate, it was to be the start of a journey that would take him to Greece, then Egypt, and finally to house arrest in Kenya. It was whilst there that the months of tension for him gave way to severe depression and it did not help that the British authorities were to allocate him the home of the murdered peer, Lord Errol, whose bizarre lifestyle and mysterious death have recently been retold in the film *White Mischief.* However, in the immediate aftermath of defeat he sought to safeguard Yugoslav interests and decline the offer of military support from Croatia. Civil war had been avoided at a time of world conflict and he was successful in his attempts to get Croatia to participate in the rebel government.

In the interests of national unity, King Petar also accepted the new government but at eighteen years of age he was open to manipulation. One of the more bizarre episodes of the coup was a radio broadcast in which a rebel army officer impersonated the king. The broadcast gave the impression that the army had acted on the orders of the crown, and appealed to people to rally around the throne and the new government. Nevertheless, with the removal of the prince regent the monarchy was to lose control of active government and those close to the king wondered whether he would have the stamina to survive such a turbulent period in the country's history. Prior to the coup, there had been talk of extending the regency for the duration of the war as it was recognised that King Petar was lacking in a number of attributes that might otherwise have stiffened his resolve.

For example, a stable upbringing. His father had been killed when he was only eleven years of age and his mother had since gone to live in England. Maturity was also an issue. His tutor was worried that he was more interested in the cartoons that appeared in the newspapers than the affairs of state. Finally, he lacked experience of Balkan politics. Prince Paul had provided the king with some tuition, but as Yugoslavia was gradually drawn into the orbit of the Axis Powers, so the prince sought to protect the king's reputation by distancing him from such business. In all it made for a somewhat withdrawn head of state but the king was to act with remarkable courage in the days and months that followed his accession. Just as Prince Paul had been proved right when he said that he would not survive in power six months if he signed the Tripartite Pact, so too was Adolf Hitler when he launched Operation Punishment and directed German forces against Yugoslavia.

On Sunday 6 April 1941, 200 German aircraft bombed Belgrade with the loss of 17,000 lives. By coincidence their targets were the same as those of the coup leaders with a heavy concentration of attack around such installations as the radio station. The royal palace was another target and the king was to be thrown to his bedroom floor by the blast of a bomb. Hearing a terrific scream, the king had got out of bed to go to the air raid shelter when there was a flash of light and a rush of hot air that knocked him over and shattered the windows in his room. As he was later to confide in his memoirs 'War had begun!' It was, however, to be a short-lived campaign and by 15 April King Petar had followed Prince Paul to Greece. His departure was to be no less traumatic than the outset of hostilities, and as he flew into exile his Italian built plane was mistaken for the enemy and buzzed by Allied aircraft. Fortunately radio contact was made in the nick of time.

Significant to the German victory was the air superiority of the Luftwaffe. Yugoslavia had a small but modern air force with aircraft built in Italy, Germany, and Great Britain. However, in the general chaos of war it was not uncommon to find Yugoslav Hurricanes fighting their own Messerschmitts. Support for their ground forces was therefore limited and within the army ethnic rivalry was also to play a part in the kingdom's downfall. Whereas the Serbian army fought with the tenacity for which they were renowned from the First World War, the other ethnic groups offered only muted resistance. This denied the king a cohesive resistance movement following the unconditional surrender on 17 April. The situation was further exacerbated by the Axis partitioning of the country. Serbia and Northern Slovenia fell under German control. Croatia gained independence under the puppet rule of the Ustase leader, Ante Pavelic, whilst Northern Slovenia, Montenegro, and Dalmatia went to Italy. Bulgaria and

Hungary were also rewarded for their membership of the Tripartite Pact with Macedonia going to Bulgaria and the Voyvodina Region to Hungary.

Several resistance movements were therefore to emerge from the ashes but they all came from different ethnic and religious backgrounds and with nothing to unite them, not even the excesses of the occupation forces, there was to be considerable infighting. Indeed, life in Yugoslavia during the Second World War was to resemble the debacle that has more recently occurred with Serb fighting Croat and Muslim fighting Christian. Hostility towards the Axis Powers was more an afterthought as the different ethnic groups resumed their age-old struggles. However, above the local politics arose two groups with a national identity. The Chetniks under General Mihailovich who supported King Petar and the Partisans under Josip Tito who supported a communist state. There was some initial cooperation between the two forces, but they soon fell apart, and by the end of the war they were locked in open conflict.

The final battle was won by Tito. The Chetniks were reduced to 2,000 men out of a force of some 30,000. General Mihailovich was subsequently executed. Tito was the new ruler of Yugoslavia and with the ruthless apparatus of a communist dictatorship he soon forced the ethnic groups into line. His task was made all the more easy by the support of the British and American governments, who had initially favoured General Mihailovich but who became disenchanted with the Yugoslav Government in Exile. It tended to spend more time arguing over the niceties of the king's marriage to Princess Alexandra of Greece than the war effort. As a result when a son and heir was born to the couple on 17 July 1945, there was no longer a kingdom to inherit, and it was small consolation to King Petar that the British Government allowed his hotel suite to be declared Yugoslav territory for the birth.

At the end of the war, Prince Paul was still under house arrest in Africa and was not to gain his freedom until 1946. The Allies did consider putting him on trial at Nuremburg but events had vindicated his prewar policy. However, the allies were prone to bear a grudge and it is doubtful whether the monarchy would have fared any better had the regency survived the war. What is certain is that Croatia might have been spared considerable heartache had the prince regent stayed in power. Ante Pavelic was placed in charge of Croatia in recognition of his efforts to destabilise post war Yugoslavia, and the Croats were to suffer the full excesses of fascism . The accession of King Tomislav II did nothing to rally the people to the cause of independence, and it is significant that the new king never set foot in his kingdom. In fact, such memories have prevented German forces from operating a peace-keeping role in Croatia in more recent times, and it was with the greatest difficulty that the exiled Crown Prince Aleksander of Yugoslavia sought to negotiate a peace settlement.

References:
1. *The Tightrope*, Cecil Parrott.
2. *Paul of Yugoslavia*, Neil Balfour and Sally Mackay.
3. *A King's Heritage*, King Peter II of Yugoslavia.

CHAPTER TWENTY-FOUR. LIECHTENSTEIN

Sanctuary for the Cossacks

The Cossacks first came to prominence in medieval times. They were mainly grouped around the Don basin in Russia and had a reputation for ruthless fighting and excellent horsemanship. This did not escape the notice of the tsars who quickly enlisted them as bodyguards, and there they remained until the Russian Revolution in 1917. With the fall of the monarchy they transferred allegiance to Kerensky and fought against Lenin in the civil war of 1918-1921.

The Bolsheviks had hoped that the Treaty of Brest Litovsk would give them peace, and with peace the opportunity to consolidate their hold on Russia. In their haste, they gave away large areas of the empire and this inspired a counter revolution. Bolshevism was well established in Central Russia, but it had to fight for supremacy in other regions. Former tsarist officers, most notably Generals Denikin, Yudenich and Admiral Kolchak, led the so-called white armies against the newly establish Red Army in the Crimea, the Baltic and Siberia. The fact that the civil war lasted for three years showed that the white armies fought with some success and the arrival of expeditionary forces from countries like Great Britain, France, America and Poland also strengthened their attack. At one point a white army was within 200 miles of Moscow. The Red Army was quickly reorganised to meet the challenge and a well disciplined, politically controlled, force of 5,000,000 men eventually secured victory for Lenin. Some Cossacks stayed and received a rather rough time of it, whilst other fled to Constantinople.

It was not without some difficulty that the Bolsheviks reintroduced and maintained conscription. The revolution had been fuelled by war weariness from the First World War and a new secret police force called the Cheka was forced to apply ruthless measures to ensure adherence to Bolshevik measures. Conscription disrupted the fragile economy and the requisitioning of foodstuffs for the Red Army brought renewed hunger. This prompted widespread industrial and social unrest which needed a strict response. It was the start of a class war that was to see the imprisonment or execution of tens of thousands of Russian people, and one that was to reach a crescendo under Josef Stalin, despite dramatic improvements to the economy.

The Second World War which brought about the German occupation of the Don region, gave the Cossacks another opportunity to overthrow the Bolsheviks. Eager to exploit the collaboration of the Cossacks, if for propaganda and not military purposes, Adolf Hitler created a Cossack army to fight alongside his own forces. In the event of a German defeat in the Soviet Union, Hitler undertook to give the Cossacks asylum elsewhere. The German-Cossack Army also attracted many exiles. This was on the assumption that

Germany would keep Western Europe, but fascism suffered total defeat, and as the Germans began to concede territory so the Cossacks fell into Allied hands. Great Britain and the United States of America agreed to a Soviet request for the Cossacks to be handed back to them, and by all accounts they were given a rather unpleasant welcome home.

A Cossack division of 500 men therefore crossed uninvited into neutral Liechtenstein, although on a technicality the principality was at war with Germany, having sided with Austria-Hungary in the Austro-Prussian War of 1866, and having been mistakenly excluded from the peace terms. The Cossacks hoped that with Liechtenstein unaligned to the Soviet Union, they would feel less obliged to hand them over. Otherwise, the principality was an odd choice because it had disbanded its small army in 1868 and could not meet a military challenge from the mighty Soviet Union. Fortunately, the Red Army did not flex its muscles but the Soviet government did bring considerable diplomatic pressure to bear on Liechtenstein.

Prince Franz-Josef II, who ruled Liechtenstein from 1938 to 1989, still refused to evict the Cossacks but he did accede to Stalin's demands for a Soviet delegation to visit the army. Some were lulled into a false sense of security by the delegation and went home with them only to be shot for collaboration with the enemy. Others stayed in Liechtenstein in barracks specifically built for them by the local people and in some cases married the local girls and lived to a ripe old age.

Should the Cossacks not have arrived in Liechtenstein, the war would have passed the principality by. There were food shortages to contend with but apart from that it was calm enough for Prince Franz-Josef to marry Countess Georgine von Wilezeck in 1943. The prince had once met with Adolf Hitler and his people would say that it was at this meeting that the dictator decided to leave them alone. The topic was not mentioned during the courtesy visit, but it might be possible that Hitler was sympathetic to the last German-speaking principality to remain in Central Europe. However, it was probably more to do with Liechtenstein's lack of strategic value.

The House of Liechtenstein had been loyal to the Habsburgs since the Holy Roman Emperor Rudolf II (1576–1612) had bestowed the principality upon them for services rendered on the battlefield. In recent times, Prince Franz I of Liechtenstein (1929–1938) had been a former Austro-Hungarian ambassador to St Petersburg and Prince Franz-Josef II could count the venerable Kaiser Franz-Josef a godfather, and the ill-fated Archduke Franz-Ferdinand an uncle. This link did ensure that the prince was to come through the war entirely unscathed.

The family had in this time acquired extensive property in the former Austro-Hungarian Empire and when the Red Army marched into Czechoslovakia and Austria at the end of the Second World War, so Prince Franz-Josef lost all his property there, some 30-odd palaces in all. He did manage to remove his vast art collection to the safety of his one remaining home, Schloss Vaduz in Liechtenstein. This collection included some rare paintings by

Rembrandt, Rubens and van Dyck. Treasures normally kept behind elaborate alarm systems but which were hung in the Prince's study as everyday pieces of the furniture. Initially he was only given permission to remove 100 paintings but none were specifically named and the Prince was able to make off with further masterpieces by using the same pass time and again. It proved another bone of contention between Prince Franz-Josef II and the communist authorities.

The Prince lived in the expectation that the property would eventually be restored to its rightful owners, and with the decline of communism in Eastern Europe, so his successor Prince Hans Adam III has attempted to reclaim their lost palaces but to date he has received little more than an apology.

CHAPTER TWENTY-FIVE. BULGARIA

The King is Dead

'Typically Balkan', was how one observer described the sudden demise in 1943 of King Boris III of Bulgaria. The official cause of death was heart disease but there were many people who consider the king to have met a more sinister end. The world was at war and a dangerous place in which to live. The major players in the conflict, Germany, Italy, America, Great Britain and the Soviet Union, were all suspected of his murder. There were also many theories as to how the king died, from an assassins bullet to a lethal dose of snake venom, to exposure to poisonous gas. His death was therefore to become one of the greatest 'whodunits' of the Second World War.

Bulgaria was a junior member of the Axis but that did not prevent Germany from becoming the prime suspect. For behind the show of comradeship there existed a strained, almost artificial, relationship. Continued Anglo-French resentment of Bulgarian opposition in the First World War had forced King Boris into a virtual economic partnership with Germany. Adolf Hitler had then exploited his hold on the Bulgarian market place to achieve political control, and to smooth ruffled feathers along the way, he made to Bulgaria such gifts as the return of the province of Dobrudja, which had been ceded to Roumania following the Balkan Wars of 1913-1914, an extremely popular move with the Bulgarian people.

Circumstances, and not ideology, had therefore forced King Boris to join the Axis Powers. He was not fully committed to the alliance and exercised an independence of mind that Adolf Hitler found uncomfortable. He did declare war on Great Britain and the United States of America, and he did send Bulgarian troops to police German-occupied territory in the Balkans but he did not declare war on the Soviet Union and would not send soldiers into frontline action. However, by the summer of 1943, Italy was out of the war and Hitler was looking to Bulgaria for a more positive contribution, asking King Boris to visit German Headquarters at Rastenburg in East Prussia.

The king was a skilful diplomat and had previously been successful in his dealings with the Führer. He would not provoke the kind of scandal his father, King Ferdinand, had caused when on a visit to Germany he caught Kaiser Wilhelm II leaning out of a window and promptly slapped him on the bottom. Nevertheless, he sensed that time was against him and he was alarmed to receive Hitler's latest invitation, so much so that he delayed his journey by two days so as to avoid travelling on Friday 13 August. However, it is doubtful as to whether this helped his situation, for when he did arrive he found himself in an underground bunker that was hardly conducive to a friendly tête-à-tête, and from the moment he walked through its steel doors the remaining two weeks of his life were to be shrouded in mystery. No one is sure as to what took place. Bulgarian aides who were not privy to the negotiations simply spoke of faces getting longer and longer as the two-day conference went on.

Reports from around the world spoke of a violent confrontation and a less than happy return to Bulgaria. Some had the king travelling home by train only to be shot and wounded en route. Others had him flying back in a German aircraft and falling ill through one of three means: poison in the guise of a travel sickness tablet, high altitude flying and the inhalation of poisonous gas through his oxygen mask; and finally, erratic flying that caused the aircraft to climb and dive at such frequent intervals as to prompt a heart attack. Prime Minister Filov attempted to clarify matters in a statement to the Bulgarian parliament but in reality did little to dampen speculation. 'The purpose of this meeting was to review the general military and political situation as well as to discuss the part of Bulgaria during the war. The king returned to Bulgaria in excellent health, tired from the flight which was unpleasant and uncomfortable.'[1]

Court officials were to confirm the safe return of the king and testify to an energetic programme of hunting and mountain climbing in the days that followed but there was a remoteness about him that unnerved them. He spent the first evening back home in isolation away from the royal family and the next day was found precariously perched on a mountain top with the strain of the events clearly etched upon his face. A week later he had taken to his bed and was fighting for his life. German physicians were sent to Sofia to treat the king but their presence was to arouse further suspicion, especially as amongst their number was Doctor Hans Eppinger who used concentration camp victims as human guinea pigs in his medical research. Nevertheless, the Germans maintained that it was Eppinger and his colleagues who spotted the first signs of poisoning. Acute pain, the disintegration of internal organs, and the appearance of blemishes on the skin, led them to believe that it was a rare snake venom that took weeks rather than hours to kill. Certainly, no one seemed able to attempt to save King Boris and he died on 28 August 1943.

Hitler blamed the Italian royal family. He would not forgive them for the overthrow of his friend Benito Mussolini and their capitulation to Allied forces. Il Duce was not a well man and Adolf Hitler was now convinced that he too had been poisoned. He blamed the actual deed upon Princess Mafalda of Italy, the wife of Prince Philip of Hesse, and his hatred of her knew no bounds. He called her the 'trickiest bitch' in the Italian royal house. The princess was the sister of Queen Ioanna of Bulgaria and for this very reason it is unlikely that she would have murdered the king even if their relationship granted access to him. However, Hitler may well have had reason to suspect some form of collaboration. Italy had after all demonstrated that there was life outside the Axis and there was every reason to believe that King Boris was looking for a way to extricate Bulgaria from the war. Indeed, Hitler was so convinced that something was afoot that he ordered the arrest of Queen Ioanna but prudent voices among his advisers prevailed.

No evidence exists to suggest that the United States of America was involved in a conspiracy to murder. Diplomatic missions to prewar Bulgaria were to comment favourably on the king and throughout the fighting the Americans were sympathetic towards him but the British took an altogether different line for the very reason that they could not forgive the Bulgarian Crown for siding with Germany in the First World War, let alone the second. The British Embassy in Washington was to inform the state department:

> His Majesty's government cannot have any dealings with King Boris, whose fate they regard as a matter of indifference, any more than they can have with the present government. The king is a man of no mean ability and cunning, but morally weak and incapable of courageous decisions, a true son of his father.[2]

Upon the king's death Winston Churchill went even so far as to say 'What happened to King Boris will also happen to others who side with Germany!'[3] It was an obituary that Hitler was quick to exploit and he did not hesitate to point the finger at Great Britain in the propaganda war that followed, but again there is nothing to substantiate his claim.

It had been a constant source of frustration to King Boris that he was unable to achieve a reconciliation with Great Britain. At times it looked as if he had succeeded. In the autumn of 1938 he certainly won praise from Churchill's predecessor, Neville Chamberlain, for helping to persuade Adolf Hitler to meet him at Munich and settle German territorial ambitions towards Czechoslovakia without resorting to war. The British Embassy in Sofia wrote the following letter to the king.

> Mr Chamberlain fully appreciates the value of His Majesty's own contribution to the cause of peace during his visit to Germany. In speaking as he did to Herr Hitler and other leading members of the German Government His Majesty showed himself a true

friend of Europe, and Mr Chamberlain is convinced that His Majesty's intervention was an important factor in the final settlement of the crisis.[4]

The message was, however, from another prime minister writing from another world, one of peace and not of war, and despite every effort war was to come again.

On a visit to Sofia in 1936, King Edward VIII had been amazed to find that King Boris spent his leisure time driving the locomotives of the Bulgarian State Railway. It was often said that King Boris did not fear dethronement because he could always move to the United States and become an engineer, but in reality the threat of revolution was never far from his mind. The king was particularly anxious of his next door neighbour, the Soviet Union, and the threat communism posed to the world order. His misgivings were of course to be fully justified at the end of war when Stalin took over Eastern Europe, including Bulgaria. The Soviet Union therefore had a motive to remove King Boris from the scene and was perhaps responsible for his death. Certainly, it had no qualms about the execution in 1945 of his brother Prince Kyril, who had been appointed regent to his nephew the six-year-old King Simeon II. Could one of the many agents working in Bulgaria have poisoned King Boris? Many of the people who might have been able to give us the answer were liquidated alongside Prince Kyril.

One person does, however, survive and that is Queen Ioanna. Looking back on events she is certain of one thing and that is that her husband did not die of natural causes, adding that during the thirteen years of their marriage he was never ill. Perhaps the fall of communism will reveal what really happened to him but in the meantime there are many questions to be answered. Was he murdered? If so, how was he killed? What was the motive and who was the murderer ?

The king's last resting place also remains a mystery. He was initially buried amid much solemnity at the Rila Monastery. Later at the insistence of the communist authorities the queen had his remains removed to the privacy of their country estate at Vrana but with the abolition of the monarchy the body was removed once again to an unknown location. However, his heart had been embalmed and buried separately from his body. This has now been found in the grounds of the former royal palace, and tests show that if it did belong to the king he would indeed have died of a heart attack but is it the heart of King Boris? Some people already suspect it may have only recently been buried to conceal the truth. Old loyalties to the monarchy are beginning to resurface and people are beginning to ask searching questions of their former communist masters.

References:

1 and 4. *Boris III of Bulgaria*, Pashanko Dimitroff.
2 and 3. *Crown of Thorns*, Stephane Groueff.

CHAPTER TWENTY-SIX. ROUMANIA

From the Frying Pan Into the Fire

Roumanian independence was likewise compromised by Axis supremacy in the Balkans. King Carol II had recognised the threat to his country, and in the prewar years had sought to preserve the Roumanian soul in the creation of a youth movement called the Straji Tarii, or Guard of the Realm. Young people were automatically enrolled in the Straji at the age of seven, and remained there until they were eighteen to twenty-one years of age. The aim of the movement was to develop a national conscience with education in morality and religion; social and civic duties; and physical exercise.

Youth leaders were trained in ideology, psychology of the young, social and national service, individuality through Straji methods, moral training, hygiene, drill in physical education, and the needs of the Roumanian village. Together with their charges they undertook not only conventional youth activities such as signalling, camp preparation and first aid, but also practical work in folklore, national dances, rural architecture, social research, fire fighting, veterinary principles, agronomy and farming, topography, aviation, and music. Through the application of these techniques they planted trees, built churches, cultural centres, roads and bridges.

The king was the Supreme Commandant of the Straji, and often appeared before his young army dressed like a glorified boy scout with knee length shorts. He was a great-grandson of Queen Victoria with one childhood memory of the great Queen-Empress, a soft, thick carpet, a plump little lady whose hands he had to kiss, and a tin of toy soldiers. It was not therefore odd to find Saint George and the Dragon as a Straja emblem.

There was, however, the king's German ancestry and in many other respects the Straja leaned towards the Hitler Youth. Traditional youth movements such as the Scouts were absorbed into the Straja. Only the Archers of Bucovina retained a unique identity, but with their white embroidered tunics, fur caps, and peculiar swagger, they embodied the ideals of Roumanian youth, much as the blond-haired brownshirts did in Germany. There was also compulsory membership, and a fascist style salute, although in Roumania it was based on an ancient custom. A sign of welcome used by a warrior was to raise his right arm, with palm extended, to show there was no weapon in his hand.

King Carol was in agreement with authoritarian rule and he invested absolute power in the monarchy. Throughout 1938 and 1939 he outlawed political parties and restructured parliament. The old parties were replaced with the Roumanian Political Renaissance Front. This new body shared the principles of the Straji: the idea of the nation; respect for the family; Christian faith; the dignity of labour; and the role of the élite. Parliament became a vocational assembly with representatives from agriculture, manual labour, commerce and industry.

In the end such close similarities to Axis rule made Roumania suscep-
tible to fascism. The revision of the constitution certainly backfired and King
Carol found himself outwitted by pro-German forces most notably Marshal
Antonescu, who forced the king from his throne in 1940 and assumed the
royal powers. Nevertheless, he was cautious to retain the facade of monarchy,
and as King Carol sheltered from gun fire in an iron bathtub aboard a high
speed train his son Prince Mihai, the Grand Voevoda of Alba-Julia, was sworn
in as king.

It was Mihai's second spell upon the throne. He had originally
succeeded his grandfather, King Ferdinand, in 1927. His father King Carol
had a liking for women and his wedding to Princess Helen of Greece in 1921
in the aftermath of his hastily annulled marriage at the end the First World
War did not prevent him from having extramarital affairs. These led to disin-
heritance, divorce, and exile. His most famous mistress was Magda Lupescu,
whose popularity can best be described by the name for which she was known
throughout the country, the 'She Wolf'.

Mihai was a small boy of six when his grandfather died in 1927, and three
regents were appointed to exercise the royal prerogatives. The most prominent
regent was his uncle Prince Nicolas who had served in the British Royal Navy as
a sub lieutenant. He had a passion for the sea and as a young child his rooms
were decorated like a ship complete with a gangway leading to his bedroom and
portholes for windows. Ruling a country was not to his taste and he welcomed
his brother Carol home when he flew back to Roumania and reclaimed his
throne on 6 June 1930. Mihai was relegated to the position of crown prince and
his mother Princess Helen was required by King Carol to live in exile.

A disturbed upbringing, even by royal standards, left King Mihai sullen
and unsure of himself. In the first months of his reign, his temperament was
not improved by the intrigue surrounding Marshal Ion Antonescu. Mihai's
youth, timidity and inexperience enabled the marshal to rule without restraint
and relegate the monarchy to the sideline as he issued decrees, bestowed
honours, and made all manner of civil and military appointments without
reference to the king. Antonescu also took it upon himself to commit
Roumania to the Axis Powers and King Mihai was only to find out that his
country was at war with the Soviet Union when the local garrison commander
telephoned him. However, Antonescu was aware that the monarchy was
popular with the country and he ensured that the king retained a public
profile, especially when it could be seen as an endorsement of his regime.

This was important in the conduct of the war, because Antonescu had
two war aims. The first was the recapture of Bessarabia which had been given
to Roumania at the end of the First World War, but had been annexed by the
Soviet Union in 1939. In this he was supported by the people. The second was
to reclaim the area of Transylvania taken by Hungary in 1940. Antonescu
needed German support to accomplish this and was prepared to fight German
battles in the Ukraine in order to achieve it; in his own words, to pay Germany
for Transylvania 'in blood and sacrifice'[1]. Had he taken the Roumanian Army

into the region he might have won popular support but to lead the Army there the long way around did not unite the people behind him. This was why he wanted the country to believe he enjoyed the support of the king.

This propaganda weapon had a double-edged blade. The king did not support his military plan and his public outings arranged by Antonescu to the front line gave the ammunition Mihai needed to fire at the dictator. His tours of the Bessarabian Front demonstrated the outdated mentality of Marshal Antonescu who followed First World War strategy in throwing wave after wave of troops at strong enemy defences with heavy, and unnecessary cost to human life. This caused unease within the army, and coupled with the contempt Antonescu displayed towards the officers and men, it was clear that he did not have the devoted support of the military. On one occasion in the king's presence Marshal Antonescu halted a column of troops and humiliated an officer before his men for riding on horseback whilst they marched. He would not accept the officer's explanation that at over 50 years of age he could not march as briskly as the younger men in his command. A little later Antonescu came across the same column and the officer approached the dictator to admit that he had been wrong, but rather than accepting the apology he humiliated the officer further with abusive language.

When Roumanian troops moved into the Crimea, the king resisted pressure to visit the front because he thought it wrong for the army to be there. Once again he was denied news of the capture of Odessa until Adolf Hitler sent him a telegram congratulating Roumania on the victory. Only upon the request of the soldiers did he venture out for a quick tour of inspection. His worst fears were soon realised because at the airport he was met by film crews and an Axis propaganda coup. Cameras were there to provide outward proof of his support for Marshal Antonescu's Crimean adventure. The king, however, could not have been further apart from Antonescu when in response to a partisan attack on Roumanian Army Headquarters in Odessa, thousands of Jews in the city were rounded up and executed.

Such brutality led to harsh retribution when the Soviet army hit back following the German loss of Stalingrad. A counter-offensive removed the Roumanian army from Soviet territory, and retook Bessarabia. By August 1944, the Soviets were on the Roumanian border and, to spare the country a nightmare, King Mihai was resolved either to force Antonescu to make an about face and surrender to the Allies, or to remove him altogether and find someone who would. Antonescu now found himself up against a king who had greatly matured in four years. Although the dictator had called Queen Mother Helen home to be with her son and help while away his time at the Castle of Pelesh outside the capital, the king had not been as idle with his time as Antonescu might have thought. The king had busied himself with a study of constitutional law. This only added impetus to his challenge to Antonescu and he established secret contacts with civil servants, opposition party leaders, and loyal military commanders. Together they hatched·a plan to extricate Roumania from the war.

On 23 August 1944, Marshal Antonescu answered a call to the palace. In the audience that followed King Mihai requested Antonescu to arrange an armistice with the Allies. The marshal refused to do so. If necessary he intended to turn the Carpathians into a fortress and continue the fight from there. To abandon the rest of the country did not meet with the king's approval and he asked for Antonescu to resign. Antonescu rejected the call in a way that demonstrated his dismissive attitude towards the king. 'Do you think I shall hand the country to you, into the hands of a child?'². The king had anticipated his refusal and signalled for four armed officers to enter the room and arrest him. As they searched him for arms his indignation quickly turned to rage. It was often said that the king's criticism would prompt Antonescu to go home and furiously jump up and down on his cap, but he now expressed himself by spitting in the faces of the arresting officers as they led him to a makeshift cell, an enormous wall safe previously used by King Carol II to store his valuable stamp collection.

One by one Antonescu's henchmen were summoned to the palace where they joined him in his incarceration. It was an amazing feat undertaken without a single shot being fired, and under the very noses of secret police headquarters opposite the palace. However, it was not very long before the Germans got to hear of developments, and the king was moved to safety outside Bucharest. Although Adolf Hitler had decorated the queen mother for her Red Cross work, he had grown to mistrust the monarchy and there had been talk of replacing Mihai with his Habsburg cousin, Archduke Stefan, but Antonescu would not believe that the king was resolute enough to oppose him. German military leaders therefore hastened to the palace to ascertain events. The loss of Roumania undermined their position in the Balkans and they were astounded to hear the king and his new government call for them to withdraw peacefully. Hitler's reaction was predictable and violent in the extreme with German bombers pounding at the capital. A particular target was the royal palace which was destroyed in the attacks.

Hitler's distrust stemmed in part from King Mihai's friendliness towards Allied airmen shot down over Roumania. The king impeded the removal of these prisoners to Germany. He also made sure they were comfortable in Roumania visiting them in prison to ensure their wellbeing. He certainly could not resist a chat with them about their aircraft. Aviation was a pet hobby of his, and he had his own plane. They received him with a good deal more respect than Antonescu afforded him. When this was noticed the visits were stopped but, on his travels around the country, King Mihai occasionally came across a captive. He met one American airman in a village police station. The airman mentioned that a photograph of his girlfriend was inside the grip of his gun, and the king arranged for this to be returned to him. The king also gave him the ring taken from a dead pilot of another plane shot down nearby, and telling him the aircraft number, asked that he pass the ring to the pilot's family upon his eventual release. These were courtesies not normally extended to the enemy by the Axis leaders.

Great Britain was involved in the coup. British intelligence had one tentative link with Roumania, and that was a wireless set left behind by British diplomats at the beginning of the war. It had passed into the hands of British sympathisers, and assumed an important role in the planning of the coup d'etat. Coded messages which saw Antonescu called the tram driver in deference to his self proclaimed title of Conducator, culminated in British acceptance of a request to bomb German military installations around Bucharest on the day planned for the coup. Unfortunately, there was no time for the bombing raids to be brought forward when Antonescu forced an earlier date upon the king by announcing his imminent departure for the front. Consequently the capital was left to the mercy of the German bombers until the British arrived to the original time schedule four days later. After that they played no great part in Roumania which was left to the tender care of the Soviet Union.

Germany was forced to abandon Roumania and King Mihai returned to Bucharest for the arrival of the Soviet army. Although the communists had promised not to change the status quo in Roumania, they did move to impose communist rule. Moscow employed various methods to accomplish this. In the first instance, the Roumanian army was neutralised in defeat and the officer corps purged of monarchist or liberal officers. Communist agents then created political insecurity by orchestrating a ministerial crisis every ten days, until a communist prime minister was appointed. His name was Petru Grozo, a wealthy landowner of Hungarian birth, who had served in the Austro-Hungarian army as a corporal, and previously led a minor political party in Roumania called the Ploughmans Front. The third tactic was the wide scale looting of property, and terrorisation of the people. The economy was crippled by the theft of industrial equipment which forced the closure of factories, resulting in high unemployment and social discontent. All this created the perfect environment for the communists to enlist the support of the people.

When the people failed to cooperate there was violent retribution. Workers of the Malaxa factory in Bucharest who rejected communist work practices were attacked by stormtroopers wielding iron bars, and when they failed to bring the workers to heel, Soviet soldiers with machine-guns intervened and many of the rebels were never seen again. The stormtroopers were called the Tudor Vladimuescu, an unpleasant outfit made up of Roumanian men who had suffered under fascist rule, or had a general grievance against the state. They also intervened to curb public demonstrations of loyalty towards the monarchy. On one occasion students took advantage of the king's birthday celebrations to make a public protest about government policy. The king was not in Bucharest for his birthday and the Tudor Vladimuescu took advantage of his absence to flex their muscles with their iron bars. It is then reputed that the female students were sent home with notes telling their parents how they had been raped and it would happen again if they took part in further demonstrations.

Against such a violent backdrop, the king voluntarily chose to restrict his public appearances to a minimum. His isolation was not therefore improved by the fall of Antonescu and the rise of Grozo. He simply swapped the restrictions of one political creed for another. However, the communists did pay him more respect than the fascists; decrees were sent to the palace for the royal signature, and court etiquette was generally observed. By signing the decrees, the king did help legitimise communism in Roumania, but it was done under duress as it was not unknown for him to be threatened with confinement in a mental institution if he objected to government policy. The king realised that his days in Roumania were numbered but if he could not stop the communists he could impede their advance. Many radical laws were delayed as a result. He was also inspired by the support of the people, which had been strengthened by the coup d'etat in 1944. His popularity certainly prevented the Soviet Union from disposing of the monarchy until three and a half years after the Soviet troops marched into Roumania.

Since the coup d'etat the king had sought support against Soviet intimidation from America and Britain, but with the Red Army firmly entrenched in Roumania they were powerless to bring about democratic government. The most they ever achieved was a broadening of the Grozo administration to include two non-communist leaders. However, the final days of the monarchy were in part to be played out in London. King Mihai's first cousin Philippos of Greece married the Princess Elizabeth on 20 November 1947. The communists allowed the king to attend in the hope that he would decide not to return, and at the wedding there was some family pressure for him to remain in exile where he would be safe. However, the king could not easily set aside his responsibilities and he went home. To add to communist disappointment he took with him the news of his engagement to Princess Anne of Bourbon-Parma, whom he had met in London. The engagement was well received by the Roumanian people. The communists knew that if they allowed a royal wedding to take place it would demonstrate the popularity of the monarchy to a worldwide audience, and harm the communist myth that the peasants of Roumania wanted a people's republic.

A replay of the Antonescu meeting therefore took place in the king's study. Present were King Mihai, Queen Helen, Prime Minister Grozo and the Secretary General of the Communist Party Gheorghiu-Dej. Grozo wasted no time with preliminaries and told the king and queen mother that the time had come for a 'friendly separation'[3]. There was no longer the need for a King of Roumania. Conscious that the prime minister had only recently told him that the monarchy would be needed for another 50 years or more, the king pressed Grozo for an explanation. His response was that left to him the king could stay but Moscow did not want a monarchy behind the Iron Curtain. When Mihai drew their attention to his popularity, Gheorghiu-Dej let it be known that was why they wanted him to go, because whilst he remained there would be trouble. He then gave the king the alternative to exile, and that was arrest for allegedly plotting with Great Britain and the United States of America against his own government.

The king withdrew to consult palace advisors who persuaded him that he could best oppose communism in exile, rather than in imprisonment and possible death. Outside, communist troops had disarmed the royal guard and tanks patrolled the surrounding streets. There seemed little for the king to do but sign the abdication document prepared by Grozo. The document itself added insult to injury by implying the king had chosen to leave the country of his own free will:

> We Mihai the First, King of Roumania, to all present and in the future, greetings! During recent years in the life of the Roumanian State, deep political, social and economic changes have taken place, which have created new relations between the components of government. These relations do not satisfy the present conditions of our State, as laid down by our constitution. The monarchical institution is a serious obstruction in the way of the development of our country. I have considered this situation, and in full agreement with responsible authority, I hereby abdicate in my name and in the name of my descendants, from all prerogatives which I have so far exercised as King of Roumania. I leave to the Roumanian people the freedom to choose their new form of State. Given in Bucharest, this day, 30th December 1947.[4]

A far more fitting tribute were the words of President Truman when he honoured the king with the American Legion of Merit for his part in the downfall of Antonescu:

> By his superior judgement, his boldness of action and the high character of his personal leadership, King Mihai I has made an outstanding contribution to the cause of freedom and democracy.[5]

References:
All quotations are taken from *Crown Against Sickle* by Arthur Gould Lee.

CHAPTER TWENTY-SEVEN. GREECE

A Bitter Legacy

King Mihai and Queen Anne were married in Athens on 10 June 1948. King Pavlos and the royal household in Greece provided all the royal pomp it could muster but times were hard. Greece was still recovering from an Italo-German occupation. Mussolini had sent his troops in on 28 October 1940. They came via Albania and quickly penetrated the outer defences of the

Greek Army. However, wet and cold weather prevented the Italian air force from providing effective air cover and slowed the advance, leaving time for the Greeks to reinforce and counter-attack. A week later the Italian army was defeated at the Battle of Mount Morova and pushed into retreat. The Greek army followed into Albania and made similar inroads into Albanian territory as those made by the Italians in Greece.

Crossing the border turned out to be the undoing of the Greek army. The Greek mountains, a natural fortress defence, gave way to the Albanian plains where Mussolini's tank corps gained the upper hand over a Greek army with no modern armour. In another about face in fortunes, poor communications lines, bad weather, and Italian reinforcements brought the Greek army to a crawl, if not a halt. Nevertheless, the fact that they were on Italian territory proved they were not a quick pushover. Germany was therefore forced to intervene and invaded Greece through Yugoslavia. Greek fortifications at the Rupel Pass held the German advance for a time, much better than the French defences but, when they fell, total defeat was quick to follow. The Rupel defences had been the scene of bitter recrimination in the First World War when Greece handed the forts to the Central Powers.

The occupation of Greece by Germany and Italy provided for communist resistance that was actually aided and abetted by the Allies. In their determination to defeat the Axis powers, political ideology did not feature in their calculations and the British even went so far as to attach military missions to the different guerrilla movements. This strategy undoubtedly worked and the occupation forces were certainly given a hard time but there was a price to pay, and the Allies first awoke to the situation when the Greek fleet mutinied whilst at anchor off Egypt. This was the revolutionaries' traditional call to arms; one that had signalled the Russian, German and Austrian uprisings at the end of the First World War. The British were therefore sufficiently worried to intervene and check the rise of communism in Greece but it came too late to prove anything other than a damage limitation exercise. Greek communism was to survive to fight another day but its next move was to be far less crude and so subtle as to once again enlist British support.

Republican sentiment had always existed in Greece and exile was nothing new to the monarchy. The communists therefore successfully harnessed the more moderate republican groups to their cause and, somewhat hiding behind them, presented the king and the Allies with what looked like a respectable opposition to monarchy. So much so, that Great Britain and the United States brought pressure to bear upon the king for a plebiscite to determine whether or not he went home after the war. He agreed under duress and not without some bitterness towards the Allies. He had, after all, been on their side throughout the war but even when vindicated by a yes vote, the Allies continued to distance themselves from his regime.

King Giorgios II was the unfortunate monarch called upon to bear the burden of invasion and exile, and as with our own King George VI, the strain of war caused his premature death at the age of 56 years. He died on 1 April

1947, and was succeeded by his brother Crown Prince Pavlos. He was to bear the burden of a civil war against communism. A conflict which came out of a world war against fascism and which had seen the latest enemy strengthened by the western allies.

It was certainly considered desirable in British circles for Prince Philippos of Greece to renounce his nationality before his wedding to the Princess Elizabeth on 20 November 1947. She was therefore engaged to Lieutenant Philip Mountbatten and not a prince of Greece. Philip was already an officer in the British Royal Navy but during the war he did not turn his back on Greece. As an officer aboard HMS *Valiant* he had escorted troop convoys in and out of Crete. When the Germans launched an all out attack on the island, HMS *Valiant* had been in the thick of it, and like a good many other Royal Navy ships there, she had sustained sufficient damage to force a withdrawal to Egypt. Philippos had later been promoted to first lieutenant, and aboard HMS *Wallace*, the prince had seen action off Sicily in 1943. His transfer to HMS *Whelp* meant he was in Tokyo Bay for the Japanese surrender in 1945.

The royal oath was not lost upon King Pavlos as he swore to uphold: 'To Guard the Constitution and the Laws of the Greek Nation, and to preserve and defend the national independence and territorial integrity of the Greek State.[1]' His first line of defence was the adoption of a more open style of monarchy. King Giorgios had been a sincere, hard-working monarch but also a remote figurehead, and although he had secured 69 percent of the vote in the plebiscite, a further 20 percent had voted for the monarchy but not the return of King Giorgios. This message was not lost on King Pavlos who needed all the support he could muster and he spent more time away from the palace meeting his people. At 45 he was that much younger than his brother and had that much more zest about him. Certainly, if it had been left to Pavlos, King Giorgios would have ignored Allied pressure for a plebiscite and gone home.

The new king also had another advantage over his brother and that was the able support of his even younger wife the 30-year-old Queen Frederika, a daughter of the Duke and Duchess of Brunswick and a grand-daughter of Kaiser Wilhelm II of Germany. The queen became a Greek citizen upon her marriage and from that day on she worked in the service of her new country. Unfortunately a wartime incident helped her enemies brand her a Germanophile, a label that was to remain throughout the rest of her life. The royal family had yet to leave Athens for Cairo and the army was still fighting Italy in Albania. Hitler wanted Greece out of the war but before he sent in his troops he attempted a palace coup through Frederika. Germany wanted Pavlos to replace King Giorgios who was an Anglophile. Pavlos was said not to get on with Prime Minister Metaxas who was waging the war against Italy, and Hitler hoped that a change of monarch would result in Metaxas' removal from office. A letter from the Duke of Brunswick was used by a German emissary to gain access to the crown prince and princess. In their presence he outlined the Nazi plan. Both were indignant that the Germans thought them worthy of treason and the emissary was rapidly sent from the palace. Despite their obvious rejection of the plan, the involvement of the Duke of Brunswick tarnished Frederika's reputation.

The king's out-and-about policy did not come easily to postwar Greece. The road and rail networks were in an awful mess and the king and queen had to rely on a jeep to get about the country. Dust in the summer and snow in the winter made it a far from comfortable mode of transport, and it amused them to think that there were people still around who thought they wore crowns throughout their daily lives and went about with the utmost ceremony. In many respects people could have been forgiven for such thoughts. The whole world would have seen Queen Frederika at her most regal for the royal wedding in London but few would have seen her return home and brave mines on the road to visit troops in the mountain fortress of Konitsa. Such was the end to 1947.

Konitsa had fallen to the communists on Christmas Day but had been retaken by the Greek army in time for the New Year. It was a hard-fought battle and the royal visit was in recognition of the courage and determination of the officers and men who had achieved victory. The king and queen retained close ties with the military. At Easter, the most important occasion in the Orthodox Church, King Pavlos could be found not only in church but also in the barracks distributing eggs to the troops. Their loyalty was shown time and time again during the civil war. On one occasion an over zealous pilot dipped his wings in salute to the king and brought enemy artillery fire down upon the position. However, Pavlos and Frederika did not repeat the mistake of the queen's grandfather and allow their vision to become so blinkered as not to see beyond the soldiers who guarded the crown. For they could see that beyond the barrack room there existed the poverty upon which communism could feed, and they did not ignore the suffering of their people.

Soon after his accession, King Pavlos instituted the National Foundation with the aim of raising moral, social, and educational standards of the Greek people. The Second World War had left the Greek economy in tatters and the work of the foundation was made all the more difficult by the communist war which kept a frightened population from the fields and sowed dissent amongst the factory workers. The war also struck at the very heart of a family by targeting the children. Over 28,000 were kidnapped by communist guerrillas and taken behind the Iron Curtain to neighbouring countries such as Yugoslavia and Albania. There each was to be indoctrinated and brought up either as a party faithful, or at worst a hardened fighter willing to continue the struggle in his former homeland. Queen Frederika therefore founded the Royal Welfare Institute to build childrens' homes, to act as safe houses for the youngsters, and schools to give them an unbiased education.

The king also initiated a scheme to rehabilitate the young people who had been captured by the authorities and had returned to Greece to fight the communist cause; in many cases after they had committed murder, rape and arson. A special school was established on the island of Leros and the prisoner of war camps were emptied of the young people who were committed to reform. Fourteen months later the first inhabitants were reintroduced to Greek society. Each went away with a diploma signed and presented by the king. Back in their villages this made each not an outcast but a rather special person. The rehabilitation of girls was much more difficult. It was almost impossible to get a village to take back a girl who had served with the communist forces, whether it had been of her own choosing or not. It was a question of morality and the strict code of conduct that governed a girl's upbringing. Attempts were therefore made to move them from Leros to a childrens' school, or if appropriate a housekeeping school elsewhere in the country.

Greece was not a welfare state and the monarchy sought to improve the quality of life with many other schemes. All provided for practical assistance and national reconciliation. The latter was of equal importance to the king and queen. The island of Leros was one example of what could be achieved, the island of Macronisos was another. Housed on this second island were members of the armed forces who had displayed left wing sympathies, something like 20,000 servicemen in all. Against advice King Pavlos and Queen Frederika went to visit them and delivered an emotional appeal for their support. Concentrating on the orthodox image of a king as the father of his people, he spoke to them as if they were his children and stated his wish for them once again to be entrusted with their weapons in the defence of their country, and their family at large.

In the last decade of the twentieth century it is difficult to envisage the impact of a father and child relationship between a monarch and his people but just as it was of considerable significance in tsarist Russia at the beginning of the century, so too was it of value to Greece in the 1940s. The soldiers and sailors present at Macronisos simply broke ranks and in a wave of enthusiasm carried the king and queen upon their shoulders. Not all could be persuaded but many went on to play a vital role in the civil war and just as the young people of Leros had received their diploma from the king's own hand, so too was he present to give the men of Macronisos their weapons back.

The personal contact was essential at such a critical time. The queen was to comment that she must have danced in every village in Greece and their tours throughout the country were by and large happy events. A royal smile, a friendly gesture, did much to raise spirits, and prompt people to momentarily forget the trials and tribulation of war. Nevertheless, their travels could not be entirely carefree and it was at times very difficult to smile. Stress was a side to a royal tour that few got to see but one that very much existed. Queen Frederika was often moved to tears by what she saw and heard. At one point she was on the verge of a nervous breakdown but there was no question of giving up the struggle, the fight had to go on.

A certain area of Salonika was known for its communist credentials. A 'no go' area for many in government but not for the queen. She insisted on visiting the town, spending time with the ordinary people in the street chatting about everyday things and overnight her photograph appeared beside those of Josef Stalin. However, with perseverance, the day came when only the queen's face graced the walls of Salonika and Greece was at peace. On New Year's Day 1950, the king was able to deliver the broadcast he had so long wanted to make :

> Hellenes,
>
> I send you all my warmest good wishes for the New Year.
> My life and my thoughts are dedicated to my people, and I feel the joys and the sorrows and the hopes of you all as if they were my own.
> May God forgive me when I say that I am a happy king, because my happiness springs from the hearts of my people.
> On Greek Independence Day nearly two years ago I declared our country to be in peril.
> A year ago I asked the nation to declare 1949 the Year of Victory.
> Today I am proud and grateful to my people that they have once again performed a miracle and made 1949 indeed the Year of Victory.[2]

The civil war was to leave a bitter legacy. It was not easy to forget that nearly 28,000 people died in the infighting, nor that over 42,000 were reported wounded or missing.

In 1963, passions were still running high and on a visit to London Queen Frederika and her daughter Princess Irene were chased through the streets of London by communist sympathisers. They had just left their hotel when an English woman with a Greek husband imprisoned for crimes committed during the civil war set upon the queen. When the bodyguard intervened he was knocked to the ground by men wielding some very large sticks. In the confusion the queen and the princess broke free and moved down the road with all due speed but not enough to lose the mob and before long they were obliged to abandon all decorum and run. Cornered in a cul-de-sac, they could do little but ring on door bells and take refuge in the first house to answer their call.

In 1967 with her husband dead and her son, King Konstantinos II, upon the throne, Queen Frederika was forced to make another escape and this time from Greece. The victim of a right wing coup that had seized power to frustrate what was perceived to be a threat from the left. The young king left to avoid another civil war and remains in exile to this day.

References:
Both quotations are taken from *No Ordinary Crown* by S. Hourmouzios.

EPILOGUE

Greece was not the only country to suffer the psychological scars of the Second World War. Belgium remained in turmoil beyond the referendum of 1950 which allowed for King Leopold III to return home. Powerful left wing demonstrations brought renewed violence to the streets and forced the king to abdicate in 1951. The 'Royal Question' divided society from top to bottom and it said something of the situation that the aristocrat, the Comte de Looz Corswaren, should turn anarchist and disrupt the passage of the Abdication Bill by exploding a smoke bomb inside the Belgian House of Lords. Nevertheless, constitutional propriety was maintained and the monarchy survived with the accession of Leopold's eldest son King Baudouin. He healed the wounds allowing the Belgian people to reflect calmly upon the war, and when King Leopold III died in 1983, his reputation had been largely restored.

King Baudouin had 6,000,000 Flemish speaking subjects in Flanders and 4,000,000 French speaking subjects in Wallonia. A conciliatory role was therefore, and still is, a mainstay of the Belgian monarchy. By the time of King Baudouin's death in 1993, the country was finally responding to the aspirations of a multi-linguistic, multi-cultural society that were expressed as far back as the First World War. A move to a federal system of government saw the king lose some of his traditional powers and questions were raised as to where federalism would leave the monarchy, but the public sorrow at King Baudouin's death and the enthusiasm with which his brother King Albert II has been received, suggests that there is a future for the crown. With the extra responsibilities assumed upon his accession, King Albert passed the presidency of the Belgian Red Cross to his daughter Princess Astrid who has been busy helping to relieve the suffering of the civil war in the former Belgian colony of Rwanda.

Wartime memories blighted the wedding of Crown Princess Beatrix of the Netherlands to the German diplomat Claus von Amsberg in 1966. Queen Juliana, who had occupied the throne since the voluntary abdication of Queen Wilhelmina in 1948, tried to reassure the people that the marriage was good for the country but that did not stop the appearance of a protestor nor his smoke bomb on the streets of Amsterdam. The couple have since defied their critics. Beatrix became queen in 1980, and is a popular and well respected monarch. Contrary to belief, the queen is sensitive to the feelings of wartime veterans and she won their admiration when on a visit to Emperor Akihito she told Japan that for the Dutch to overcome the bitterness of their wartime memories the Japanese had to demonstrate the error of their ways. Meanwhile Prince Claus does not cut a Nazi figure. By his own choice he does not hold military rank and is more comfortable with his role as Inspector General of Cooperation with Developing Countries.

This kept him free of the Lockheed scandal that befell Prince Bernhard in the 1970s. Lockheed was an American company which sold a fighter aircraft called the Starfighter. The company was actively bribing European officials to accept the aircraft and Prince Bernhard in his role as Inspector General of the Netherlands Armed Forces was caught in the web of intrigue. There was no evidence to suggest that the prince received the $1,000,000 payment earmarked for him but the scandal forced Bernhard to resign his military commissions in 1976 and that year he attended the state opening of parliament in a morning suit. However, it was impossible for the Dutch people to forget his otherwise positive contribution to the country and he was back in uniform for his 80th birthday celebrations in 1991. This enabled Prince Bernhard to present his grandson, Crown Prince Willem-Alexander, with his air force 'wings'. Willem-Alexander is the first male heir born to House of Orange for over a century. Since achieving his wings the prince has flown relief missions to Bosnia.

Unlike his European counterparts of the post war years, the British Duke of York has fought for his country. As a naval helicopter pilot he went into action during the Falklands War of 1982. This saw him act as a decoy for Exocet missiles. He brought home a sober message. War is terrifying, lonely and very sad. Three years later the British royal family was hit by a wartime scandal when it came to light that the father of Austrian-born Princess Michael of Kent was a former SS official. Princess Michael, formally known as Baroness Marie-Christine von Reibnitz, was accused of a cover up but the princess was equally surprised by the revelation and was reduced to tears at a public engagement. Satisfied by her frank response to questions about her father, press interest declined and the crisis came to an end.

A frequent visitor to Great Britain is Grand Duke Jean of Luxembourg who holds the honorary appointment of Colonel of the Irish Guards. When his state duties allow he takes part in the ceremony of Trooping the Colour and rides on to Horse Guards Parade alongside the other royal colonels, the Duke of Edinburgh, the Prince of Wales and the Duke of Kent. The Grand Duke served in the Irish Guards during the Second World War under the pseudonym of Lieutenant Luxembourg. His mother the Grand Duchess Charlotte had arrived in London so as to avoid the charges of complicity levelled against the Grand Duchess Marie-Adelaide in the First World War. She later moved on to Canada where in common with the other royal exiles she made a valuable contribution to the Allied cause. This paved the way for a significant role in postwar Europe, and today, the Grand Duchy of Luxembourg is home to the Secretariat of the European Parliament and other bodies of the European Union. The pocket size state has returned to the heart of Europe.

The objective of some European Union officials and statesmen is the creation of a federal superstate. As power shifts to the European Parliament so the usefulness of the remaining monarchs is brought into question. However, if in the future everything is standardised down to the little green men at our pedestrian crossings, then the crowned heads may offer the one distinction in national identity. One man who has embraced European union is Crown Prince Otto of Austria-Hungary, or Doctor Otto von Habsburg as he is known in the European Parliament. The crown prince has turned member of the European Parliament for a Bavarian constituency. He hit the headlines during the miners' strike in Great Britain when he took exception to a British Labour MEP waving a miners' banner in the debating chamber. Otto attempted to remove the banner and the tussle that followed prompted the Speaker to suspend the debate. Otto von Habsburg is not a firebrand by nature and his royal pedigree was apparent when Austria briefly witnessed the grandeur of empire with the Viennese funeral of Kaiserin Zita. The empress was taken to her last resting place aboard a museum piece, the horse-drawn hearse last used for the funeral of Kaiser Franz-Josef.

Swedish monarchy is less likely to be disrupted by European union than most. Sweden moved to a purely titular monarchy in 1975. King Carl XVI Gustaf is now removed from the day-to-day government of the country. He does not take a role in government appointments, nor the enactment of legislation. The constitution even allows for Swedish politicians to dethrone the king if they consider he has failed to fulfill his duties. Nevertheless, King Carl Gustaf retains the right to advise and warn on government policy. This will help Swedish governments in the long term because the longevity of life enjoyed by his predecessors suggests that he will survive many a political career. King Gustaf V who ruled Sweden from 1907 to 1950 and King Gustaf VI Adolf who occupied the throne from 1950 to 1973 both lived into their 90s. The latter's second wife was Queen Louise, a Mountbatten, and the aunt of the Duke of Edinburgh.

King Carl Gustaf has continued the scout tradition set by Count Folke Bernadotte. He is the President of the World Foundation of the Scout Movement, and is seen in the distinctive Swedish scout uniform of a blue shirt and yellow scarf which conforms to the national colours. The king's uniforms have proved a contentious issue. The reformists have deterred the king from attending the State Opening of Parliament in uniform. It was considered that it promoted militarism at the time when the country was committed to a long-established policy of peaceful neutrality. Yet their neutrality in the Second World War continues to trouble the national conscience. The prime minister has in recent years questioned the justification of sitting back whilst fellow Scandinavians suffered in Norway, Denmark and Finland. In Norway the bitterness of the war was expressed in their own war crime tribunals that led to the execution of 25 Nasjonal Samling officials, Vidkin Quisling included. Swedish neutrality was not exactly popular within these countries but the traditional friendly ties of the Scandinavian countries is now very apparent.

Family ties helped in the process. Princess Ingrid of Sweden became Queen of Denmark in 1947 when her husband King Frederik IX succeeded the wheelchair-bound King Christian X. In 1972, the throne passed to their daughter Queen Margrethe II. Princess Martha of Sweden represented the Swedish royal family in Norway but she died three years before her husband became King Olav V in 1957. Until his death in 1991, King Olav was a frequent visitor to Sweden and in 1983 he was with King Carl Gustaf in Stockholm for the unveiling of a monument to the Norwegian Resistance in the Second World War. King Harald V and Queen Sonja of Norway are godparents to Crown Princess Victoria of Sweden who came of age in 1995.

Until shortly before his death King Olav was also a frequent visitor to Britain, especially to attend Remembrance Day events and services in each November. He maintained close ties with the British royal family especially Queen Elizabeth the Queen Mother, widow of George VI.

The stability of postwar monarchy has prompted a reappraisal of the institution in Eastern Europe where the fall of the Iron Curtain has revived a certain freedom of action. Restoration is encouraged by the re-emergence of the Spanish monarchy in 1975. King Juan-Carlos is the grandson of King Alfonso XIII. Their reigns were interspersed by the right wing dictatorship of Generalissimo Francisco Franco. He was the one time associate of Hitler and Mussolini and survived the Second World War through a policy of neutrality, albeit one inclined to the Axis Powers. He abhorred communism and this aided his survival in the postwar years as a useful ally to the United States in the struggle with the Soviet Union during the Cold War. Franco orchestrated the restoration and King Juan Carlos was initially branded his stooge. However, the king dismantled the totalitarian regime of his predecessor and brought democracy to Spain.

His commitment to the reforms were tested when in 1981 Civil Guards in their tricorn hats seized the Spanish parliament and held the deputies hostage. This included the entire government. King Juan-Carlos chose not to forsake democracy and with the authority vested in him as commander-in-chief of the armed forces he brought the rebel guards to heel. The king was enthusiastically acclaimed by the people and from that moment the restoration was judged a success.

It is argued that the exiled monarchs of Eastern Europe could smooth the transition from communist dictatorship to democracy. King Simeon II lives in Spain and the example of the Spanish monarchy is often used in Bulgaria. Initially, hopes were high for a restoration. Queen Mother Ioanna and her daughter, the king's sister, Princess Maria-Luisa, both made highly successful visits to Bulgaria, as did Simeon in May 1996. Monarchists had decided that the heart found in the gardens of the old royal palace did belong to King Boris III and have reburied the heart with all due reverence. The queen mother was in Bulgaria to visit the new grave and attend a religious service in memory of her husband.

With Queen Ioanna being over 80 years of age, her schedule of engagements was limited. Not so for her daughter who spent nine days visiting various parts of the country. The princess honoured old and new cultures with visits to the Rila Monastery and the National Football Stadium. It is estimated that 50- to 70,000 people turned out to cheer Princess Maria-Luisa. The visits encouraged plans underway in Bulgaria for a referendum on the return of the monarchy but growing support for King Simeon unnerved the authorities and the vote was cancelled. King Simeon therefore remains in Madrid but he is no longer an obscure exile. Bulgarian wine growers are certainly advertising his presence by once again displaying the royal warrant on their merchandise.

King Simeon may well have been deterred from a hasty return to his country by the treatment meted out to King Mihai of Roumania when he attempted to go home to a country now called Romania without the letter 'u'. Following the Romanian revolution which led to the downfall of communism in 1989, and the execution of President Nicolae Ceausescu in favour of a more moderate left wing government, the king was given his passport back. He had previously held a British passport from his days as a chicken farmer outside London. However, it did not represent a ticket home and when he attempted to visit Romania for Easter 1990, he was turned back en route at Zurich Airport. A further attempt made that Christmas did get him to Bucharest airport and beyond but his motorcade was stopped by the police and he was escorted out of Romania amid a blaze of publicity.

At the time of the revolution, demonstrators had torn the communist emblem from the Romanian flag and the authorities clearly feared that the royal coat of arms would fill the void. Demonstrations in favour of King Mihai were reported to have been subdued by armed police, and in another flashback to the past, workers wielding iron bars were employed elsewhere to end rallies against the government. Not until the Easter of 1992 was the king allowed home unmolested. He was well received by the people. Many could remember him from the Second World War and they implored him not to leave.

King Mihai is the greatest strength to the monarchist cause but at 74 years of age time is running out for a restoration. The authorities are aware of this and are playing a waiting game. Not that the monarchist cause would be at a total loss without the king. His eldest daughter, Princess Margarita, does have freedom of entry to Romania and through the Princess Margarita of Romania Foundation she undertakes work to improve health and social provision in Romania.

The treatment of King Mihai is only rivalled by that of his second cousin King Konstantinos II of the Hellenes. The political establishment in Greece has always felt insecure towards the monarchy following its formal abolition in 1974. Ten years later at the Olympic Games in San Francisco the socialist government of Andreas Papandreou created quite a rumpus when King Konstantinos, a member of the Olympic Committee, was announced as the king of Greece at a gold medal presentation he made to an athlete. Later with the election of the conservative government of Konstantinos Mitsotakis, a nephew of the First World War statesmen Eleftherios Venizelos, there was an improvement in relations between state and the king. A longstanding feud over the royal estates was resolved, the king was allowed to transfer artifacts from the palace at Tatoi to his London home, and he was granted a Greek passport. In return Konstantinos acknowledged the validity of the republic.

Notwithstanding these developments Mitsotakis despatched two gunboats and an air force plane to harass the king on a cruise of northern Greece in 1993. The politicians accused King Konstantinos of a restoration bid. The king replied that he simply wanted to show his children their Greek heritage. Whatever the reason the consequences were dire and the present socialist administration has once again stripped him of his citizenship and by implication barred him from entering the country.

Curiosity about the royal family still exists in Greece and there was considerable media coverage of the wedding in London in 1995 of Crown Prince Pavlos and Marie-Chantal Miller. The value of monarchy goes far beyond the glamour of royal weddings, but they are occasions of consequence as the Prince and Princess of Wales have found to their cost. The recent wedding of the Portuguese pretender Dom Duarte, Duke of Braganza influenced an opinion poll in which 88 percent of the participants supported a restoration of a throne abolished as far back as 1910. Crown Prince Pavlos did not wear uniform to his wedding although he did serve in the Royal Scots Dragoon Guards before a serious car accident on the A303 in Hampshire nearly killed him. It would appear that exiled royalty also value a military education for their would-be heirs.

Crown Prince Aleksander of Yugoslavia served in the British Army with the Royal Lancers and saw service in Northern Ireland. Aleksander declined the title of King when his father, King Petar II, died in exile in 1970. Nevertheless, he would favour a restoration of the monarchy but he has failed to persuade the warring factions in Yugoslavia that he offers their best chance of keeping the country together. All sides appear hell-bent on going their own way, and when he introduced himself to the people of Belgrade he was unwittingly drawn into Serb nationalist propaganda. Whilst the crown prince has joined in diplomatic attempts to end the civil war, his wife Crown Princess Katherine is making every effort to relieve the suffering of the war through her charity SOS Yugoslavia. A recent appeal has been for the donation of gold jewellery to finance anaesthetics for Yugoslav hospitals.

In contrast to Aleksander of Yugoslavia, Crown Prince Leka of Albania did assume his father's title when King Zog died in France in 1961. However, he went on to attract some unfortunate publicity when he was expelled from Spain in 1978 for owning a private arsenal. Nevertheless, by the time King Leka settled in South Africa he had no apparent interest in a mercenary army called Delta Force which offered to bring about a restoration in Albania. He is confident that his time will come, his hopes being partly based on a dream his father had shortly before his death. In the dream Queen Geraldine returns to Albania aboard a ship; the port of arrival is very similar to Durazzo harbour today. Queen Geraldine lives on, so there is hope for the future. King Leka is certainly keen to enhance the future for his heir and namesake, Prince Leka, who was born to the royal house following the king's marriage to his Australian queen the former Miss Susan Cullen-Ward.

An Albanian restoration will not come easily but King Leka does stand a better chance than Prince Vittorio Emanuele of Italy, whose country deposed King Zog. The male members of the House of Savoy are still barred from Italian soil lest they take advantage of the political instability and corruption there to mount a comeback. Italy has seen in excess of 40 governments since the end of the Second World War. It was the last wish of King Umberto II that he be allowed to return home to die but his request stirred such emotion that the Italian parliament was still debating the issue when the king died in 1983. The prestige of his family was not enhanced when in 1991 his son, Prince Vittorio Emanuele went on trial in Paris for manslaughter. He was accused of the 1978 shooting of a German teenager by the name of Dirk Hamer over the theft of a dinghy from the prince's yacht. The court went on to acquit Vittorio Emanuele of the charge but the sight of the would-be king in handcuffs has done little to further his cause in Italy. Not surprisingly, monarchist hopes are ever more concentrated on the next generation and in particular Emanuele Filiberto, the dashing Prince of Venice.

Germany has a healthy democracy and there is little incentive to restore the Hohenzollern monarchy. The once mighty Prussian Empire is now restricted to the walls of Schloss Hohenzollern where the current pretender, Prince Georg-Friedrich of Prussia brings youth to an otherwise ancient tradition. The one consolation for his late grandfather, Prince Louis-Ferdinand, was the reunification of Germany. By the time the Berlin Wall came down the prince had enhanced the reputation of his family and he was not totally ridiculed for holding out the monarchy as an aid to the reunification process. Prince Louis-Ferdinand was all for reconciliation and he brought the Hohenzollerns and Romanovs together again with his marriage to Grand Duchess Kira of Russia.

Kira's brother was the Grand Duke Vladimir, the leading claimant to the Romanov throne. He was invited to Leningrad when it was renamed St Petersburg and attracted the sympathetic attention of a media and public taught to despise the Romanovs. When he died in 1992 whilst on a lecture tour of the United States of America, his body was taken back to the city for what was virtually a state funeral. His will named the new claimant to be his only child the Grand Duchess Maria. This sparked off a fresh bout of infighting within the Romanov family and a meeting of the surviving grand dukes sought to discredit her claim.

The grand duchess had previously made another dynastic match with Germany when she wed Prince Franz-Wilhelm of Prussia, but the marriage was not a success and they went their separate ways following the birth of their son Grand Duke Georgij. Meanwhile there is talk of another royal funeral in Russia following the discovery of the remains of Tsar Nikolai II. The discovery of the remains has rekindled considerable interest in a bygone age. Whether a restoration can be staged appears to hinge upon a monarchist pressure group which is busy collecting signatures to a petition which it hopes will force a popular vote.*

* Genetic tests have now identified the remains found in a wood outside Ekaterinburg to be those of the tsar, tsaritsa and three of their four daughters. Blood samples taken from living relatives, such as the Duke of Edinburgh, and bone matter taken from the remains of Grand Duke Georgij Alexandrovich in his St. Petersburg tomb, have greatly aided the process, which in part was undertaken by British scientists at the Home Office Forensic Laboratory at Aldermaston, England. The remains of the tsarevitch and one of the younger grand duchesses have yet to be found, but the Bolsheviks testified to the incineration of two bodies, and there is now little reason to doubt this account. Murder most foul was indeed committed.

Great Britain	Albania	Austria Germany	Belgium France Luxembourg	Bulgaria	Denmark Norway Sweden	Greece	Hungary	Italy	Monte-negro	Nether-lands	Roumania	Russia Yugoslavia	Spain
Adolphus		Adolf	Adolphe		Adolf								
Alexander	Leka					Alexandros						Aleksander	
Andrew						Andreas							
Charles		Karl			Carl						Carol		Carlos
Constantine						Konstantinos							
Cyril				Kyril								Kyrill	
Emmanuel								Emanuele					
Eric		Erich											
Ernest		Ernst											
Francis		Franz											Francisco
Frederick		Friedrich			Frederik								
Frederica		Frederika				Frederika							
George		Georg				Giorgios						Georgij / Jord	
Harold					Harald								
Helen								Elena	Elena				Elena
Henry		Heinrich	Henri										
Humbert								Umberto					
John			Jean		Johan								Juan
Joseph		Josef										Josip	
Margaret					Margarethe				Margriet	Margarita			
Michael											Mihai	Mikhail	
Nicholas						Nikolaos	Miklos		Nikola		Nicolas	Nikolai	
Paul						Pavlos							
Peter												Petar	
Philip			Philippe			Philippos		Filiberto					Felipe
Rupert		Rupprecht											
Stephen		Stefan								Stephanus			
Victor		Viktoria						Vittorio					
Victoria													
William		Wilhelm	Guillaume		Wilhelm					Willem			

BIBLIOGRAPHY

Alexander, John T., *Catherine the Great*, Oxford University Press Ltd., 1989.

HRH Princess Alice, Countess Of Athlone, *For My Grandchildren*, Evan Brothers, 1979.

Aronson, Theo, *The Coburgs of Belgium*, Cassell, 1968.

Balfour, Neil and Mackay, Sally, *Paul of Yugoslavia*, Hamish Hamilton, 1980.

Bradford, Sarah, *George VI*, Weidenfeld & Nicolson, 1989.

Broch, Theodor, *The Mountains Wait*, Michael Joseph, 1943.

Brook-Shepherd, Gordon, *The Last Habsburg*, Weidenfeld & Nicolson 1968.

—, *Victim of Sarajevo*, Harvill Press, 1984.

Buchan, John, *Greenmantle*, Hodder & Stoughton, 1916.

Bullock, Alan, *History of the 20th Century*, Phoebus & BPC Publishing, 1976.

Calmes, Christian and Reuter, Raymond, *Jean Grand-Duc de Luxembourg*, 1986.

Cammaerts, Emile, *The Prisoner at Laeken*, Cresset Press, London, 1941.

—, *Albert, King of the Belgians*, Nicholson & Watson, 1935.

Carpenter, Clive, *Kings, Rulers & Statesmen*, Guinness Superlatives.

Carey, John, *The Faber Book of Reportage*, 1987.

Castellani, Aldo, *Microbes, Men and Monarchs*, Victor Gollancz, London, 1960.

Churchill, Winston S., *The World in Crisis*, Thornton Butterworth, 1915.

Constant, Stephen, *Foxy Ferdinand, Tsar of Bulgaria*, Sidgwick & Jackson, 1979.

De Szinyei-Merse, Antionette, *Ten Years, Ten Months, Ten Days*, Hutchinson, London, 1940.

Denholm, Decie, *Behind the Lines – One Woman's War 1914–1918*, Jill Norman & Hobhouse, 1982.

Dimitroff, Pashanko, *Boris III of Bulgaria*, The Book Guild, 1986.

Erskine, Stuart, *The Reign of King Alfonso XIII of Spain*, Hutchinson, 1931.

The Infanta Eulalia Of Spain, *Courts & Countries After the War*, Hutchinson, 1925.

Fenyvesi, Charles, *Royalty in Exile*, Robson Books, 1979.

Queen Frederica of The Hellenes, *A Measure of Understanding*, Macmillan, London, 1971.

Galet, Lieutenant General E., *King Albert in the Great War*, Putnam, 1931.

Gilbert, Martin, *The Routledge Atlas of the First World War*, Routledge, 1994.

—, *The Illustrated London News – Marching to War, 1933-1939*, Bracken Books, 1989.

Gould Lee, Arthur, *Crown & Sickle*, Hutchinson, 1953.

Grant, A. J. and Temperley Grant, *Europe in the Nineteenth & Twentieth Centuries (1789–1938)*, Longmans Green, 1939.

Greve, Tim, *Haakon VII of Norway*, Hurst, London, 1983.

Groueff, Stephane, *Crown of Thorns*, Madison Books, 1972.

Hall, Angus, *The Queen Mother – 75 Glorious Years*, Phoebus & BPC Publishing, 1975.

Hambro, C. J., *I Saw it Happen in Norway*, Appleton-Century, 1941.

Hanbury-Williams, Major General Sir John, *The Emperor Nicholas II as I Knew Him*, Arthur L. Humphreys, 1922.

Harding, Bertita, *Imperial Twilight*, Harrap, 1940.

Hatch, Alden, *HRH Prince Bernhard of the Netherlands*, Harrap, 1962.

Hazelhoff, Erik, *Soldier of Orange*, Hodder & Stoughton, 1972.

Hewins, Ralph, *Count Folke Bernadotte*, Hutchinson, 1948.

Hibbert, Christopher, *Benito Mussolini*, The Reprint Society, London, 1963.

Hindenburg, Paul von, *Out of My Life*, Cassell, 1920.

Hoptner, J. B., *Yugoslavia in Crisis*, Columbia University Press, 1963.

Hourmouzios, Stelio, *No Ordinary Crown*, Weidenfeld & Nicolson, 1972.

Hoven, Baroness Helena von der, *King Carol of Roumania*, Hutchinson, 1940.

Jonas, Klaus W., *The Life of Crown Prince William*, Routledge & Kegan Paul, 1961.

Judd, Dennis, *King George VI*, Michael Joseph, 1982.

—, *Prince Philip*, Michael Joseph, 1980.

Katz, Robert, *The Fall of the House of Savoy*, George Allen & Unwin, 1972.

Kaufmann, J. E. & H. W., *Hitler's Blitzkrieg Campaigns*, Combined Books, Pennsylvania, 1993.

Kerensky, Alexander, *The Kerensky Memoirs*, Cassel, London, 1966.

Keyes, Roger, *Outrageous Fortune*, Secker & Warburg, 1985.

Kiste, John van der, *Windsor and Habsburg, 1848–1922*, Alan Sutton, 1987.

Lacey, Robert, *Aristocrats*, Hutchinson, 1983.

Laffan, R. G. D. *The Serbs*, Dorest Press, New York, 1989.

Legge, Edward, *King Edward, the Kaiser and the War*, Grant Richards, London, 1917.

Longford, Elizabeth, *The Royal House of Windsor*, Sphere Books, 1976.

Loring, Ulrick and Page, James, *Yugoslavia's Royal Dynasty*, Monarchist Press, 1976.

Makin, W. J., *The Life of King George the Fifth*, George Newnes, 1936.

Queen Marie of Roumania, *The Story of My Life*, Cassell, 1935.

HH Princess Marie-Louise, *My Memories of Six Reigns*, Evan Brothers, 1979.

Macmillan, Harold, *Harold Macmillan War Diaries. The Mediterranean, 1943-1945*, Macmillan, 1984.

—, *The Blast of War, 1939-1945*, Macmillan, 1967.

Massie, Robert K., *Nicholas & Alexandra*, Leisure Circle, 1967.

Massock, Richard G., *Italy From Within*, Macmillan, 1943.

Matanle, Ivor, *World War II*, CLB Publishing, 1994.

Mountfield, David, *The Partisans*, Hamlyn, 1979.

Muir, Olive, *Why I Defended a King's Honour*, Hudson & Son, 1955.

Muggeridge, Malcolm, *Ciano's Diary 1939-1943*, William Heinemann, 1947.

Muller, George von, *The Kaiser and His Court*, Macdonald, 1961.

Newman, Bernard, *Inquest on Mata Hari*, Robert, Hale, 1956.

HRH Prince Nicholas Of Greece, *My Fifty Years*, Hutchinson, 1926.

—, *My Political Memoirs*, Hutchinson, 1928.

Nicolson, Harold, *King George V*, Constable & Co. Ltd., 1952.

The Letters of the Tsar to the Tsaritsa, 1914–1917, Bodley Head, London, 1929.

O'Shaughnessy, Edith, *Marie Adelaide Grand Duchess of Luxembourg*, Jonathan Cape, 1932.

Overstraeten, General R. van, *The War Diaries of Albert I*, William Kimber, London, 1954.

Page, James, *Leopold III*, Monarchist Press.

Paleologue, Maurice, *An Ambassador's Memoirs*, Hutchinson, London, 1923/25.

Pakula, Hannah, *The Last Great Romantic*, Weidenfeld & Nicolson, 1985.

Palmer, Paul, *Denmark in Chains*, Lindsay Drummond, 1942.

Paneth, Philip, *Queen Wilhelmina*, Alliance Press.

Paola, Princess of Saxe-Weimar, *A King's Private Letters*, Eveleigh Nash & Grayson, London, 1925.

Pares, Sir Bernard, *Letters of the Tsaritsa to the Tsar, 1914–1916*, Duckworth, London, 1923.

Parrott, Cecil, *The Tightrope*, Faber & Faber, 1975.

Pavlowitch, Stevan, *Yugoslavia*, Ernest Benn, 1971.

King Peter II of Yugoslavia, *A King's Heritage,* Cassell, London, 1955.

HRH Princess Pilar of Bavaria and Chapman-Huston, Major Desmond, *Don Alfonso XIII*, John Murray, London, 1931.

Ponsonby, Sir Frederick, *Recollections of Three Reigns*, Oldham Press.

Popperwell, Ronald G., *Norway*, Ernest Benn, 1975.

Ramm, Agatha, *Beloved and Darling Child*, Alan Sutton, 1990.

Robertson, Reverend Alexander, *Victor Emmanuel III, King of Italy*, George Allen & Unwin, London 1925.

Robyns, Gwen, *Geraldine of the Albanians*, Muller, Blond & White Ltd., 1987.

Stone, Norman and Obolensky, Dimitri, *The Russian Chronicles*, Random Century Group, 1990.

Quaroni, Pietro, *Diplomatic Bags: An Ambassador's Memoirs*, Weidenfeld & Nicolson, 1966.

Trewin, J. C., *Tutor to the Tsarevich*, Macmillan, London, 1975.

Vansittart, Peter, *Voices of the Great War*, Jonathan Cape, 1981.

Vare, Daniele, *Twilight of the Kings*, John Murray, London, 1948.

Viereck, G. S., *Spreading Germs of Hate*, Duckworth, London, 1931.

Vitaliev, Vitali, 'The Day the Russians Came and Stayed', *The European*, 22/25 April 1993.

Wake, Jehanne, *Princess Louise*, Collins, London, 1988.

Whitlock, Brand, *Belgium Under the German Occupation*, William Heinemann, London, 1919.

HRH Princess Wilhelmina of The Netherlands, *Lonely But Not Alone*, Hutchinson, London, 1960.

Williams, Ian, *Newspapers of the First World War*, David & Charles Reprints, 1970.

HRH The Duke Of Windsor, *A King's Story*, Cassell, 1953.

Wolden-Raethinge, Anne, *Queen in Denmark*, Gyldendal, 1988.

Wulff, Louis, *Silver Wedding*, Sampson Low, Marston, 1948.

—, *Queen of Tomorrow*, Marston, 1949.

Zee, Henri Van Der, *The Hunger Winter, Occupied Holland 1944-5*, Jill Norman & Hobhouse, 1982.

INDEX